Dialectic of Romanticism: A Critique of Modernism

Dialectic of Romanticism: A Critique of Modernism

David Roberts and Peter Murphy

continuum
LONDON • NEW YORK

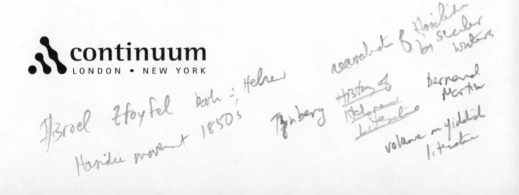

Continuum

The Tower Building
11 York Road
London SE1 7NX

15 East 26th Street
New York
NY 10010

www.continuumbooks.com

© David Roberts and Peter Murphy 2004

British Library Cataloguing-in-Publication Data
A catalogue record for this book is available from the British Library.

ISBN: 0-8264-7204-4

Typeset by Acorn Bookwork Ltd, Salisbury
Printed and bound in Great Britain by Biddles Ltd, *www.biddles.co.uk*

To Agnes Heller and György Markus

Contents

Introduction: Three Modernisms

Our title deliberately sets itself against Max Horkheimer and Theodor Adorno's *Dialectic of Enlightenment*. We take issue with the authors' challenging but deeply flawed vision of the trajectory of the West from Greek beginnings to totalitarian conclusions, and with their one-dimensional equation of enlightenment and myth. This conflation is symptomatic of the hidden romantic roots of Horkheimer and Adorno's critique of enlightenment. By assimilating antiquity to modernity, and modernity to domination, their negative idea of progress robs them of any counter-balancing or constructive conception of civilization.

At the same time as Horkheimer and Adorno unmask enlightenment ideas as dangerous myths, they appeal to romantic dreams of reconciliation with a nature that is at once innocent, archaic and redemptive. It is this romantic myth that allows them to picture the history of technology as the self-traumatizing drive of human beings to dominate nature. *Dialectic of Enlightenment* depicts the relentless power of progress that is one with the progress of power. Human beings adapt themselves to ever more commanding powers that demand self-sacrifice in the name of self-preservation. Progress is achieved, not as dream but as nightmare. It is a black vision but no less 'all consuming' for this. There is no escape from progress, no point outside of it.

Horkheimer and Adorno's reading of history as an ever-accelerating spiral of calculation and abstraction, sacrifice and resignation is the perfect expressionist trope of love-to-loathe the machine. Their bleak indictment of progress betrays their fascination. In this manner, Horkheimer and Adorno reproduce what we call, in this book, 'the divided unity of modernism'. This is the attraction of the two poles that beguile modern personalities – attraction to the romantic critique of modern society on the one hand and attraction to futurist technology and progressive techniques on the other hand. We are sceptical about both these poles of attraction.

We argue that both romanticism and enlightenment have proved fatal genies in modernity. Romanticism's redemptive myths celebrating original genius and archaic origins, aesthetic politics and aesthetic gods provide justification for retrograde totalitarian fantasies. Equally, aesthetic progress, like industrial progress, encourages fantasies of a 'rational society' marching joylessly to the tune of the master technologist. Progress, not least an avant-garde progress left to its own devices, stands for an image of the future that breaks decisively with human continuity. It is contemptuous of the durability and transmitted qualities of civilization. In contrast, romanticism offers an image of the future in which the future is a creation anew of a mythical past of organic harmony, aesthetic gods, heroes and geniuses. Both the romantic future and the progressive future are unbearable. Both are enormously influential in modernity. Both are frequently at war with each other. Both participate in equal measure in the constitution of modernity and modernism.

This is our fundamental proposition: European modernism – the two hundred years from 1750 to 1950, more exactly the long nineteenth century from the French Revolution to the 'German Revolution' of the Nazis – was co-constituted by romanticism and enlightenment. Much of the *Dialectic of Romanticism* is concerned with arguing against the notion that modernism is simply a movement of enlightenment or that it is simply a movement of romanticism. Both are part and parcel of modernism.

Our critique of modernism takes account of but does not share the late twentieth-century postmodernist mood of cultural and critical theory. If the great merit of postmodernist revisionism is that it helped to dissolve the unthinking equation of modernism and modernity, its great weakness is that it has all too easily seen itself as outside or beyond modernity, while it is in fact another of modernity's modernisms. Its historicist self-understanding indicates its multiple entanglements with basic assumptions of modernism. Postmodernism's equation of modernism with the grand narratives of enlightenment progress and emancipation, and of modernity with the dialectic of enlightenment is unconvincing. Postmodernism represents the continuation of a largely unquestioned romantic critique of the modern world. Our critique of modernism is thus also a critique of a postmodernism which has lost the sense of the internal tensions and contradictions of European modernism at the same time as it silently appropriates and dubs postmodern a romantic discontent with disenchanted modernity.

Historically this discontent found its sharpest and most sustained articulation in Germany. Just as the philosophical and aesthetic discourse of the whole modernist epoch was in large measure defined and determined by German thinkers,[1] so German romanticism can lay claim to being the fundamental romanticism.[2] For the same reason Heidegger and Adorno figure prominently as recurrent points of reference in our argument. They are the inheritors (along with such thinkers as George Lukács, Ernst Bloch and Walter Benjamin) of the German romantic tradition. They radicalized this tradition and its negative vision of modernity into totalizing, not to say totalitarian, critiques of Western civilization. These critiques of logocentric reason and of technology, complemented by the appeal to nature and art as the redemptive other of domination, made them godfathers of postmodernism.

The German source of modernism and postmodernism is the primary focus of our enquiry. This enquiry takes us from central Europe to the United States. Between the poles of German romanticism and American postmodernism lies the flight across the Atlantic of German and Austrian artists, architects and intellectuals from National Socialism. This forced migration marked a sea change in European modernism. California sharpened the critical gaze of European theorists for the dystopian but also utopian potentials of the alliance between technology and nature. Conversely, translation to the New World prompted leading pupils of Heidegger, notably Hannah Arendt and Leo Strauss, to return to antiquity to recover – against the master – the idea of a perennial modernity, distinct from any historicist versions of modernism – or postmodernism.

The distinction between enlightened, romantic and classical modernisms and their antagonistic conceptions of modernity is integral to our argument. Modernity as such can be defined most succinctly as the consequence of the historical break that Bruno Latour terms the 'Modern Constitution'. This break results from the separation of society and nature, subjects and things. In depriving society of its divine origins, and nature of its divine presence, 'the Crossed-out God' set in train the paradoxes of a nature and society that we comprehend as an immanent construction and at the same time as something that transcends us infinitely.[3] These paradoxes of nature and society, transcendence and immanence, permeate the dialectics of enlightenment and romanticism. Our third – classical – modernism functions here in a double guise. It stands on the one hand for a regulative idea of the city and civilization. It offers a vantage point and perspective outside and opposed to modern historicisms. At the same time, it denotes a stream within aesthetic modernism, represented most signally by the constant reinventions and renewals of tradition that characterize the lifework of Picasso and Stravinsky.

Classical modernism thus offers a standpoint outside of the warring poles of romanticism and progress from which one can tell the story of modernism. This 'third stream' does not have a neat, simple name like romantic or progressive. We sometimes call this the 'civilizing' stream. We do so simply because the image of 'the city', the *urbs* or the *civitas*, is a key part of its symbolic make-up. Unlike either progress or romanticism, the third stream is continuous with the past – in its modernity, it self-consciously re-creates and re-utilizes and renews aspects and forms of the Greek-Roman-Latin-Renaissance past. This is sometimes characterized as 'neo-classical', although such terminology can be confusing when romantics and progressives each have their own versions of relations with antiquity. The romantics find in antiquity inspiration for the idea of archaic genius and mythical powers, while progressives admire its revolutions in engineering and communications and political technologies (and forever curse its failure to industrialize the labour power of the slave).

The third stream that we talk about does not interpret modernity as the creation of society anew in the name of the most advanced techniques or the most potent archaic fantasy. It does not seek re-creation in order to better dominate nature or to resurrect a fallen nature. The third stream does not see human emancipation as due to the fulfilment of the desideratum of either technology or mythology. The 'civilizing' stream is simultaneously purposively modern and classically inspired, metropolitan and cosmopolitan, and presents itself as a counter to organic and aesthetic romanticism, and to enlightened models of progress and futurism.

The third stream emerges out of the culture wars of modernism and into self-consciousness, roughly speaking, in the 1950s. We see how a cohort of figures such as Mies van der Rohe, Hannah Arendt, Leo Strauss, and Igor Stravinsky – all of them in exile in America – distanced themselves from romanticism and progressivism. In their different ways, they postulate an image of nature, self and society that is neither progressive nor romantic, but draws on a fusion of classical rationalism and modern dynamics. In their work, architectonic qualities – such as form, structure, rhythm, proportionality, constitutionalism, balance of powers, geometric nature and so on – replace romantic genesis and innovative technique as core intellectual concerns.

The mature Stravinsky offers a case in point of what we mean. He distanced himself from the youthful radical-cum-archaic 'rite of spring' but he did not accept the notion that Arnold Schoenberg's serialism was an advanced technique of aesthetic production superior to all other techniques, as alphabetical writing is superior to the pictogram. This view damned Stravinsky in the eyes of Adorno. From the 1920s on, the mature Stravinsky embraced neither romantic reconciliation with archaic nature nor the progressive history of artistic technique. Indeed, he viewed the serialism that Adorno espoused not as a superior artistic technology but as simply another musical form, one civilizing form among many, which would never die out like a technological fossil, and yet which he never pretended was anything but the work of human artifice and human ingenuity of a very high order. Stravinsky was happy to re-create and renew, and inventively construct, all kinds of musical forms. His modernism was the mastery of form and of architectonic ordering. Adorno charged that this modernism was retrograde – a bad rhythmic-spatial modernism, as opposed to a good expressive-dynamic modernism. Stravinsky lost no sleep over the matter. He knew that the warring twins of romantic expressivism and technological dynamism were not the sole constituents of modernity, and that Adorno's clever synthesis of them was not the last word on the nature of modernism.

In the spirit of Stravinsky, *Dialectic of Romanticism* proposes a threefold critical revision of modernism. Its critique is internal, external and retrospective. Part One – *Mytho-Logics of Modernity* – traces, through the German discourse of aesthetic modernism an unfolding mytho-logic of romanticism from Schelling to Adorno, and from Hölderlin to Heidegger via Wagner and Nietzsche. Central to this romanticism is the redemptive vision of the archaic

Greek polis as *Gesamtkunstwerk*. Part Two – *Modernism and Civilization* – introduces the counter-vision of the city as metropolis and cosmopolis. Bridging antiquity and modernity, the city offers an (Archimedean) point from which to weigh and interrogate the claims of enlightenment and romanticism. As a trans-historical model and an 'architectonic' fashioning, the city is the carrier and repository of a philosophical conception of nature, art and social life that is distinct from enlightenment functionalism and romantic revivalism, and opens a perspective onto an alternative modernism. The city embodies the 'classical' idea of nature – nature as artifice – as against the mechanicism of progress and the organicism of romanticism. Part Three – *Modernity's Utopias* – sets the architectonic utopia of 'classical' modernism against the aesthetic utopias of enlightenment and romantic modernisms. Aesthetic modernism is revisited in the light of the crucial but neglected distinction between the idea of the 'avant-garde' and the idea of the 'total work of art' to pose the question of the future of modernism. We note how already in Wagner's idea of the total work of art there is a fusion of romanticism and progress – the interlocking of mythic drama with an appetite for the development of the aesthetic means of production. We suggest that, when translated from Europe to America, this fusion is massively compounded, and the multiple dialectics of modernity enter into new relationships bringing about a reduction of the antagonism between enlightenment and romanticism, mechanicism and organism, and the beginning of a new phase of modernity.

Part One
Mytho-Logics of Modernity

Introduction: The Retreat and Return of the Origin

If the enlightenment defines itself through the break with tradition, romanticism draws its self-understanding from the quest to recover a living relation to tradition. As the critique and counter-movement to the project of modernity as conceived by the enlightenment, romanticism opposes to the *denaturalization* of man the call for his *renaturalization*. Robert Legros's reconstruction of the romantic idea of humanity[1] is governed by this opposition, which points to what may be called the original paradox of romanticism. On the one hand there can be no return to the closure of tradition from which we are separated by disenchantment, by the withdrawal of spirit from the world, leaving only intimations of its lost presence and the lost origin. On the other hand, how can there be a renaturalization that is not instituted as closure,[2] a renaturalization that formulates its paradoxical task as that of an original repetition? The origins of romanticism lie in this quest for the sources of originality, which we want to approach through Legros's reading of the romantic idea of humanity.[3]

For the enlightenment man is the maker of his own humanity. His task is to free himself from the closure of all historical naturalizations, rooted in the particularism of tradition. The emancipation from tutelage, the passage from nature to freedom (Kant) raises autonomy to the supreme norm, to be realized through the refusal of external authority and the self-critical use of reason. The traditional confusion of the 'natural' and the human order of things in particularism stands in the way of the recognition of the idea of universal humanity, which can only be understood as an open-ended project since the idea of autonomy exceeds all determinations and calls for the cease-

3

less critique of all forms of renaturalization. The criticism of religion, morality, law, history, economics and politics is thus the condition of the advance of knowledge and progress to a better, more civilized and more rational society, based on the universal rights of man.[4]

The romantic idea of man by contrast springs from the sense of our irreducible embeddedness in a particular humanity.[5] This sense of embeddedness as the key to the truly human rejects the empty autonomy of the enlightenment subject, the subject of transparent consciousness and will. Against the primacy of the cognitive and instrumental faculties romanticism privileges sensibility, free of the domination of reason. The romantic comprehension of sensibility, which gives expression to tradition, culture and epoch, is that of a sensibility penetrated by spirit, for which the sensible and the intelligible are one. This sense of the living unity of the sensible and the non-sensible represents a radical subversion of the dualism of western thought because it rejoins what Platonic metaphysics and modern subjectivity have split apart: body and soul, matter and spirit, the one and the multiple, the eternal and the temporal, the divine and the human, the infinite and the finite. The universal is thus realized in and through particularity; its image is the symbol, its essence the synthesizing powers of the productive imagination, romanticism's answer to the analytic powers of reason.[6]

From the enlightenment's abstraction of man from all particular contexts flows the romantic critique of the metaphysics of subjectivity. The romantics criticized the idea of man as self-determining subject and the corresponding project of founding a new society of autonomous individuals. The failure to recognize that man and society are products of history results in what Adam Müller, in the wake of Burke, identified in his *Elemente der Staatskunst* (1809) as the three prejudices of the enlightenment: that the individual can create his society, that we can extract ourselves from history and treat it as a political experiment, that politics is a means in the service of individual interests.[7] This abstract humanism finds its complement in a dualistic epistemology, which places the observer outside of the world and reduces the sensible to indifferent matter and the non-sensible to pure intelligibility. Not only is the natural world cut off from its given meaning but also from the human-historical world. The purely rational and technical attitude reduces human institutions – language, law, religion, politics and art – to a question of their function. Such a reconstruction defines meaning in terms of means and ends.

In asking how romanticism can reverse the denaturalization of the world – how, in other words, naturalization can be conceived as original – Legros poses the question of what is specifically modern in the romantic counterimaginary to the project of enlightenment. His answer is that naturalization acquires a new meaning with the romantics. The second nature of particularization is in fact primary in relation to human nature and is to be thought of as the origin and not the alienation of man's humanity. Given that the universal can only realize itself in the particular, it defines romanticism's holism as the incarnation of the universal in the particular. The romantic conception of life as the union of body and soul thus underlies the principle of particularization, embodied in the spirit of a people, its history, customs and traditions, which alone give meaning to the individual. Only through the acquisition of a particular language does man accede to his universal humanity.

The meaning of creation accordingly is to be sought not in innovation but in giving expression to the spirit at work in nature and history. Once communion with the living spirit is broken, tradition dies and nature becomes disenchanted. Creation is thus centred in the romantic idea of life, the mystery of incarnation, which spiritualizes nature and naturalizes history and defines originality as contact with the animating spirit that is both transcendent and immanent. Nature speaks to us because it is an original revelation, the manifestation of the infinite in the finite, of the invisible at the heart of the visible. The romantic ideas of religion (Schleiermacher) and of art (Schelling) converge in this intuition of the infinite in the finite.[8] The romantic exaltation of subjectivity, evident above all in the cult of genius, thus stands at the opposite pole to the enlightenment's conception of the subject as foundation. Subjectivity is inscribed in a natural and historical world that transcends it. It is in this sense a consciousness traversed by the unconscious, such that the creativity of the genius is to be understood not as autonomous subjectivity but as nature in the subject, that is to say, as the privileged medium of that which exceeds the intellect and concepts.

But again we must ask with Legros: where does originality come from in a disenchanted world, what is originality if it expresses the longing to recover a lost tradition? Both romanticism and enlightenment are separated from the premodern closure of tradition. And this means that the call for renaturalization contains the seed of its own dialectic. If renaturalization is not to be instituted as closure, its opening to the world must also include an opening to the enlightenment. This means the recognition that naturalization and denaturalization are both products of history and in this sense equally original.[9] Here, however, we must register a reciprocal failure of dialogue. Two imaginaries, two concepts of origin and foundation confront each other across the great divide of the French Revolution. Nowhere is this division of modernity, this crisis of foundation registered more acutely than in Germany. The very question of a dismembered Germany's existence, its political unity and cultural identity, was at stake.[10] The intellectual hegemony of French civilization, reinforced by the imperialism of the revolutionary nation-state, overdetermined the critique of a soulless, mechanical enlightenment and the appeal to organic particularism against abstract universalism. If for Georges Gusdorf or Isaiah Berlin German romanticism is the fundamental romanticism,[11] it is not least because the critical reaction to the dominant western model of enlightenment was closely linked to the search for an alternate redemptive vision of modernity, through which an as yet unborn Germany would attain its essential destiny as the heartland of Europe.

Here too the paradox of romanticism, more exactly the paradox of romantic historicism, appears. Like the enlightenment, romanticism is informed and carried by a reflexive historical consciousness born of the break with the closure of tradition. The quest for renaturalization is that of a historicism divided against itself; it discovers on the one hand the organic originality of particularism, while calling on the other for the recovery of the lost origin. Romantic historicism[12] is haunted by this sense of presence and absence, which is reflected in the distinction between *organic* and *aesthetic* historicism. Herder is the father of organic historicism.[13] Organic historicism grasps the second nature of naturalization as the living spirit of a people that informs all its institutions. The collective creations of community, custom and tradition form the natural unity of historical life. Organic historicism comprehends history as nature, as natural development. Its doctrine of development and decline expresses an original vitalism, later challenged by Nietzsche's more radical concept of life and of history in the service of life.

The vitalist current, which defines the code of organic historicism in terms of living and dead spirit, leads to the fatal opposition of life and mind in life philosophy and cultural pessimism, and to a correspondingly radicalized 'naturalization' of history, culture and society. Nietzsche's call for cultural renewal places him at the same time in the line of aesthetic historicism, which grasps origin, foundation and creation more originally, more profoundly as the very spirit of the living spirit. That is to say, it grasps it in terms not of a naturalization of history but of a spiritualization of nature, whose highest manifestation is the creative imagination. Myth, as realized in the collective genius of a people, and art, as the product of the individual genius, express the essential relation between nature and history because they spring from a common source, the productivity of *natura naturans*. Aesthetic historicism represents a higher potency of organic historicism. Against the natural products of development (language, tradition, community, historical institutions), it sets the productivity of nature itself, figured in the aesthetic act of creation. This programme of renaturalization is summed up by the invocation of a *new mythology*, to be brought to life by the polytheism of the imagination. A new mythology promised the reunion of nature and spirit.

Organic and aesthetic historicism both respond to the *querelle des anciens et modernes*. For all its privileging of the childhood of the human race, organic historicism defuses the *querelle* through its recognition of the unique individuality of peoples and cultures. Aesthetic historicism by contrast seeks to sublate the *querelle* in an aesthetic comprehension of modernity, predicated not on the neo-classicizing 'imitation of the moderns' but on the original and hence redemptive repetition of the Greek origin.[14] In returning to Greece as the 'constitutive Other' of national identity,[15] the new mythology reinforces the dilemma of a historicist consciousness, confronted by what Foucault speaking of the modern order of knowledge calls 'the retreat and return of the origin': 'in setting itself the task of restoring the domain of the original, modern thought immediately encounters the recession of the origin'.[16]

What Foucault is describing here is the inescapable effect of the transition in the course of the eighteenth century from a transcendent to an immanent conception of origin, the transition from created to self-creating nature, and correspondingly from an instituted to a self-instituting society. Out of this transition, out of the death of the transcendent God, there emerges the modern world, which – whatever else it is – is born with and from historicist consciousness and is forced to grapple with the conundrum of self-origin: 'It is no longer origin that gives rise to historicity, it is historicity that, in its very fabric, makes possible the necessity of an origin which must be both internal and foreign to it.'[17] The paradox of the origin, which is both internal and alien, spells out the consequences of the death of God. The internalization of the externalized origin means that henceforth origin can only be thought as paradox, whose recurrent figure is the circle. The romantic thinking of origin from Herder to Heidegger circles around the mystery of *divine immanence*, the *circulus vitiosus deus* (Nietzsche). To quote Foucault again: 'European culture is inventing for itself a depth in which what matters is no longer identities ... but great hidden forces developed on the basis of their primitive and inaccessible nucleus, origin, causality and history. From now on things will be represented only from the depths of this density withdrawn into itself.'[18] Origin is to be comprehended as the manifestation of the deep, inaccessible forces of being, the being whose mode of being is historicity. The god of the philosophers has been transformed into the living god of History, the coming and becoming God, the Dionysus of romantic mythology, mythic embodiment of the forces of self-creation. If the owl of Minerva announces the twilight of European culture, the night of the departed gods conceals a coming dawn. To Hegel's completion of the circle of history in the self-recollection of Absolute Spirit, Heidegger opposes the call for a more original repetition of the Greek beginning, the *ricorso*, the re-volution of time, which brings back the past as future possibility and makes the future past of repetition the paradoxical chiffre of the retreat and return of the origin.

The paradox of future past origin defines German romanticism from the beginning. Its founding gesture – the idea of a new mythology – embraces the circle of origin and repetition in the quest for re-foundation against the revolutionary rupture of modernity. Re-foundation stands under the sign of retreat and return: the thinking of modernity as the loss of the divine and loss of community is drawn irresistibly to the image of the original community, the organic totality of Greek culture and its mythical self-representation. The appeal of mythic origins masks, however, the origin of 'myth'. Like the idea of community, mythology is a modern invention, or more exactly, a modern re-invention: the lost community and the lost function of myth come together in the romantic project of a new mythology. Since this project is not only pre- but also post-enlightenment, it presents itself from the beginning as a mythology of mythology, as the very schema of the circle of creation, in which community and myth appear as mutually engendering. Just as myth's founding purpose lies in articulating the relation between nature and history, the divine and the human, so romanticism seeks to renaturalize man by re-embedding him in a natural-historical world prior to the modern illusions of a self-grounding subjectivity.

Foucault's circle marks the return of time in a double sense; the return to the native ground of finitude negates the time of progress and re-inscribes history within nature and nature within history. This idea of natural history, which binds the *telos* of history to the retreat and return of the origin, is central to the imaginary of romanticism. The Christian myth of paradise, fall and redemption returns in secularized form to appropriate the historical space vacated by the withdrawal of the divine.[19] The search for a transcendence immanent to history and its ground in nature has its roots in Herder's organic historicism. From it comes romantic nationalism, the religion of the people, comprehended in terms of its natural origin – the divinity expressed in the living spirit of a national-popular culture, its language, customs and institutions. The organic cycle of natural history cannot escape, however, the recession of the origin. What Herder, the father of the 'German movement', began Spengler completes.[20] Nineteenth-century historicism is haunted by the spectre of the decadence and decline of culture, but where organic or religious romanticism clings to the origins, to the old mythology, aesthetic romanticism seeks to captures the presence and the absence of the gods – their withdrawal and immanence – in the idea of a new mythology. This mythology's redemptive re-volution will bring the succession of time to completion in a new higher synthesis of nature and history, that is, a synthesis of the ancients and the moderns (Schelling). The radical historicism of the romantic mythology of mythology already points, however, to a third more comprehensive vision of the retreat and the return of the origin. This vision combines organic and aesthetic historicism in what we may call a meta-historicism, inspired by Heraclitus's world game, played by the god of time.[21] This onto-poetics of history conceives of the world as a work of art giving birth to itself. It seeks to grasp the originary as such, oscillating between the quietism of organic historicism and the voluntarism of aesthetic creation. Nietzsche's *amor fati* and Heidegger's *Ereignis* share this ambiguity of attentisme and activism.

Metaphors of creativity play a leading role in German thought from Herder to Nietzsche.[22] Whether it be expression (Herder), production (Schelling, Marx), revolution (Marx, Wagner) or life (Schopenhauer, Nietzsche), they all revolve around the relation between nature and history, the unconscious and the conscious, the instituting and the instituted. For the romantics the circle of creation lies at the very centre of the mythology of historicism. But original creation carries with it, as we have seen, opposed meanings of origin. Jean-Luc Nancy can thus define romanticism as the scene of the invention of the founding myth and as the simultaneous awareness of the loss of this power.[23] If the work of art alone can adequately present and re-present the poetic-religious re-foundation of modernity – the birth, the origin of the community from its myth – such a re-foundation stands under the imperative of original imitation. The quest for the aesthetic state[24] – from Schiller to Heidegger – articulates the retreat and return of the origin in terms of Germany's Greek mission. The tyranny of Greece[25] over a Germany in search of its future past identity would be better understood, however, as a tyranny in reverse, which makes Greece the screen onto which Germany projects its own historical-political dilemmas. The more original dionysian Greece, discovered by romanticism, breaks with the classicizing imitation of antiquity to affirm

Germany's own original aesthetic-cultural self-understanding as a nation without a state against the western political model of modernity.

In rejecting the modern imitation of the Roman imitation of the Greeks and all that it entails – renaissance, humanism, classicism, rationalism and civilization – Germany announces its double agon with the ancients and the moderns. The task is this: to transform national belatedness into the overcoming of a modernity, which has not yet been attained, through an act of self-creation, which can be figured only as an original imitation. This programme of 'national aestheticism'[26] translates the contradictions of a divided, unborn Germany, the theoretical but not the practical contemporary of the West (Marx), back into the original contradiction of the new mythology. The return of the origin re-inscribes its recession: community in search of its lost myth, myth in search of its lost community. The very desire to fathom the mystery of origin, to gain conscious access to the unconscious sources of creativity, leads Wagner to declare that the highest achievement of the poet lies in the invention of new myths. Such creativity contains its own dialectic, which remains to be disengaged from the dominant logic of enlightenment.

The disenchantment of romantic nature is already evident in its reversal into Schopenhauer's blind Will. This reversal lays bare the negative implications of the romantic appeal to nature and art. Odo Marquard articulates the regressive consequences of Schelling's philosophy of nature, when he reads transcendental idealism as opening the way to the empowering of extra-rational and extra-historical, natural forces.[27] The turn to natural forces abandons history to the other of reason and evades the political through the turn to aesthetics and mythology. The empowering of the extra-rational brings with it the empowering of the sublime, the experience of history as nature. The sublime offers perhaps the ultimate figure of the retreat and return of the origin. It surges forth from the void left by the withdrawal of the divine and testifies to the abyss of foundation and the 'dark ground' (Schelling) of being. In Wagner's *Ring*, redemptive nature collapses into the fundamental ambiguity of natural history. The romantic invocation of a mythology of reason reverses with Nietzsche into the return of tragic myth that destroys the illusions of enlightenment.

If the 'dark ground' of existence ungrounds the sovereign reason of the enlightenment, it signifies at the same time the abyss of being, history and psyche. The romantic circle of origin, which is meant to resolve all contradictions of thought, also contains its identical Other – a vicious circle within the virtuous circle of return. The circle functions indifferently as the figure of infinite resolution and of bad infinity. It is the symbol of completed history and of the fatal repetition of the ever same. This figure of the convergence of progress and regress points to the mythical closure within which the thinking of historicism revolves and which it cannot escape. The mytho-logics of modernity give rise not only to a dialectic of enlightenment but also a dialectic of romanticism.

1 The Idea of Natural History

The entwinement of myth and enlightenment is the theme of Horkheimer and Adorno's *Dialectic of Enlightenment*. Viewed through the perspective of enlightenment, myth is transformed into allegory. *Dialectic of Enlightenment* presents the melancholy allegory of the 'original history of subjectivity': the journey of the prototypical subject through the world of myth towards self-consciousness and identity. *The Odyssey* recounts the mythical story of the exit from myth. At its centre is Odysseus's encounter with the Sirens. Horkheimer and Adorno call this encounter the 'anticipatory allegory of the dialectic of enlightenment'. Odysseus, the prototype of modern man, is cut off from the past – the song of the Sirens – by the fear of regression. The sacrifice of the past to the future sets in train a progression which will reveal itself as blind progression without progress, driven by the separation from nature – the forgetting of nature in the self – whose trace is preserved solely in art's echo of the song of the Sirens. Art thus functions as the impotent promise of the fulfilled moment – the moment of present experience that will reconnect past, present and future.[1] From this 'separation from nature' springs time – time as temporal succession. It is the empty, homogeneous time of progress.

Heidegger's *Being and Time* sets out to destroy the metaphysical, scientific and vulgar conception of time as a temporal succession of present instances, which divide lifetime into past, present and future. This is the time of *Historie* (the history of historiography) to which he opposes, as its true ground and origin, the historicity of *Dasein*, lived and living time. The analysis of *Dasein* uncovers the transcendental horizon of temporality, made up of the three temporal ecstasies, which, by setting us outside of chronological time, reveal the fundamental unity of past, present and future. Heidegger reverses the vulgar perspective of progress. The essence of *Dasein*'s temporality is repetition. The human condition is future-oriented because it is being unto death. The future, that is, our future possibility, comes to meet us as a coming back of our past, that is, our past possibilities. The unity of the three dimensions of temporality is disclosed by decision, resoluteness in the face of death. Resoluteness unto death accepts and assumes the thrownness of human being into finitude. It transforms inauthentic existence, divided between past, present and future, into authentic fate.

The resoluteness of decision is conceived purely formally. Its disclosure of the original temporality and historicity of *Dasein* points the way, however, to a conception of history open to political appropriation. Individual fate (*Schicksal*) coexists with the general or collective fate (*Geschick*) of its 'generation', which is that of the community or the people (*Volk*).[2] This formal structure of decision in *Being and Time* is filled with historical content in 1933 by Heidegger's decision for National Socialism and the German Revolution.[3] We cannot understand Heidegger's fateful leap, however, without reference to the formal structure elucidated in *Being and Time*. Two points need to be stressed. First, only 'future past' *Dasein* can accede to presence, that is, to the presence of the here and now, the *Da* of the authentic moment (*Augenblick*), through which *Dasein* becomes present for 'its time'.[4] This time strikes for Heidegger and for the German people in 1933. Second, this moment of fate is the moment of repetition, defined by Heidegger in his 'Rectoral Speech' (1933) as the challenge to Germany to repeat the Greek origin of the history of the Occident. Let us say, somewhat facetiously, that Heidegger has heard the song of the Sirens. By this we mean that decision has found its historical hour – the decision through which past, present and future are to be reunited. This essential time of history comprises on the one hand the eschatological time of the first and last things, and on the other hand, the mythical time of repetition.

In contrast, Adorno and Horkheimer's origin of history is inaccessible, repressed. Human history is to be understood as the history of this original repression, which unconsciously perpetuates the blind power of nature. We can escape the compulsion to repetition – the eternal return of the repressed – only by remembering the origin. Only by liberating ourselves from the forgetting of nature in the subject can we escape the blindness and violence of enlightenment. Heidegger's origin inaugurates by contrast the space-time of history. As opposed to Horkheimer and Adorno, the Greek beginning remains incomparable for Heidegger because it constitutes the original opening of Being, the 'birth to presence' that manifests the mystery of creation, the mystery of the origin. History does not develop from inconspicuous beginnings. On the contrary, all greatness belongs to the beginning and all that follows is decline. Heidegger therefore insists that the authentic greatness of historical knowledge lies in the understanding of the mystery of the beginning, and that the knowledge of original history (*Ur-Geschichte*) is the province not of science but of mythology.[5]

Horkheimer and Adorno and Heidegger give us two opposed versions of origin, repetition and fate. In the one, inaccessible origin operates behind our backs to turn enlightenment into ever-repeated mythical fate. In the other, origin is the past that comes to meet us as fate, i.e. the destiny we assume in repetition. The loss of the origin is called (by Horkheimer and Adorno) the forgetting of nature in the subject and (by Heidegger) the forgetting of Being. Thus for all their differences they are repeating the same romantic story, the story of the Fall, that Rousseau made the founding myth of romanticism. The original myth of paradise, fall and redemption returns through an exchange of terms: the fall from nature into history points to the redeeming reunion of nature and history, myth and enlightenment. The founding text of German romanticism, the fragment called 'The Oldest Systematic Programme of German Idealism' (1797) – written by Hegel but the co-product of Hegel, Hölderlin and Schelling – envisages the coming synthesis of nature and history in the form of a mythology of reason, the new religion that will be the last and greatest deed of humankind.[6]

The negative counterpart to this mythology of reason is the dialectic of enlightenment, unfolded in Horkheimer and Adorno's history of the West and in Heidegger's history of Being – two mythical histories, which recount the catastrophic consequences of the forgetting of the origin in terms which are well known: the domination of nature, the devastation of the earth, the will to power and nihilism. Accordingly, it is a matter of indifference whether we speak with Horkheimer and Adorno of the destruction of history by nature or with Heidegger of the destruction of nature by history. In each case the vanishing point of judgement is provided by what Adorno in his Lecture of 1932 calls 'The Idea of Natural History'.[7] 'Natural history' certainly translates 'Naturgeschichte', but it conveys none of the resonances and complexities of the original, which expresses in the most concentrated form the question of history – the relation between nature and history – central to German thought since Herder and Kant. In the symmetry of its co-equivalence, *Naturgeschichte* can be read in three ways: nature as history, history as nature and the synthesis of both, just as each of its terms, in and by virtue of their division, is open to a triadic reading: original, fallen and resurrected nature, mirrored in original, fallen and redeemed history. The resurrection of nature and the redemption of history – *Naturgeschichte* in its full meaning – constitute the mythical other to the allegory of the dialectic of enlightenment.

The German romantic critique of the enlightenment culminates in Horkheimer and Adorno but also in Heidegger. Here we observe close, if antagonistic, parallels. The germ of *Dialectic of Enlightenment* and the defining theme of Critical Theory are formulated in Adorno's 1932 Lecture. The idea of natural history developed there is expressly conceived as a response to Heidegger's idea of historicity in *Sein und Zeit*. The parallels are even closer after 1945. Adorno and Heidegger's histories of the West end in the quietism of negative theology. If Heidegger declares that only a god can save us, Adorno rests his case with Beckett's endgame, *Waiting for Godot*.

In 'The Idea of Natural History' Adorno defines the task of philosophy as the overcoming of the division of the world into nature and history (spirit).

He welcomes Heidegger's ontological turn in *Sein und Zeit*: i.e. the bringing together of ontology and historicity in a fundamental ontology of *Dasein* which reveals the basic ontological structure of history. The price, however, which vitiates Heidegger's solution to the reconciliation of nature and history, and makes it merely an apparent solution, is the reduction of history to the structure of Heidegger's ontology. Ontology alone is insufficient. What is required is a further step: the ontological reorientation of philosophy of history, which Adorno develops from Lukács's *Theory of the Novel* (1919) and Benjamin's *Origin of German Tragic Drama* (1922). Lukács grasps history as nature: the reified world of social convention is a frozen second nature, which awaits resurrection. Benjamin conversely grasps nature as history: 'The word "history" stands written on the countenance of nature in the characters of transience.'[8] The sign language of transience, in which nature and history converge, is the language of allegory. Natural history signifies the interweaving of natural and historical being in the second nature of the social, whose 'death's head' is the emblem of allegory. Philosophy's task can now be understood as allegorical: the awakening and resurrection of the petrified world through allegorical interpretation, which lays bare the identity of first and second nature, rooted in original history. Natural or original history overcomes the idealist division of the world, in which nature is understood as self-alienated spirit (Hegel), by means of a materialist concept of spirit as self-alienated nature.[9]

Philosophy's task is thus dialectical. It must demonstrate that concrete history partakes of nature, and that nature is historical, by deconstructing the antithesis between nature and history. Adorno's starting point is the definition of nature as mythical, i.e. the fateful predetermined being underlying history, and of history as the qualitatively new. In the archaic-mythical and the historically new we recognize the two key terms of *Dialectic of Enlightenment* – myth and enlightenment. Read dialectically, the archaic-mythical reveals its inherent dynamic, which Adorno elucidates through the strife of the old and the new gods in (Greek) tragedy: 'tragic myths contain at one and the same time subjection to guilt and nature and the element of reconciliation that transcends the realm of nature'.[10] Conversely, the historically new belongs inescapably to the mythical, since the second nature of the social as illusion or semblance (*Schein*) carries with it the (ideological) illusion of a meaning beyond the allegorical.

Adorno's ontological transformation of philosophy of history into the idea of dialectical nature substitutes for idealism's division of the world a materialism which appeals to concrete history against the tautologies of Heidegger's ontology. But if the petrified world of 'second nature is, in truth, first nature',[11] this first nature is in fact already a double nature. First nature comprises both the historicity and facticity of transience and the promise of reconciliation, just as history is constructed in the light of this double image. Adorno's 'Idea of Natural History' thus represents the vanishing point of philosophy of history, the last stage of the search for a synthesis of nature and history in response to the ratification of their division by Kant, a search which runs from Schiller and Schelling to Hegel and Marx, and whose characteristic tendency – the humanization of nature and the naturalization of history – appears most clearly in Schelling, is echoed in the young Marx and renewed in Ernst Bloch's philosophy and eschatology of nature.[12] The 'resurrection of nature', which will redeem history from the mythical cycle of the compulsion to repetition, replaces the original Kantian division by a 'dialectical' doubling of nature and history, underpinned by Marx's distinction between the realm of necessity and the realm of freedom, prehistory and history. Marx's distinction brings out clearly the double concept of *Naturgeschichte*. On the one hand, we have the romantic-utopian project of the young Marx; on the other, especially after 1848, the scientific-materialist insistence on the economic laws of motion of modern society.

Ludger Heidbrink distinguishes four meanings of natural history in Marx. First, man's metabolism with nature, which transforms nature as raw material into the second nature of human self-objectivation, thereby unfolding the progressive humanization of nature and naturalization of man. Second, its negative counterpart: the blind development of modern society in thrall to capitalism. To this opposition corresponds after the failed revolutions of 1848 the liberation of humanity through the science of history, which in turn can be seen as the scientific reduction of history to natural history.[13] From the beginning to the end of the tradition of a dialectical philosophy of history in German thought – from Schiller's *Naive and Sentimental Poetry* and the *Letters on the Aesthetic Education of Man* through to Marcuse's *Essay on Liberation* and Adorno's *Aesthetic Theory* – nature must function in this double guise. It is here that we can locate the origin of the 'performative contradiction'[14] of *Dialectic of Enlightenment*. When Horkheimer and Adorno state: nature is 'neither good, as the old, nor noble, as the new romanticism believes. As model and goal, it signifies anti-spirit, lie and bestiality, only as recognized does it become the impulse of existence to peace',[15] history appears in the light of a nature that is divided, like reason, into the negative and the normative, moreover, in such a fashion that nature is called upon to rescue us from nature. Threatening nature produces civilization just as civilization reproduces threatening nature. Adorno and Horkheimer complete the whole idea of a dialectic of enlightenment in a short circuit of the dialectic of nature and history, above which floats the song of the Sirens, the echo of the realm of the non-identical, the call of unreconciled nature.

If the idea of natural history is central to the German idea of history, it is not least because of Kant's dual legacy. On the one hand, his division between pure and practical reason, nature and freedom, sums up enlightenment thought and defines the problem and the challenge to post-Kantian philosophy. On the other hand, his third Critique, in seeking to bridge the gap between nature and freedom, becomes both the bridge and the break between enlightenment and romanticism. The outcome of Kant's dual legacy is a fourfold conception of nature: 1. nature as the object of possible experience, the object of science; 2. teleological nature, i.e. nature as the organism which exceeds the capacity of the understanding, to which we must add nature in its two natural-aesthetic manifestations; 3. beautiful nature, i.e. the beauty of living form; and 4. sublime, destructive nature. The philosophy of nature and the philosophy of art, developed in Kant's *Critique of Judgement*, converge in an aesthetic vision of the organic to give what Odo Marquard calls 'romantic nature'.

Marquard proposes an illuminating distinction between three conceptions of nature central to modernity: *controlled nature* is nature as understood by enlightenment science; *romantic nature* is the aesthetic-creative nature of romanticism; *drive nature* stands for the Hobbesian civil war of all against all, that is to say, the natural history uncovered by the death of god in the modern period, prefigured in the English Revolution, and fully manifested in the French Revolution.[16] Now the key point of Marquard's argument is that both controlled nature and romantic nature have the primary function of defending us from the threat of drive nature. Each defines, in opposite ways, the relation between nature and history in the paradoxical terms of nature against nature: tamed, objectified nature against threatening nature; and creative nature against destructive nature. What is Schiller's answer in his *Letters on the Aesthetic Education of Man* to the terrifying nature of man revealed by the French Revolution? Beautiful nature. It is clear that controlled nature and romantic nature, precisely by virtue of their defensive function, contain a dialectic. In Horkheimer and Adorno's natural-historical deduction: the controlled nature of self-preservation and instrumental reason is only the other face of drive nature, which leaves romantic nature – the song of the Sirens preserved in art – as the impotent witness and other of the always already completed *negative* short circuit of nature and history.

The 'nature' of romantic Idealism is conceived as the identity of origin and goal, as the *positive* short circuit of nature and history in the Absolute. Art becomes, in Schelling's *System of Transcendental Idealism*, the organon of philosophy because it is living form – the sensuous manifestation of the infinite in the finite and the aesthetic pledge of the synthesis of nature and history. This pledge is to be sealed by the new mythology, which will be the last and greatest deed of mankind. Two points need to be made. The romantic synthesis embodies not only the synthesis of nature and history, but equally that of philosophy and history. Philosophy finds its historical fulfilment, and history its philosophical fulfilment in the union of Greek nature and Christian history. The new mythology stands as the symbol – not the allegory – of the dialectical completion of history, through which a self-alienated modernity comes to fulfilment and redemption. The new mythology thus symbolizes the completion of the allegorical odyssey of philosophy through which philosophy returns to the 'ocean of poetry', in which poetry, philosophy and myth are once again one (Schelling).

Heidegger's more original repetition of the origin also envisages the 'completion' of history – but now as a Spenglerian 'Decline of the West', the inescapable theme of the 1920s, which clears the way for the new beginning, for Germany's 'Greek-German mission'. Heidegger's repetition reverses the *telos* of dialectical history. Modernity can be neither completed nor rescued. It must be overcome, and this demands the liberating of the greatness and power of the origin – the Greek conception of *phusis* – from its denaturalization in the 'second nature' of its Roman, Christian and modern scientific translations. The task of Heidegger's history of philosophy is to undo the dialectical conception of history. Heidegger's own philosophy of history is thus accomplished by the ungrounding of metaphysics in order to lay bare its abyssal ground in original history. Looking back in the light of the sun setting over the *Abendland*, the land of evening, which conceals the coming dawn, Heidegger constructs his allegory of the West as the story of the forgetting of Being. The driving force of this history springs from the imperative to repeat the beginning, to bring back an original revelation of Being, in which philosophy and poetry will be reunited in a new mythology, whose prophets are Heidegger, the poetic thinker, and Hölderlin, the philosophical poet.[17]

The most concise presentation of the history of Being, 'the hidden essential history of the Occident', is to be found in Heidegger's lectures on Parmenides, given in the winter semester 1942/43. Occidental history can be summed up under the three titles: Being and Word, Being and *ratio*, Being and Time. In the Greek beginning, Being reveals itself through the mythopoietic word, which is transformed by Plato and Aristotle into *logos*, thereby inaugurating the history of metaphysics, in which *logos* becomes *ratio*. The break with this history is announced in *Being and Time:* 'time' points to the origin of the Greek origin. As the primordial ground of the world, time announces the more original beginning, destined for the Occident, the event and advent (*Ereignis*) that can occur only in an occidental-historical people of poets and thinkers. The German people thus incorporate the site of the destiny of the Occident, which holds concealed a world fate. Heidegger is speaking in the shadow of German defeat in Stalingrad. Even if 'victory' is denied us, he declares, the people of the poets and thinkers has already conquered because it is invincible.[18]

Being and time, nature and history meet in the *Ereignis*. Heidegger's conception of history is that of the eschatology of Being. The god of this eschatology is the god of time. Time reveals Being as the temporality, the transience that transmutes, as in Adorno's 'Idea of Natural History', history into nature and nature into history. And just as Adorno's allegory of fallen nature and fallen history is framed by mythical remembrance, so Heidegger's allegory of *Seinsvergessenheit* is framed by the myth of origin. The genealogy of Germany's more original repetition – the genealogy of its new/old mythology – is traced by Heidegger in his Hölderlin lectures of 1934/35. It runs from Heraclitus via Meister Eckhart to Hölderlin, Hegel and Nietzsche. In the beginning is Heraclitus's World Time (Fragment 52): 'World Time – it is a child, a playing child, moving the pieces here and there, [such] a child is master [over Being].' Heidegger comments: original history is the great game that the gods play with peoples and with a people. The great times of World Time are the great times of world-historical turning, the advent in which the earth becomes home and opens itself to the power of the gods. 'Both are the same and include in themselves the third: that the earth stands in the storm of the divine and is torn open in its foundations and abysses [Gründe und Abgründe].' 'The great times of turning of peoples come from the abyss, and to the degree that a people reaches down into it, that is, its earth and possesses home.'[19] In the beginning the divine lightning strikes and opens the earth to history. The originary leap (*Ursprung*) of the work of art holds fast this strife of earth and world, of nature and history, of the old and the new gods, and it is the thinking of this original strife that Hölderlin has bequeathed to the Germans as the essential opposition within and between Greek and German *Dasein*.

The most familiar expression of this essential opposition is that symbolized by Apollo and Dionysus. Reframed in Nietzschean terms, Hölderlin's thinking of the essential opposition within and between Greece and Germany can be formulated in the following way: Greece achieved its identity through the Apollonian mastering of the Dionysian; Germany, the West, will attain its identity when its occidental Apollonian endowment of order and organization is infused with Dionysian power, when as Heidegger puts it, it is seized by Being.[20] And this mythical refoundation of history in nature, in the abyss of the native earth, will be one with Germany's nativity. Germany will give birth to the coming god, Dionysus, and the coming god, the seizure by Being, will give birth to Germany. Heidegger thus situates himself in the hour of Germany's destiny, the great time of the world-historical turning of the Occident, in the tradition of the new mythology. This tradition reaches from the French Revolution to the German Revolution, and conceives Germany's birth, identity and mission in terms of a twofold struggle with antiquity and modernity.

Out of this twofold struggle between Greek nature and art and modern history springs the quest for the aesthetic state:[21] the coming god of the new mythology is also the god of the aesthetic state, the total work of art (*Gesamtkunstwerk*) that will redeem modernity. Thus, at each stage of Franco-German history between 1789 and 1933, the coming birth of Germany is announced. This is the response of Schiller, Hölderlin, Schelling and Friedrich Schlegel to the French Revolution, of Heine to the July 1830 revolution in Paris,[22] of Wagner to 1848/49 (*Art and Revolution*), of Nietzsche to the Franco-Prussian war of 1870/71 (*Birth of Tragedy*), of Ernst Jünger to the First World War. As the title of Jünger's most famous book, *Storm of Steel*, indicates, the Great War is experienced as the sublime Dionysian return of history to nature from which the new man, the mythical figure of the Worker, is born.[23] Jünger's *The Worker* (1932) projects the coming military state as a total work of art, imbued with the spirit of Nietzsche's 'great style', and dedicated to the cult of power and death – a vision that finds its appropriate cultic representation in Leni Riefenstahl's film of the 1934 Nuremberg Rally of the Nazi Party, *Triumph of the Will*. After 1934 Heidegger draws back from his fascination with Nietzsche and Jünger and his own proclamation of the triumph of the will in his Rectoral Address. He turns to Hölderlin and Germany's Greek-German mission in the lectures of 1934/35 and presents his version of the aesthetic state in *The Origin of the Work of Art*.

Behind Heidegger's *The Origin of the Work of Art* – the central, over-determined text of the 1930s – stands the question of Germany's Greek mission, which sets Hölderlin's originality not only against Hegel but also against the aesthetics of Wagner and Nietzsche and their Nazi instrumentalization. Hölderlin's poetic opening of the space-time of advent places German *Dasein* and with it the politics of national aestheticism at the very centre of the History of Being. With Hölderlin's poetic politics, Heidegger contests the ground he shares with National Socialism – the romantic ground of myth, the source of the 'original' identity of art and politics – in the name of the Nazi movement's 'inner truth'.[24] What is at stake is 'the unique historical destiny of the German people in the face of the nihilism of modernity, a destiny articulated by the poet Hölderlin', which grows, as Villa writes, out of the romantic vision of the state as artwork. 'Appealing to Hölderlin Heidegger poetizes the vision, bringing the romantic concept of the aesthetic state to fulfilment in his conception of the political community as vehicle for the disclosure of Being.'[25] The choice of Hölderlin as the subject of his 1934–5 lecture series thus represents, Heidegger states, a 'historical decision'.[26] This decision, according to Lacoue-Labarthe, signals the return of a repressed romanticism.[27] More exactly, it must be understood as Heidegger's repetition of romanticism's obsession with the future past of the new mythology. The return of philosophy to poetry brings the conception of Being as Time back to its once and future origin: Being and the Word, the undivided unity of mythos and *logos*. Poetry advances to the highest instituting power that founds the historical Being of a people: to live poetically is to dwell historically *in the origin*.

2   A New Mythology

Kant prepares the romantic enthronement of art and the artist. He points the way in his Third Critique. Kant seeks to build a bridge between pure and practical reason by means of the reflective faculty of judgement. Moreover, reason itself becomes creative in Kant. As the product of the transcendental imagination, the phenomenal world can be regarded as our creation. The 'hidden art of the imagination' can be readily extended to the synthesis of unconscious and conscious productivity realized in the work of art. Art breaks free from its inferior cognitive status as imitation to become the creative source of truth, which becomes not only the complement of the truth of science but also the very organon of philosophy with Schelling. The sensuous presentation of the infinite in the finite, i.e. the aesthetic intuition of the absolute, relegates science to a secondary position.

The romantic turn to art and the philosophical elevation of the aesthetic also register the unsolved problem of Kant's critical philosophy: the lack of any rational mediation between nature and spirit leaves Kant with only the path of indirect reason, that is, the appeal to aesthetic and teleological judgement.[1] The beautiful appears as a symbol of morality while teleological judgement can claim only a reflective status as a critical principle. The assumption of purpose in nature responds to the self-organizing being of the organism, whose unity and parts are reciprocally the cause and effect of its form. The end purpose of man – the realization of moral freedom in history – is entrusted, however, to the antagonism of interests as the means to the infinitely distant goal of eternal peace and the world republic. In the space opened up between exact reason and moral reason, between metaphysics and philosophy of history, art and nature must take the place of the realization of reason in history.[2] The *Critique of Judgement* becomes the founding text of the romantic conception of nature and art, since romantic nature is nature viewed aesthetically, and romantic art is the product of nature in the subject (the genius).

The *Critique of Judgement* can also be seen as standing between enlightenment and romanticism because it lacks the historicist frame, which transforms the union of art and nature, central to the romantic paradigm, into a reading of history. It is Schiller in his *Letters on the Aesthetic Education of Man* (1795) who brings together Kant's philosophy and historicist reflection through the comparison of the ancients and the moderns with the aim of realizing political philosophy by other means.[3] Schiller's response to the course of the French Revolution is to argue that nature and freedom can only be reconciled aesthetically: practical reason (the form drive) and sensuous nature (the material drive) must be synthesized in the play drive, the free harmony of form and matter in beauty. This third mediating principle – the path of indirection – is necessary if the twin dangers of the direct political goal of transforming the state in its natural form into a moral state – anarchy and tyranny – are to be avoided: 'There is no other way to make sensuous man rational other than first making him aesthetic' (letter 23).

The political goal thus presupposes a total revolution in man's way of feeling (letter 27),[4] which requires the recovery of man's true social character. The progress of civilization has been achieved at the price of the alienation and fragmentation of the individual, who can become whole again only through play. The programme of aesthetic education – the bringing of the understanding, will and feeling back into harmony – is informed by the contrast between the natural humanity of the Greeks and the divided state of modern man (letter 6). Kant's dichotomy between nature and freedom is translated into the prototype of a dialectical philosophy of history, which seeks to combine Greek nature and modern freedom in a new higher totality. The dialectic as formulated by Schiller – we must become nature again through reason and freedom[5] – remains suspended, however, in Kantian indirection. At the beginning of the *Letters on Aesthetic Education* the construction of genuine political freedom is described as the most perfect work of art (letter 2); by the end the most perfect work of art, the aesthetic state, no longer functions as the means to the end of political freedom but has become an enclave of beautiful illusion for the happy few. Moreover, as Marquard stresses, Schiller operates with a dual concept of nature: *real* nature, which blocks the way to the rational realization of freedom, is overcome by *true*, aesthetic nature.[6] The opposition implies two opposed conceptions of 'natural history': history as nature, i.e. freedom in thrall to 'real' nature, and nature as history, i.e. the harmony of nature and freedom realized in 'true' nature.

Schiller's *Letters on Aesthetic Education* are eloquent testimony to the quest for the aesthetic state, which plays such an important role in the German philosophical discourse of modernity and by the same token in the German ideology. The turn to the aesthetic, in search of an answer to the alienation of modern society and the crisis of political foundation in the French Revolution, is integral to the imaginary of cultural and national renewal, aptly characterized by Lacoue-Labarthe as 'national aestheticism'.[7] Its 'mythological' expression is to be found in the two seminal texts of German romanticism: the fragment, known as 'The Oldest Systematic Programme of German Idealism' and Friedrich Schlegel's 'Discourse on Mythology', which forms part of the 'Conversation on Poetry', published in the third volume of the journal of the Jena romantics, the *Athenäum* (1800).[8]

Although it now seems established that Hegel and not Schelling was the author of the 'System Programme', it is nevertheless clear that it must be understood as the joint product of Hegel, Schelling and Hölderlin's symphilosophizing. Each is the author in the sense that each is imbued with the consciousness of the crisis and the challenge of the present and the philosophical-poetic task of creating a 'world-historical synthesis' of antiquity and modernity.[9] The programme finds its philosophical continuation in Schelling's philosophy of art and its poetic continuation in Hölderlin. Hegel breaks, however, with the dream of the aesthetic reconciliation of modernity by declaring the Greek 'art religion' a thing of the past,[10] whose dissolution by Christian subjectivity prepares the way for the philosophical reconciliation of modernity to itself. But, as Heidegger says, Hegel looks back and closes the way; Hölderlin looks forward and opens the way.[11] Despite Hegel's verdict on the end of art in the modern world as the negative counterpart to the programme of a new mythology, the idea of a world-historical synthesis as the answer to the *querelle des anciens et modernes* continued to exert its fascination with its promise of Germany's unique and uniquely privileged Greek mission of the aesthetic redemption of modernity. The idea of a new mythology with its inherent paradox of 'original imitation' thus opened the way to the onto-poetic historicism, unfolded by Nietzsche and Heidegger.

The 'Systematic Programme' is a text of extraordinary density,[12] which envisages the unification of the moral, physical and historical worlds in the idea of freedom. The transformation of thought into reality, and metaphysics into ethics, calls for the construction of a system of ideas that involves at the same time the construction of the world as an act of absolute freedom. The first idea is given by *my* self-representation as an absolutely free being. From it there emerges a whole world – conceived as the only true *creatio ex nihilo* – and the question: how must the world be constituted for a moral being? The question of the relation between nature and freedom – which points to the need for a new physics, a new philosophy of nature to satisfy 'our creative spirit' – poses in turn the problem of the realization of freedom in history. The idea of humanity – 'the absolute freedom of all spirits, who bear the intellectual world in *themselves*' – calls for an organic principle of human history. The state with its constitutions, government, laws and priesthood is a machine, which must give way to the organic community, united in and through the idea that combines all the ideas – the idea of *beauty*. The highest unifying act of reason is accordingly an aesthetic act, which synthesizes truth and goodness in beauty. From this highest act flows the necessity for the philosophy of the spirit to become aesthetic, thereby completing philosophy through the restoration of poetry to its original dignity as the teacher of humanity: 'there will be no more philosophy, no more historiography, poetry alone will supplant all other sciences and arts'. The monotheism of reason and the heart must be united with the polytheism of the imagination and art – if philosophy is to become aesthetic and mythology rational. This is the task that falls to an entirely new idea, the creation of a new mythology, a mythology of reason. Only when mythology becomes philosophical – in order to make the people rational – and philosophy mythological – in order to make the philosopher sensuous – will there be unity without coercion and the *equal* development of *all* energies in freedom. 'A higher spirit, sent from heaven, must found this new religion among us, it will be the last, greatest work of humanity.'

This last and greatest deed as the goal of history defines the present as both end and beginning. For Friedrich Schlegel, the situation of modern civilization is summed up by its absent centre – the lack of a mythology.[13] The consciousness of this lack is already the sign of a present that is pregnant with new possibilities, heralded by the great phenomenon of the age: the birth of idealism, as it were, out of nothing. This wondrous emergence, the anticipation of the self-production of a new mythology from the innermost depths of the spirit, indicates the 'secret coherence and inner unity of the age', manifested in the revolutionary crisis, whose outcome will be either the downfall or renewal of humanity. At the centre of the spirit's struggle for self-renewal stands the idea of a new mythology, the unifying focus of romantic knowledge, in which philosophy and poetry, physics and mysticism will converge. Schlegel's new mythology of art, like the mythology of reason of the 'Systematic Programme', is a mythology of the self-creative spirit. Both are informed by a radical historicism and in this sense present a mythology of mythology. As opposed to the single, indivisible and completed poem of the ancients, Schlegel's new mythology announces itself as the most artificial of artworks, as an infinite poem. Whereas the old mythology was the work of art of nature, the new mythology will be the art of nature come to consciousness of its own productivity, a new nature whose self-creativity is figured as a *creatio ex nihilo*. From the 'original chaos of human nature', symbolized by the 'colourful throng' of the ancient gods, a new pantheon will arise. This new pantheon will draw its inspiration from Spinoza and the new physics, which offers the 'holiest revelations' of the mysteries of nature.[14] Behind the mysticism of Spinoza *sub specie aeternitatis* we discern, however, the theosophy of Jacob Boehme,[15] mentioned only in passing by Schlegel. Boehme supplies the subterranean link between the idea of a new mythology and the onto-poetic horizon of the romantic imaginary of creation. Schlegel's formulation – 'All holy games of art are only distant copies of the endless play of the world, the eternally self-shaping work of art' – directly anticipates Nietzsche's aesthetic cosmogony of the world as a work of art giving birth to itself.

The common features of the 'Systematic Programme' and the 'Discourse on Mythology' are readily apparent: the sources in Kant, Schiller and Fichte[16] on the one side, Spinoza and Boehme on the other; the sense of revolutionary crisis; the comparison between the ancients and the moderns; the tension between nature and freedom, to be overcome through the appeal to the self-productivity of nature and spirit and the voluntarism of an original creation. Above all, both texts are seeking a socially binding force, which will provide a unifying spiritual centre against the corrosive effects of analytic reason and will open the way to the recomposition of society beyond the mechanical state through an 'organic' bond between mythology and community. Although the 'Systematic Programme' invites a political reading, its politics – to be sanctioned by a higher heavenly spirit – represents rather a meta-political vision. Insofar as it is a political statement, it is, as Chytry observes, a manifesto for the aesthetic state.[17] Similarly, in a fragment from the *Athenäum*, Schlegel sees the chemical ferment of the revolutionary present as preparing a coming organic age, which will find its legitimacy only through a new mythology. The philosophical critique of modernity and the historicist deduction of a new religion thus meet in the idea of an aesthetic synthesis of the ancient and the modern, which will inaugurate a third redemptive age of history. Inauguration is carried by an exoteric and an esoteric concept of foundation. The one, the exoteric, defines foundation in terms of the reciprocity of mythology and community and opens onto the quest for the aesthetic state. The other, the esoteric, defines foundation onto-genetically in terms of the relation between nature and spirit in history, such that the world is grasped as a self-creating work of art. They find their common reference in the idea of natural history and its thematics of origin, the origin that is at the same time the goal of history, symbolized by the return of philosophy to poetry in a new mythology. Like the organism, mythology as a work of art of nature manifests the circle of creation. It is both cause and effect of origin, presenting and representing in one the encounter of gods and mortals, earth and world, the instituting and the instituted symbolic.[18] Romanticism unfolds an imaginary of creation, which takes Schelling beyond the synthesis of the philosophy of nature and of spirit in his system of transcendental idealism – the paradigmatic fulfilment of the 'Systematic Programme' – to the theogony and cosmogony of Boehme's living god.

Schelling and Schlegel represent the philosophical and the aesthetic poles of Jena romanticism in their contrasting conceptions of system, the absolute and art. Schlegel's celebration of the infinite poem, of the universal progressive poetry of the moderns, springs from an understanding of the 'literary absolute'[19] that is mystical in inspiration. Literature's infinite programme of potentiation follows the 'artificial' path of the self-critical destruction of all finite literary forms through the self-nihilating act of ironic sovereignty. It is a programme of 'infinitization' that Kierkegaard will turn against ironic, aesthetic existence and employ to ground the paradox of religious existence. In Kierkegaard's wake Heidegger will use it to destroy inauthentic existence and to ground authentic *Dasein* in the abyssal paradox of the leap of origin. Schlegel's oscillation between the impossible alternatives of system and chaos – which becomes in Kierkegaard and Heidegger the complete hostility to Hegel's system – stands in sharp contrast to Schelling's identification of system and the absolute. Schelling's *System of Transcendental Idealism* unfolds the circle of origin. As he writes in the introduction and conclusion, a system of knowledge is only completed when it returns to its starting point. Philosophy's recovery of unconscious origin – the transcendental 'natural history' of consciousness realized in the identity of unconscious and conscious activity – must turn to art to demonstrate this identity.

> The ideal world of art and the real world of objects are therefore products of the one and the same activity; this concurrence of the two (the conscious and the nonconscious) *without* consciousness yields the real, and *with* consciousness the aesthetic world.
> The objective world is simply the original, as yet unconscious, poetry of the spirit; the universal organon of philosophy – and the keystone of its entire arch – *is the philosophy of art.*[20]

The work of art is thus accorded the central place in the system because it incorporates the solution to the world riddle: the manifestation here and now of the absolute, which lifts the invisible dividing veil between the real and the ideal worlds to rejoin in the one flame what is separated in nature and history. As the sensuous pledge of this identity of origin and goal, art becomes 'the only true and eternal organon and document of philosophy'.

> Art is paramount to the philosopher, precisely because it opens to him, as it were, the holy of holies, where burns in eternal and original unity, as if in a single flame, that which in nature and history is rent asunder, and in life and action, no less than in thought, must forever fly apart. The view of nature which the philosopher frames artificially, is for art the original one.
> But now if it is art alone which can succeed in objectifying with universal validity what the philosopher is able to present in a merely subjective fashion, there is one more conclusion to be drawn. Philosophy was born and nourished by poetry in the infancy of knowledge, and with it all those sciences it has guided toward perfection; we may thus expect them, on completion, to flow back like so many individual streams into the universal ocean of poetry from which they took their source. Nor is it in general difficult to say what the medium for this return of science to poetry will be; for in mythology such a medium existed, before the occurrence of a breach seemingly beyond repair. But how a new mythology is itself to arise, which shall be the creation, not of some individual author, but of a new race, personifying, as it were, one single poet – that is a problem whose solution can be looked for only in the future destinies of the world, and in the course of history to come.[21]

With the elucidation of mythology as the medium of art in his lectures on the philosophy of art (1802),[22] Schelling modifies his system. If, as Cassirer writes, Schelling's idea of the creative productivity of nature and history is modelled on the autonomy of artistic creation,[23] it finds its fullest articulation in his lectures on the philosophy of art, in which it is now the philosopher who constructs the universe in the form (*Gestalt*) of art. In this construction the unconscious poetry of nature comes to self-consciousness in art, but art itself comes to self-consciousness in the philosophy of art. Since for art the *real*, living and existing, ideas are the gods, the universal and absolute content of art is given by the symbolism of mythology, which refracts the universe and life through the prism of the human imagination.

In the highest archetype of this poetic world, the mythology of the Greeks, we witness the emergence of gods and men from the original chaos of night and darkness (§30). As the product of the original genius of a people, mythological creation is indeed the work of a god, which brings back, on the highest level of production, nature in art (§42). Only such a divine art can effect the harmony of the individual and the species but equally only a people which is one can bring forth such an art. Although the moderns can no longer comprehend this perfect collective individuality, it nevertheless remains the highest idea for the *whole* of history, and provides the key to Schelling's comparison of the ancient and the modern worlds. In the Greek conception of the universe as *nature*, the species are individuals; in the Christian conception of the universe as *history* there are only individuals. The modern world thus begins with the separation of man from nature. Symbolic realism – the 'in-forming', the imagining (*Einbildung*) of the infinite in the finite – has been replaced by the allegorical idealism of Christian mythology – the *Einbildung* of the finite in the infinite. Greek religion, based on mythology, gives way to Christian mythology, based on religion (§52). The relation between the real and the ideal is reversed: in the ancient world nature was revealed in mythology as opposed to the mysteries of the ideal world, in the modern world nature withdraws into mystery behind the revelation of the ideal world (§51). The Christian separation of the real and the ideal, compounded by scientific disenchantment, has desacralized nature. We have lost the creative bond between visible and invisible spirit, manifested in the mythological self-creations of humanity, where the gods, anthropomorphic symbols of the forces of nature, embody the hidden unity of man and nature. The return of the gods in a new mythology will thus signify the resurrection of nature and the final absolute identity of nature and history (§60), being and becoming, space and time (§44). Although Schelling must concede that this final poetic totality remains the task of the future, it is not in order to dwell on the lack and negativity of the present, since the new world is already visible beyond the opposition of the ancient and the modern. The historical epoch of Christianity can already be grasped as transition, as the one side of the coming synthesis, in which the temporal succession of the modern age will come to rest.

However, Schelling soon felt compelled to go beyond the closure of his system to pose the circle of origin more originally in his *Philosophical Investigations on the Essence of Human Freedom* (1809), a text of great importance for Heidegger. This more original questioning takes Schelling from Spinoza to Boehme, from the indistinction of nature and God in Spinoza's system to the distinction between nature and existence in God. Schelling posits the *ground* of God's existence – 'the unconscious will of his longing' – as distinct from and yet in God. The relation between ground and existence in God is explicated by means of the analogy in nature between gravity and light: 'gravity precedes light as its eternally dark ground, which is not itself *actu*, and withdraws into the night as the light (the existing) appears' – and by means of an anthropomorphic analogy: 'it [the ground] is the longing, which the Eternal One feels, to give birth to himself'.[24] Origin is thus comprehended as the circle of ground and existence. In this eternal play of appearance and withdrawal, the illumination (*Verklärung*) of the ground through existence, we recognize Heidegger's concept of *alētheia* as the happening of the truth of Being and the lighting (*Lichtung*) of beings.[25] Heidegger stresses the importance of Meister Eckhart and Boehme for Schelling's thinking of the becoming God. Here we may note that already in the 1920s Jaspers identified Eckhart and Schelling as key elements of Heidegger's philosophy.[26]

The historical presupposition of the new mythology is the death of God, that is to say, the age of crisis and revolutionary transition that announces the end of the Christian era. The coming God of the new mythology is a historical god, or rather we should say, the god of historicism and finally, with Heidegger, the god of historicity. In giving birth to himself, Boehme and Schelling's God infuses historicism with a dynamic of becoming. As Gusdorf writes, Boehme's originality lies in the idea of the living god as opposed to the god of the philosophers, the theo-logical god. The godhead beyond revelation stands for the absolute as such, the abyss of unfathomable freedom and will, the divine nothing out of which god creates himself, the world and man. This, the deepest and most secret idea of German mysticism[27] is deeply congenial to German romanticism, and makes it for Gusdorf the essential romanticism. Boehme's reconnection of metaphysics with mythology – cosmic life as eternal struggle and genesis – appealed to the romantics' renewal of the occult tradition, which had been displaced by the mechanical worldview of the enlightenment.[28]

Two interrelated aspects of Boehme's theosophy are important for the coming god of onto-poetic historicism. The one is the comprehension of freedom as primordial potentiality: the freedom which wills self-creation expresses the original 'metaphysical voluntarism' (Berdiev),[29] taken up by Schelling and Heidegger. The other is Boehme's mythical vision of the eternal self-creation of god as an endless tragic struggle between light and darkness. In this vision nature appears as unsatisfied longing and unconscious suffering, as the demonic cycle of self-creation and destruction, which anticipates Schopenhauer's blind, ceaselessly striving Will.

3   The Disenchantment of Romantic Nature

The birth of a new mythology from the spirit of nature completes Schelling's system of transcendental idealism. It is a completion that involves a double circle of creation. The recognition that 'the objective world is simply the original, as yet unconscious poetry of the spirit' finds its higher confirmation in the primordial productivity and poetic gift of the imagination.[1] Mythology symbolizes the very idea of natural history. The identity of the one unconscious and conscious activity in nature and history provides the answer to the riddle of history. If organic nature is itself unconscious reason, demonstrated in the harmony of means and ends, then the history of the human spirit is rational because it is grounded in nature. In turn, the creativity of the imagination raised to the highest power in the work of art rests on the same circular argument: philosophy of nature takes art as its model just as the philosophy of art, whose medium is mythology, takes nature as its model. The aestheticization of nature and the naturalization of aesthetics form two sides of the in-forming power of what Marquard calls *romantic nature*, that is, the organic viewed in the light of the aesthetic.[2]

What is the price of Schelling's aesthetic synthesis of nature and history? It is for Marquard the price of indirection. The appeal to the indirect reason of nature and art leads unwittingly to the empowerment of extra-rational and extra-historical natural forces. Transcendental philosophy's task of anamnesis – the recovery of the unconscious history of consciousness – blocks the way forward. History is defined not in relation to its political future but its natural past.[3] Genealogy replaces dialectics and mythology replaces philosophy of history. Marquard accordingly locates transcendental idealism between a dissolved metaphysics and an unattainable philosophy of history. Its position of suspension and possibility is that of a historicism which participates in the historicization of metaphysical concepts (being, substance, thing-in-itself) without advancing to a philosophy of history. The problem of a post-metaphysical foundation of modernity is tackled through regression: the unconscious creativity of nature and the imagination (the genius) makes the unconscious the central theme of transcendental philosophy and leads to an interpretation of history in natural as opposed to political terms.[4] In sum: philosophy of history is reduced to remembering the unconscious history of consciousness thereby abandoning history to the other of reason. Since the 'I' as principle between being and history lacks an adequate theory of the end purpose of history and the means to its realization, the outcome is historical pessimism, the evasion of the political and the turn to theological, aesthetic and mythological history.[5]

For Schelling the complementary and sustaining other of reason is given by romantic nature, conceived as the defence against 'real' nature and as the answer to the Christian-modern split between nature and history. Beautiful nature contains (in both senses of the word) the sublime, the latent possibility of the reversal into the irrational other of reason and history. Marquard traces this reversal – the disenchantment of romantic nature – through to Freud's reduction of history to biology, the eternal struggle of the life and death drives. The dialectic runs from Schelling to Schopenhauer, Nietzsche to Freud, from romantic nature to *drive nature*. It involves the collapse of the romantic-idealist idea of *Naturgeschichte* into Schopenhauer's 'natural' concept of nature as the Will and the reduction of history to nothing but 'natural history'. The dialectic is set in train by the turn to the rescuing powers of romantic nature against the enlightenment's scientific conception of nature as *controlled nature* and its version of natural history. Precisely the desire to rescue 'rescuing nature' from scientific domination, organicism from mechanism, leads to blindness to the other of romantic nature. Marquard identifies this blindness as a recurrent trait of German thought up to Heidegger.[6]

Important as this dialectic of romantic nature is for an understanding of the dialectic of romanticism, Marquard's reconstruction takes as its conclusion Freud rather than Heidegger, even though their common recourse to genealogy is acknowledged as the legacy of transcendental idealism's failure to reconcile metaphysics and philosophy of history.[7] Heidegger points back to Schelling rather than Freud, who was to discover that his metapsychological speculations had led him back to Schopenhauer. Freud furnishes Adorno and Horkheimer with the fundamental figure of the dialectic of enlightenment – natural history as the eternal return of the repressed. If we are to locate the dialectic of romanticism between metaphysics and philosophy of history, then this also defines the place of the dialectic of enlightenment. Heidegger and Adorno's opposed but complementary interpretations of 'progress' 'take back' not only modernity but also the whole of western history since the Greek beginnings. Both mark the 'completion' of the philosophical discourse of modernity. Both end in a gnostic theology in the twin forms of a negative metaphysics and a negative philosophy of history. This convergence in a negative historicism stands at the very opposite pole to Schelling's aesthetic synthesis. Nevertheless this negative historicism is intimately linked to romanticism, openly proclaimed in Heidegger's identification with Hölderlin and his indebtedness to Schelling, but no less evident in Adorno's call for the remembrance of nature in the subject, which echoes the intention of Schelling's transcendental philosophy. What makes Heidegger and Adorno so critically attentive to the modern project of unlimited mastery blinds both of them at the same time to the romantic roots of totalitarianism.

Marquard's reconstruction of the disenchantment of romantic nature helps us to understand this blindness. In the passage from Schelling to Heidegger three post-metaphysical concepts of nature emerge: drive nature, as the natural condition of humanity after the death of god; controlled nature, as the object of the natural sciences; and romantic nature, based on the organism and the object of imagination and poetry. Controlled nature's function as a defence against drive nature calls forth romantic nature in response to its perceived inadequacy since the 'rationalization' of 'natural' interests only strengthens them. (We see this in the case of the French Revolution.) Romantic nature claims for itself the reciprocal harmony of ends and means against the antagonistic interests of drive nature (for which any means serves) and the rational means of controlled nature (for which any purpose serves).[8] The romantic vision of the organic community thus answers the enlightenment project of a rational science of society in analogy to the science of nature. Both defences against drive nature are confronted, however, with the threat of the return of the repressed. Marquard relates the dialectic of romantic nature to an aesthetic outbidding of reality in the quest for the realization of the poetic. The ensuing poeticization of reality brings out the ambivalence of redemption and destruction, registered in the doubling of aesthetics and nature into the beautiful and the sublime.[9]

If our harmony with the world is symbolized by the beautiful, the sublime by contrast manifests the loss of this harmony and leads to an aesthetics of tragic Dionysian disharmony. This tragic vision springs from the recognition of history not as Apollonian healing and rescuing nature, but as Dionysian nature, destructive but also seductive at the same time. For Marquard this ambivalence signifies the failure of the aesthetic, with a consequent tendency to nihilism.[10] Just as the fascination with dreams, death and madness constitutes the 'night side' of genius, so the disturbing, sublime experience of history as nature points to the shadow cast by onto-poetics. The 'positivity' of world-creation is shadowed by its 'negativity', implicit in Schlegel's 'Discourse on Mythology' with its Heraclitean imaginary. This is made explicit in romantic irony, where the freedom of the self-creating subject, affirmed through self-negation, is figured in the self-annihilating potentiation of the absolute work of art.

The new mythology appears in a double light. On the one hand, we have – to use Schelling's distinction – Schelling's own classical-symbolic understanding of mythology, the 'imaging' (*Einbildung*) of the infinite in the finite, which calls for a new Homer. On the other hand, we have Schlegel's modern allegorical understanding, the imaging of the finite in the infinite. Romantic mythology will be an infinite poem. In the 'Ideas' published in the *Athenäum* together with the 'Discourse on Mythology', Schlegel speaks of the enthusiasm of annihilation that reveals the meaning of divine creation, of God as the abyss of individuality, of all concepts of God as empty words. The negative way ponders the question of origin as such, the relation of Being and Nothing. The romantic fascination with the absolute exceeds all determinations and can reveal itself only *ex negativo*. In relation to this abyss of faith and knowledge, all revelation and mythologies are secondary: they both reveal and conceal the becoming god. Gusdorf accordingly speaks of an eschatology of Being, in which potentiality precedes reality, and of an eschatology of knowledge, directed to the holy mysteries of nature.[11]

Romantic non-knowledge protests against the scientific reduction of the world and nature to the knowable and rescues itself from the fascination with the other – the journey to the end of the night[12] – through the *creatio ex nihilo* figured in art. As opposed to the absolute captured for Schelling in the symbolic presence of the work of art, Heidegger's origin of the work of art manifests the truth of Being as the play of presence and absence. But here we must distinguish between the two abysses which open up on either side of the paradigm of romantic nature: the sublime in the sense of the mystical, but also the holy (Hölderlin) and the theogonic (the later Schelling), which points forward to Heidegger, and the sublime as natural history in the sense given by Marquard, which leads through Schopenhauer to Nietzsche.

In 'The End of All Things' (1794) Kant addresses the 'frightful-sublime' expectation of the end of the world, whose source he locates in our horror at the thought of a meaningless creation 'like a play that has no end and reveals no rational intention'. In *The Determination of Man* (1800) Fichte asks: 'To what purpose this circle ceaselessly returning into itself, this game ever renewed and ever the same … this monster, continuously devouring itself?' In 'On the Sublime' (1801) Schiller evokes a vision of history as a 'frightful magnificent play of all destroying change, ever creating, ever destroying'.[13] It is not by chance that these examples present the aesthetic spectacle of history as play in the dual sense of game and drama. The world as a work of art giving birth to itself can take either the beautiful form of the construction of the universe as art, as in Schelling's *Philosophy of Art*, or the frightful-sublime form of the endless cycle of creation and destruction, as in Nietzsche's *The Birth of Tragedy*. The only possibility of redemption this tragic-nihilistic vision allows is the aesthetic redemption realized by tragedy, which initiates us into the mystery religion of Dionysus – 'the mysterious god (*Rätselgott*) of the becoming world' (Bachofen). And just as Dionysus is the coming god of romantic mythology,[14] so nihilism is a word and concept that first appears in the context of German idealism and the French Revolution.[15]

The connection between the experience of the frightful sublime and nihilism is closely related to the disenchantment of romantic nature. As we have seen,

the romantic turn to nature is inherently ambivalent: the beautiful is shadowed by the sublime, the creative by the destructive. If the genius is threatened by madness, it is because the romantic personality is the aesthetic
personality, dissected most notably by Hegel, Kierkegaard and Carl
Schmitt.[16] Kierkegaard's contrast between the aesthetic and the ethical personality in *Either/Or* sums up the (self-)judgement passed on the romantic
'heroes of our time' (Lermontov), such as Hölderlin's Hyperion, Senancour's
Obermann, Benjamin Constant's Adolphe, or Pushkin's Onegin, cast in the
image of Goethe's Werther.

If the adventures of Odysseus become the allegory of the dialectic of
enlightenment, we can take the sorrows of Goethe's Werther as the symbolic
enactment of Marquard's dialectic of romanticism. As *Werther* confirms, this
dialectic is present from the beginning in the romantic turn to nature. The
original history of the subject, as traced by Horkheimer and Adorno, is
defined by the separation from nature. From this separation springs the
permanent tension of regression: 'The strain of holding the I together adheres
to the I in all its stages, and the temptation to lose it has always been there
with the blind determination to maintain it.'[17] Werther, the would-be artist,
experiences nature as an overwhelming magnificence that can no longer be
captured in beautiful imitation. And yet it is precisely this sublime sense of
the unpresentable which assures him of his artistic empathy with nature. He
does not become, however, the 'genius' of the unknown masterpiece, of the
absolute self-destroying work of art.[18] His longing is for the absolute as such,
the absolute moment of the *unio mystica* with 'the inner, glowing, holy life of
nature' that cancels the limits of individuation. Werther is thus a 'sublime'
personality, for whom the sublime is not as with Kant the confirmation of
moral freedom but an aesthetic experience, in which the beautiful appears as
'the beginning of the terrible' (Rilke). Werther's longing for the infinite
reverses into the deadly recognition of the all-engulfing destructive force of
nature. 'My heart is undermined by the consuming force which lies hidden in
the totality of nature, which forms nothing which does not destroy its neighbour and itself. And so I reel in disquiet! Heaven and earth and all the active
forces around me! I see nothing but an eternally swallowing, eternally
devouring monster.'[19]

Werther's vision is already that of Schopenhauer and Nietzsche, the philosophers of disenchanted nature. Their reduction of history to the blindness of
the self-willing Will negates the teleology of history and empowers nature as
the irrational other of reason and history. Schopenhauer and Nietzsche
reduce the subject and consciousness to epiphenomena. The devaluation of
consciousness goes together with the devaluation of the Socratic illusion that
the world and existence can be corrected by knowledge. Behind the illusion of
the principle of individuation, human life must be recognized as suffering
without purpose. It is to be endured either as punishment (Schopenhauer) or
affirmed as play (Nietzsche),[20] or, in terms of Nietzsche's critique of Schopenhauer, either as the pessimism of weakness or the pessimism of strength,
either as decadence or as the tragic heroism of *amor fati*, which transforms

inauthentic into authentic nihilism. Nietzsche's higher nihilism proclaims the religion of the death of god and the (be)coming god:

> this my Dionysian world of eternal self-creation, of eternal self-destruction, this mystery-world of the two sensual lusts, this my 'Beyond Good and Evil', without goal, unless there lies in the happiness of the circle a goal ... do you want a name for this world? A solution to all its riddles? ... This world is the will to power – and nothing else.[21]

The world as the will to power is the world of natural history, from which arises, stripped of all *telos*, the onto-poetic circle of world creation and destruction, sublime in its self-affirmation over the abyss of blind *natura naturans*. But if Nietzsche's onto-poetics asserts its identity with the world will, his historicism is rendered all the more desperate by the historicist consciousness of the nineteenth century against which he fulminates. All the anathemas Nietzsche hurls against the disappearance of greatness, the rule of the herd, the last man, the decadence of unoriginal civilization, reveal a cultural despair, which registers in acute form the contradiction of a rapidly modernizing Germany in search of identity in the context not only of European imperialism but of the perceived sterility and decline of European culture. This mood of cultural pessimism is documented by the doom-ridden diagnoses of modernity that followed German unification in 1871.[22]

Schopenhauer already accomplished the disenchantment of the romantic-idealist synthesis. But it is only after 1848 that we can speak of a decisive change of perspective. Up to 1848 the idea of a 'mythology of reason' contains and holds together the dialectical and onto-poetic strains of historicism. The disenchantment of romantic nature does not bring with it, however, the dethroning of art. On the contrary art advances with Nietzsche to the sublime manifestation of the Dionysian ground of existence.

4 Original Imitation

The new mythology of the romantics was an answer to the new science of the enlightenment. Against the Cartesian grounding of modernity in consciousness it opposed an immanent regrounding. Against the *ego cogitans* of Descartes it opposed the natural creativity of the genius. Schelling's quest for the transcendental natural history of consciousness is indicative of the romantic turn to the unconscious productivity of nature and history. The collective genius of a people – manifested in its language, institutions and culture – is the source of creativity. It is one thing to discover the unconscious sources of creativity in a nature that is already historical and a history that is natural. It is quite another, however, to posit this process in reverse: the *conscious* creation of the unconscious, that is to say, the invention of a new mythology. Romantic mythmaking is riven by this contradiction. The idea of overcoming the split between nature and spirit must perpetuate its own original sin. The paradox of the conscious recovery of the unconscious source, which makes origin the goal, must repeat itself in the split nature of the mythical in a post-mythical age. The Systematic Programme's vision of a 'mythology of reason' sought to escape the false alternatives of enlightenment or myth, but how can myth after enlightenment deny its divided nature? It is this inherent contradiction which drives the romantic protest against 'enlightened' modernity backwards in search of the instituting powers of myth and forward into the ever more radical diagnosis of the nihilism of modernity.

Origin and goal form the eschatological horizon of the new mythology, its organic politics, and its quest for the aesthetic state. The idea of the aesthetic state defines the programme of the new mythology at the same time as it reproduces its contradiction. Germany's task is that of an original imitation of the Greeks. In turn, this contradictory imperative sets into sharper focus the contradictions of Germany's situation and historical mission: the transformation of national belatedness into an overcoming and surpassing of a modernity still to be attained. Self-creation can be figured only through its projection onto Greece.

The tyranny of Greece over Germany should rather be understood as the tyranny over a Greece constructed in the image of the German quest for origin. This quest discovers a romantic Greece[1] beneath the eighteenth-century classicist image of Greece. This more original Greece serves as the screen onto which an unborn Germany projects its accession to its own essential self and history, identified with the future and fate of the West. What we have here is a historicist consciousness fascinated by the 'original' and divided against itself. The very appeal to unconscious origins against the project of enlightenment simultaneously invites and bars the way to originality. Hence Nietzsche's polemics against the stultifying effects of *historicism* in the second of his 'untimely meditations' on the uses and abuses of history, in which he proclaims the rights of the present and a coming culture against the sterility and decadence of historical knowledge.

The genesis of historicism, as described by Friedrich Meinecke,[2] is one with the genesis of German identity. The product of the 'German movement', historicism signifies for Meinecke Germany's spiritual revolution. This revolution represents one of the deepest caesuras in the history of the Occident, indeed the decisive moment in which Europe's genius attains its true individuality. It liberates historical thinking from the paralysing legacy of imitation, that is, from the whole inheritance of the natural law tradition from antiquity to the enlightenment.[3] Meinecke brings out clearly the initial dialectical impetus of the German movement: what he calls the reaction of nature to the enlightenment's emancipation of human reason. The renaturalization of man and history is to be accomplished by the awakening of the irrational forces of the soul and the overcoming of the dualism of reason and instinct in the creative idea of the inner unity and totality of living form.[4] The aesthetic perspective of art history (Winckelmann)[5] together with the new understanding of historical phenomena as products of nature (Herder), opened the way to the sense of the natural-historical, of history as *Naturgeschichte*.[6] The soul of natural history accordingly resides in the unconscious inner nature of a people, in the living form, the living god of culture. In Goethe's words: 'The divinity is active in the living but not in the dead: it is in what is becoming and self-transforming but not in what has become and rigidified'.[7] There is thus no place in historicism for the rationalistic idea of humanity or resentful normative judgement: natural law must bow in respect before the fateful and irrational forces of natural history.[8] In the organic historical totality good and evil belong together. Meinecke thus speaks of a tragic and demonic vision of history.[9] Goethe embodies for him the essence of the German sense of history: 'History was for him ultimately that part of an eternal dramatic spectacle, in which temporal succession becomes the means to the end of creation eternally giving birth to itself.'[10]

Meinecke's *Historicism* appeared in 1936. To Hitler's German revolution Meinecke can oppose only the original German revolution, despite his recognition after the First World War that the German ideology has cut Germany off from the rest of the 'modern, progressive world'. The tragic view of history beyond good and evil has become Germany's tragedy.[11] And yet this 'tragic' insight does not stand in the way of the celebration of a Goethean onto-poetics in 1936 or the return to Goethe after the Second World War in *The German Catastrophe*, where Meinecke proposes the establishment of Goethe congregations to meet on Sundays in church.[12] Meinecke's *Historicism*, written under the shadow of Hitler, clings to the idea of the holistic individuality of national culture and its organic development, without ever confronting the immanent logic of 'natural history' articulated by Spengler. Spengler insists that that which grows must die: the age of technological civilization has supplanted the age of culture. It is not by chance that Jünger's mythical *Gestalt of the Worker* is dedicated to Spengler, who declared *The Decline of the West* to be the application of Goethe's morphology of organic life to the study of history. Meinecke's pious hope in 1936 that historicism can heal the wounds it has inflicted is as blind to the genesis of the 'German movement' as it is to its demise. Schelling stated that the meaning of the beginning is revealed in its end. Heidegger echoes him in 1934 at the beginning of his Hölderlin lectures: 'The beginning [*Anfang*], the origin, appears only in the course of events and is completely there only at its end.'[13]

This obsession with the 'mystery of origin'[14] is, to repeat, the original sin of historicism. It leads Meinecke to condemn teleological history – from the French enlightenment through to the dialectical philosophy of history of Lessing, Kant, Schiller, Fichte and Hegel – as the secularized continuation of Christian providential history which sought to reduce the interplay of rational and irrational historical forces to the common denominator of reason.[15] The opposition of organic to dialectical history, of living form to rational synthesis, bequeaths a fatal legacy to the romantic quest for identity. If the divinity dwells in a living culture, the contradictory imperative of the new mythology expresses in the sharpest form the conflicting impulses of *original imitation*. Heidegger's call for the more original repetition of the Greek origin itself repeats the original constellation of romanticism just as Germany's 'metaphysical' mission defines *ex negativo* Germany's historical reality: from Hölderlin to Heidegger, the awakening of Germany remains suspended between origin and goal in the night of the absence of the gods. It is in this sense that a commentator can speak of Hölderlin as the poet of Germany's *Sonderweg*,[16] whose vanishing point is resumed in Heidegger's conjuration of *Ereignis*, the advent of the 'last god' in *Beiträge zur Philosophie* (1936–8).[17]

Like Nietzsche, Heidegger is compelled to polemicize against the fatalism of historicist thinking. In 1929 he dismisses the cultural pessimism of the postwar years, referring in particular to Spengler and Klages,[18] as nothing but a tired repetition of Nietzsche's dualism of the Apollonian and the Dionysian. Spenglerian biologism and historicist irrationalism are declared to be incapable of grasping the truly demonic, destructive malignancy of history.

The need of the times requires a deeper grounding than the opposition of 'life' and 'spirit'. And yet, when Heidegger seeks to characterize the crisis of the age in his *Introduction to Metaphysics* (1935), the topoi of Germany's ideological estrangement from western modernity are once again rehearsed: the subjection of the spiritual powers of culture – poetry and the plastic arts, state formation and religion – to calculating intelligence and conscious planning, whose outcome is the darkening of the world, 'the flight of the gods, the destruction of the earth, the massification of humanity, the rule of mediocrity'.[19] If the glow of original creation has paled to the reflected light of a deadly, demonic rationalism, this critique is deadly in a second sense. The knowledge that a culture lives only as long as it does not comprehend itself, is a fatal 'knowledge', which haunts the romantic longing for origin.

The imperative of original imitation thus produces a history of repetition in quite another sense than that intended by Heidegger. From the beginning the German ideology drew its differential impetus from the need to distinguish itself from what Lacoue-Labarthe has termed the imitation of the moderns – the need, that is, to break with the French imitation of antiquity, whether it be the neoclassicism of an absolutist national culture or the neoclassicism of revolutionary republicanism. In seeking to go beyond the French imitation of the Roman imitation of the Greeks, German rebirth hoped to draw upon the creative power of the Greek originality of origin.[20] This return to the source is confronted, however, by Germany's historical dilemma: how is a Germany that does not yet exist to define its identity against the French model? How can it be modern without first having been classical? How can it be classical if it lacks a nation and a state? How can it become a nation and a state if it lacks a classical foundation? To a people without a national culture corresponds a culture without a people – the Weimar classicism of Goethe and Schiller. It was Goethe, moreover, who pointed in his essay 'Literary Sansculottism' to the unacceptable price of revolution as the condition of a national culture.[21] Precisely this disjunction of the political and the cultural produces – from Schiller's *Letters on the Aesthetic Education of Man* onwards – an aestheticization of politics. This aesthetic politics is predicated on a cultural as opposed to a political definition of national identity. It is an aesthetic programme, which is compelled to repeat the circle of self-creation: culture must create the unity and identity of the people, which must already exist if cultural creation is to be possible. We thus have a Germany, which in western terms is neither classical nor modern, but projects the problem of its identity onto Greece, a projection whose ultimate point is attained with Heidegger's invention of a Greece that never was for a Germany that has not yet acceded to its essential destiny.[22]

Neither classical nor modern: the question of German identity and of a national culture, inescapably posed by the French Revolution, is open to two opposed readings, both of which we find in Marx. On the one hand, Germany risks becoming the contemporary of European decadence before it has become emancipated. On the other hand, by virtue of its non-contemporaneity, Germany possesses the capacity to leap over and surpass the stage of bourgeois-capitalist modernity.[23] Translated into the imperative of national aestheticism: Germany will overcome the challenge of western classicism, enlightenment and modernity, which it has neither assimilated nor attained, by the return to the Greek origins. The way forward is the way back. The result, however, is a double division of the ancient and the modern: to a divided Germany corresponds a divided Greece.[24] The Germany, which lacks a classical culture, discovers a pre-classical Greece as model for a Germany, that is not yet modern but already in its critique of modernity 'postmodern'. For Habermas postmodernity dates from Nietzsche.[25] More consistently Louis Dumont argues that Germany is already postmodern by 1800.[26] A pre-classical Greece for a 'post-modern' Germany characterizes the forced para-doxical logic of original imitation, which can sustain its agon with Greek anti-quity and western modernity only by defining both the classical and the modern more originally. This more original definition, whose task is to trans-form European decadence into the redemption of the Occident, goes beyond and behind the dialectical reading of the ancients and moderns, which ends in Hegel's recognition not only of the incomparable greatness of classical art but of the impossibility of great art in modernity.

This struggle for originality, which pits romanticism against enlightenment and art against science, is played out in terms of the rival constructions of antiquity and modernity that govern the 'imitation of the moderns'. If the dominant western model looks to Rome, the counter-model looks to Greece and proclaims the superiority of its own original imitation over Europe's translation of the beginning into the derivative languages of latinity and all that goes with this translation – renaissance, humanism, classicism, ration-alism and civilization. Romantic renewal by contrast is rooted in the linguistic originality that makes German the language of poets and thinkers and predes-tines Germany's redemptive mission. Moreover, as we have seen, this logic demands a more original Greece, in which the modern, historicist antithesis of civilization and culture returns in the discovery of the Dionysian beneath the veneer of harmonious Apollonian civilization. Nietzsche proposes a doubly tragic reading of Greek culture in *The Birth of Tragedy*. The demise of authentic tragic culture – the 'suicide' of Greek tragedy executed by Euri-pides and Socrates – symbolizes the fatal victory of civilization. The deadly confrontation of tragic and theoretical culture, of myth and enlightenment reduces the whole intervening history between a dying Greece and an unborn Germany to two thousand years of decline and decadence. It is a 'cultural' construction of European history that Nietzsche takes over from Wagner and hands on – in the radically sharpened form of a diagnosis of nihilism – to Heidegger. The other side to this reading of the history of the West – as a genealogy of the 'progressive' unfolding of nihilism – is the rejection, shared by Wagner, Nietzsche and Heidegger, of philosophy's subsumption of art under the hegemony of aesthetics. And here we might say that if Hegel's *Aes-thetics* completes the closing of the way, Kant unwittingly opens it through his recognition of the modern distinction between the beautiful and the sublime – unwittingly, because the romantic sublime cancels the moral autonomy of the subject vindicated for Kant in the experience of the sublime. The dividing line between the eighteenth and the nineteenth centuries – between a 'classical' and a 'romantic' Greece, between the Apollonian and the Dionysian – is the line drawn between a secondary aesthetics of beautiful illusion and a primal aesthetics of the sublime, manifested in the originary strife of tragedy (exemplified for Hölderlin, Hegel, Wagner and Heidegger above all in Sophocles's *Antigone*) which founds history and culture.

The conflict of the old and the new gods, the gods of the earth and the heavens, the maternal and the paternal, darkness and light, makes Greek tragedy simultaneously the aesthetic representation and objectivation of foundation and the sublime enactment and presencing of the powers of origin, such that tragedy stands as the unsurpassed paradigm of the identity of community and myth. The 'origin of the work of art' (Heidegger) holds fast the sublime strife of earth and world that founds history. When Lacoue-Labarthe identifies the idea of history as perhaps the fundamental idea of the German tradition, it is in order to place Heidegger's thinking of the relation between *phusis* and *technē* in *The Origin of the Work of Art* within this tradition – a tradition, determined since Kant by the question of the relation between nature and history.[27] Just as the new mythology inaugurates this mythopoietic tradition so Heidegger's history of Being can be seen as its most complete expression: onto-poetic historicism comprehends history in the light of origin and divides it into essential and fallen history. All greatness and creativity lies for Heidegger in the origin:

The basic fallacy underlying such modes of thought consists in its belief that history begins with the primitive and the backward, the weak and the helpless. The opposite is true. The beginning is the strangest and mightiest. What comes afterward is not development but the flattening that results from mere spreading out; it is inability to retain the beginning; the beginning is emasculated and exaggerated into a caricature of greatness taken as purely numerical and quantitative size and extension. That strangest of all beings *is* what it is *because* it harbours such a beginning in which everything all at once burst from superabundance into the overpowering and strove to master it.

If this beginning is inexplicable, it is not because of any deficiency in our knowledge of history, on the contrary, the authenticity and greatness of historical knowledge reside in an understanding of the mysterious power of the beginning. The knowledge of primordial history is not a ferreting out of primitive lore or a collecting of bones. It is neither half nor whole natural science but, if it is anything at all, mythology.[28]

The authenticity and greatness of historical knowledge is given to mythology. Here we come closest to the mysterious character of the beginning. For what is mythology other than the symbolization of the originary strife of foundation in which the union of nature and history is consecrated? The crucial question, however, is whether the 'knowledge of primordial history' is itself historical or original. Does it point backwards to the old mythology and the history of mythology or forward to the new mythology and the mythical history of the Occident? Here we can turn to Alfred Baeumler, Heidegger's successful philosophical rival in the contest for Nazi favour.[29] For Baeumler what is involved in this alternative is the question of the true romanticism. This is the guiding question of his introduction to a selection of Bachofen's writings, published in 1926.[30] In aligning himself with Bachofen[31] against Nietzsche, Baeumler arrives at a 'deeper' understanding of origin, and hence of romanticism. Behind the question of the true succession and completion of romanticism lies the subterranean struggle between nature and history, the unconscious-maternal and the conscious-paternal principles, which Baeumler identifies with the two lines of historicist thinking: religious romanticism and aesthetic or onto-poetic romanticism.

Baeumler's 'religious' concept of origin, shrouded in the 'holy darkness of prehistory',[32] excludes the active imperative of original imitation. Greece serves rather as the mirror in which romanticism discovers its essence in reaction to the eternal day of the eighteenth century's aesthetic ideas of epic and plastic beauty, which inspired German classicism from Winckelmann, Goethe, Wilhelm von Humboldt and Schiller to Hegel. This one-sided Apollonian vision of Greek beauty knows neither death nor tragedy, and is thus cut off from the true and deeper Greece: classicism sees antiquity under the sign of life, romanticism under the sign of death.[33] The return of Dionysus was accomplished, however, not by the romanticism of Jena but by the romanticism of Heidelberg. Only Hölderlin, who sensed the infinite life behind the Greek gods, is excepted from the judgement that Jena represented a last synthesis and dissolution of the eighteenth century, scornfully dismissed as the 'euthanasia of the rococo'.[34] The return of Dionysus signifies the recovery of chthonian popular religion and its cosmic consciousness of the power of life and death, which belongs to the Earth Mother and her fearful avatars, the Furies and the Fates. 'In the word *mother* is combined everything that romanticism sought, desired, strove for':[35] the combination of 'demonic sexuality, love of the night, belief in spirits, fear and longing for death, ancestral cult and submission to fate'. The romantics were led by inner necessity to the discovery of Dionysus, the god of women and tragedy, because the religion of Dionysus was the romanticism of antiquity.[36]

Baeumler's interpretation of Greek tragedy is presided over by Dionysus, the god of the dead and of nature. The cult of sacred heroes, summoned from the underworld, is directed against Nietzsche's interpretation of tragedy as ecstatic identification with Dionysus Zagreus, the dismembered god. Although Baeumler approves of Nietzsche's treatment of sexuality and assigns him to the religious line of romanticism, the whole thrust of his argument is to identify Nietzsche with the new mythology of the beginning of the century. Like Friedrich Schlegel, Nietzsche speaks of the return and rebirth of myth, whereas true romanticism knows that myth belongs to the mysteries of prehistory.[37]

Baeumler's defence of chthonian myth – the powers of earth, mother, blood and death – against the hubris of male appropriation and violation brings us to the most 'original' dimension of his understanding of romanticism: the distinction between male and female origin, male and female nature, male and female history. Its Kantian and Fichtean provenance defines the aesthetic romanticism of Schelling and Schlegel. Schelling's philosophy of nature grounds the correspondence between natural and transcendental philosophy in the idea of nature as active, productive, i.e. male spirit, the very antithesis of the unity of 'earth, people, nature, the past and night' in Görres's philosophy of nature, which is rooted in the eternal polarity of the sexes and the mystery of life.[38] Görres's recognition of the maternal side of history makes him the source of the true romanticism of the nineteenth century.[39] Against the light of origin, whose ultimate principle is pure activity, Baeumler invokes a god who is not an idea but a symbol of the living connection with the origin, transmitted through time into the present. Baeumler's religious romanticism is also a religious nationalism, in which language, law, custom and myth partake of the divine because they express the natural, mystical continuity with the origin. As the repository of the 'secret life of underworldly powers' before and beneath history, the natural unity of historical being can only be that of a people: the inner life of history comes from nature.[40]

The answer to the question of origin is thus clear for Baeumler. It lies in the naturalization of history through the return to the maternal embrace of myth. Consequently it is Nietzsche who looks forward and closes the way and Bachofen who looks back and opens the way to the origin by articulating the fundamental intention of the romantics through his romanticization of antiquity from the perspective of women, death and the symbol.[41] Nietzsche's Dionysian concept of life, derived from Schlegel and from Creuzer's suffering god of the mysteries,[42] closes the way because it springs not from Mother Nature (the Orient) but from the celebration of male creative power (the Occident). Baeumler can thus conclude that *The Birth of Tragedy* presents a 'Socratic'(!) theory of myth, composed of a combination of *logos* and mysticism, German classical aesthetics and Wagner's music, even though he must admit that Bachofen's comprehension of the unity of life and death in the mother finds its parallel in Nietzsche's union of life and orgiastic self-annihilation.[43]

Baeumler's reading of the two romanticisms throws the contradiction of the new mythology into sharp relief. Religious romanticism bars the way not only to the dialectical completion of modernity but equally to rebirth and repetition of the origin. The organic conception of natural history leads inescapably, Baeumler insists, to the decline of the West. It is Spengler who spells out the logic of romantic historicism. Above all, origin – like language – cannot be remade artificially.[44] Our detour via Baeumler brings us back to the question of original imitation. If Baeumler is indeed right to distinguish the two lines of romanticism, he fails to grasp that the fatalism of the one generates the activism of the other, precisely because they are rooted in the same ground and share the same phantasm of the powers of origin. The new mythology (the coming god) draws its dynamic from the decay of the old mythology (the death of god), but once it has lost its dialectical *telos* – the synthesis of the ancients and the moderns in a mythology of reason – religious and aesthetic romanticism enter into a process of mutual radicalization, whose outcome is a nationalization of myth[45] and a mythicization of the history of the West, conceived as the fatal decline from mythical origin. Spengler's morphology of history not only traces the logic of organic historicism, it is also inspired by the radical historicism of aesthetic romanticism. His comprehension of history as a succession of 'culture souls', that is, as a series of finite cultural imaginaries, is not so distant from Nietzsche or Heidegger's onto-poetics of history, dramatized as the mythical history of the retreat and return of the origin.

If onto-poetic historicism derives in first line from aesthetic romanticism, it is not less imbued with the pessimism and finally nihilism of organic historicism and religious romanticism. It is Heidegger who expounds in his 1934/35 Hölderlin lectures the 'intrinsic law' of the 'stages of decline of a historical *Dasein* as such in the plight (*Not*) of the absence of the gods'.[46] But in registering the intrinsic law of decline, authentic historical knowledge is impelled by the longing for advent, the *Ereignis* of the coming god. Onto-poetic historicism is thus the ultimate expression of the fascination with the powers of origin, which governs the romantic quest for self-creation and its metaphors of creativity.

5   Metaphors of Creation

The modern foundation of knowledge, based on the *ego cogitans*, method and the mathematization of nature, separated nature and spirit into distinct realms, a separation confirmed by Kant's critiques of pure and practical reason. In the *Critique of Judgement* Kant sought to bridge the gulf between the physical and moral universe through a philosophy of nature and a philosophy of art. This opposition of science and art, method and imagination, reflected opposed conceptions of history: the universal history of the enlightenment, modelled on natural law and the progress of science, and the organic history of romanticism, directed to the growth and development of individual cultural totalities as the expression of the collective genius of a people. The romantic renaturalization of man, which affirms the transcendence of historical and linguistic origins, is premised on an interpretation of history as nature, or more exactly on the contrast between 'natural' and 'unnatural' history. The understanding of culture as unconscious, organic growth distinguishes historicism's version of natural history from that of the enlightenment. It signifies not the record of superstition and prejudice (cf. Hume's *The Natural History of Religion*) but the mysterious entwinement of reason and the 'irrational depths of the soul' (Meinecke), of the conscious and the unconscious, accessible solely to intuition and not to analysis. The 'unnatural' split between nature and spirit underlies Horkheimer and Adorno's vision of history as the blind perpetuation of nature, behind which stands Freud's return of the repressed as the figure of mythical fatality. Freud's new science of the unconscious returns to Schopenhauer's disenchanted conception of nature as blind Will. Jung's depth psychology by contrast returns to the romantic conception of creative and healing nature and repeats Faust's descent to the Mothers, the source of the archetypes of 'natural history', present in the symbolism of mythologies and religion.

The romantic desire to overcome the Cartesian–Kantian division between subject and object, history and nature is driven by the search for transcendence in a modernity where the death of God demands a new relation between the infinite and the finite, the unconscious and the conscious. The universal reason of the enlightenment lacks the ground that would unite nature and spirit, the task delegated to the infinite progression of history and the progressive rationalization of social organization. Hence Saint-Simon's distinction, taken over by his pupil Comte, between organic and critical epochs in history and his call for a New Christianity for post-revolutionary society.[1] However, the modern dilemmas which the organic community is supposed to solve – the new relation between individualism and the collective, between the conscious and the unconscious – point to the contradictions of the romantic counter-conception, evident in Baeumler's double lineage of religious and aesthetic romanticism, underpinned by the distinct if intertwined lineages of organic and onto-poetic historicism, and encapsulated in the double meaning of original and origin. If the original genius – nature in the subject (Kant) – is meant to embody the synthesis of unconscious and conscious creation, if the act of creation is meant in turn to figure the refounding of a communal culture, the modern age is characterized precisely by its suspension between the lost organic totality of the past, whether of Greece or the Middle Ages, and the community to come. The eminently modern, but equally anti-modern, idea of creativity thus revolves around the reconnection on the one hand of nature and the subject and of nature and history on the other.

With his opposition of nature and civilization Rousseau set the natural goodness of man against the corrupting influences of modern culture and learning. Modern civilization teaches us to live not according to our inner impulses but according to opinion. The subjectivism of modern moral understanding is announced in Rousseau's call to follow the inner voice of sentiment as the source of truth and goodness. This notion of an inner voice, the conviction that truth is to be sought within the self, makes feelings as opposed to reason, inner participation as opposed to external observation, the key to access to the natural order. Feeling authenticates 'truth which is its own testimony'. Sentiments thus become values in their own right, leading to a blurring and dissolution of the distinction between feelings and traditional ethical codes. This fundamental change in the mode of access to truth privileges the individual subject as medium, who transforms himself through the reconnection with the inner source. Becoming attuned to nature and the cosmos brings with it a deeper and fuller experience of the self, at one with the current of life in nature. Romantic pantheism flows from the sense that we can gain access to the divine through living nature.

The conviction that we can only truly know nature through articulating our inner nature gives rise to the expressive subject,[2] that is, to the modern idea of expression as self-shaping and self-creation, i.e. the idea of self-development and *Bildung* as the manifestation of an inner power. The expressive subject is not defined in terms of rational control but in terms of the capacity for self-articulation. This places a premium on individuation, authenticity and originality, in the double sense of creative reconnection with the living source and uniqueness. Art, as opposed to natural science, is called upon to fill a central place in our spiritual life, just as the artist as genius, the highest embodiment of originality and creative imagination, comes to be seen as priest, seer and creator god.[3] The traditional doctrine of art as the imitation of nature gives way to the idea of art as the expression of nature's creativity. But here it is important to remember that the originality of genius represents the originality of the self in its individual uniqueness. The self is no longer to be understood as some impersonal form or copy but as a being capable of self-expression. It is this capacity for the expression of inner feeling which completes us as human beings and rescues us from the enlightenment's *denaturalization* of man, which at its most extreme reduces nature and life to a machine. Expressivism can thus be seen as central to the romantic programme of the *renaturalization* of man, the romantic longing for a reconciliation of nature and spirit that rests on the inner unity of the self and nature.

Leibniz is an important source of Expressivism. In *The Philosophy of the Enlightenment* Cassirer writes that, in order to grasp the intellectual structure of the eighteenth century, we must distinguish two streams of thought: the classical Cartesian form of analysis and the new form of philosophical synthesis which originates in Leibniz. 'From the logic of "clear and distinct ideas" the way leads to the logic of "origin" and to the logic of individuality; it leads from pure geometry to a dynamic philosophy of nature, from mechanism to organism, from the principle of identity to that of infinity.' This whole movement of thought (from France to Germany) is already contained in Leibniz's monadology. 'Every monad is a living centre of energy, and it is the infinite abundance and diversity of monads which constitute the unity of the world.' As such, the individual entity 'no longer functions merely as a special case, as an example; it now expresses something essential in itself and valuable through itself. For in Leibniz's system every individual substance is not only a fragment of the universe, it is the universe itself seen from a particular viewpoint.'[4] The self as universe is the autarkic source of its own inner activity. What appears causally and mechanically in natural phenomena must be understood at the same time as purposive dynamic form, 'concentrated and living' (Leibniz) in the monad.[5]

The transformation of external – mechanical – determination into inner – organic – self-determination transforms Cartesian dualism into the pre-established harmony of non-causal correspondences. The key to Leibniz's harmony and Spinoza's parallelism lies, Deleuze has argued, in the idea of expression. God expresses himself in the world in a double movement of implication and explication. The comprehension of the world as the expression of God breaks with the transcendence of the Creator to creation, and thus signifies a new ontology of immanence, based on a rediscovery of nature and its powers. The Cartesian dualism of body and soul, mind and matter, ideal representation and real causation is transformed into expression.[6] The corollary of the new ontology is the collapse of the doctrine of the imitation of nature, which denied for two thousand years any place for human creativity. Expression replaces imitation, production replaces reproduction – once the living producing force (*energeia*) is grasped as immanent to the product (*ergon*).

What applies to the subject applies equally to the realm of history. Herder's understanding of history as a natural process, as the cyclic sequence of birth, growth, decay and death, makes him, along with Vico, the father of historicism. His counter-position to the universal history of the enlightenment gives language priority over reason and the understanding. The opposition of nature and history is sublated in the idea of organic development: nature is historicized as development and history naturalized into the succession of natural events. The same laws govern both the natural and the historical cosmos, and both are the expression of divine-natural forces. Each epoch and people is therefore equally close to God in its naturally unique individuality. Herder's new vision of history in *Reflections on the Philosophy of the History of Mankind* (1774) does not escape Kant's sobering critique: the attempt to determine the spiritual nature of man and his development in analogy to the natural formation and organization of matter requires the assumption of invisible forces. What we do not understand is to be explained by what we understand even less. Despair at the objective possibility of knowing nature produces the turn to the 'fruitful field' of poetry.[7]

Kant's reminder to Herder – that it is not spirit that is to be explained from nature but nature from spirit – is equally at odds with the romantic conception of culture as the product of inner formative forces. Romantic historicism gives precedence to language over the understanding, to poetry over reason, and regards the institutions of a people as the expression of its inner soul or spirit. Herder is the father of romantic nationalism, for which the imaginary community of the nation is a creation rooted in its origins It is a collective individuality whose genesis precludes the hubris of a rational construction of the social order. German romantic nationalism, for all its emphasis on particularity and uniqueness, must be understood with Dumont as a differential expression of identity.[8] It defined itself in opposition to French intellectual and political hegemony and to the western political model of the nation-state, in both its revolutionary republican form, grounded in democratic citizenship and constitutionalism, or its liberal form, based on individualism and the rights of civil society. The cultural conception of nationalism, with its emphasis on integration and holism, appeals not to a political but to a genetic notion of nationhood, defined through language, culture and history.

The priority of genesis, which makes the past and not the future decisive for national self-definition, means that historical explanation finds its focus in unconscious organic processes. The historian Thomas Nipperday stresses that the discovery of the historical unconscious of a people was the great achievement of romanticism.[9] The heritage of the original, spontaneous expression of national spirit must be protected from foreign influences and the dangers of foreign imitation. Although romantic nationalism is modern in its dynamic, it responds to modernization primarily in terms of its perceived threats to social integration. The stereotypical opposition of organic community and mechanical society, individualism and holism, looks to the nation as the source of the reintegration of the individual. The individual finds through his birth into the community his transpersonal identity in the national religion of the people. Organic historicism and romantic naturalism are ill suited, indeed fatally constricted, in their capacity to adapt to modernization. What is experienced as the crisis of modernization – alienation, disenchantment, division of labour, social conflict, industrialization, the power of the market – and registered above all as cultural decadence and decline reflects the crisis of the pre- and anti-political organic conception of history, whose 'natural' end is cultural pessimism.

The central theme of organic historicism – from Herder to Spengler, and the ground bass of romantic nationalism – derives from the conception of history in analogy to nature and of culture as the expression of the inner life and spirit of a people. Between Herder's expressive conception of history as nature and Nietzsche's reduction of history to the natural history of the life force lies the turn to nature as *production* (Schelling) and *revolution* (Wagner). Integral to all four positions and their metaphors of creativity[10] is the relation between consciousness and the unconscious. Whereas expression and life privilege the unconscious, production and revolution spring from the creative synthesis of the conscious and the unconscious. Where Herder sees the unfolding of the source – the expression in history of God's plan of nature – romantic idealism sees the productivity of spirit. Herder's natural-divine origin becomes creation raised to the higher power of self-comprehending origin. What separates Schelling, Wagner and Nietzsche from the original model of expression and organic historicism is what we can call a second order historicism, that is to say, a radical activation of the ideas of origin and creation under the impact of the French Revolution. The philosophy of Fichte plays this role for Schelling, Hölderlin and Schlegel, the music of Beethoven for Wagner. Radical historicism replays the eighteenth-century *querelle des anciens et modernes*, under the double imperative and double-bind of national aestheticism and original imitation. It transforms Herder's model of conscious/unconscious expression and culture as organic totality into the aesthetic programme of a new mythology.

The death of God, dramatized by Nietzsche, already haunts the radical historicism of post-revolutionary romanticism. Christian history mutates into the religion of the death of God and the coming god. Revolution provides the grandest and most radical metaphor of the coming god, as the eschatological figure of the death and rebirth of culture in modernity. It makes Wagner the central figure of the nineteenth-century romantic imaginary. Situated between Feuerbach and Schopenhauer, Marx and Nietzsche, communism and nationalism, atheism and the Christian longing for redemption, he incorporates all the contradictions of the romantic-revolutionary quest for identity. His political-aesthetic manifestos after the collapse of the Dresden revolt of 1848–9 carry on the revolution by other means. They take him from revolutionary politics to the meta-politics of *Art and Revolution*, from which will be born 'The Art Work of the Future'. On the one hand, Wagner's prophecy of the coming revolution, the coming aesthetic community – the last and greatest deed of mankind – resumes the aesthetic vision and dialectical version of *Naturgeschichte*, the natural *history* of the self-realization of human nature in history (Kant, Schiller, Hegel, Marx). On the other hand, Wagner's reading of western history as two thousand years of cultural decadence and Christian despotism since the Greeks anticipates Nietzsche and Heidegger's turn to original history against the contradiction of the *unnatural* history of the West.

The ambiguities of Wagner's revolutionary utopia have their provenance in the equation of revolution and nature, articulated as the historical task of original imitation. The one true art – 'the great unitarian Artwork of Greece', the *Gesamtkunstwerk* – has not been born again, indeed cannot be *reborn* since it must be *born anew*.[11] It must be *birth* (Nietzsche), it must be *origin* (Heidegger). But what will be the origin of the artwork of the future, which will celebrate the religion of humanity, the 'glorious Tragedy of Man'? It can come only from the 'hidden depths' of humanity's great revolution, that is, from the setting free of the force of nature which is revolution: 'Nature, Human Nature, will proclaim this law to the twin sisters culture and civilization: "So far as I am contained in you, shall ye live and flourish; so far as I am not in you, shall ye rot and die!"'[12] And what is human nature but nature that has come to self-consciousness in man in the double form of science and of art? What science separates, art rejoins. In art man recognizes nature's essence as his own. In art life becomes conscious of its free harmony with nature. Such a creative synthesis of nature and spirit would be impossible, however, if thought governed life. Knowledge severed from the energy of the unconscious is mere illusion, the historical error of the intellect, of religion, science and state, which have raised themselves against the life-force of necessity and usurped the vitality of their true originators – the people (Volk). Only from the people can the work of redemption come: 'It is not the lonely spirit, striving by Art for redemption into Nature, that can frame the Artwork of the Future; only the spirit of Fellowship, fulfilled by Life, can bring this work to pass. But the lonely one can prefigure it to himself.'[13]

Wagner's revolutionary metaphor of creativity also prefigures, before his encounter with Schopenhauer, Nietzsche's appeal to life as *the* metaphor of creativity. As Hans Joas observes, the philosophy of life attempts to think creativity as such.[14] Its source is Schopenhauer's Will, the primal force of *natura naturans* prior to the world of phenomenal individuation and all and any specific goals of action and consciousness. But where Schopenhauer saw only the eternally unsatisfied, ceaseless, senseless striving of the Will, Nietzsche identified with the life-force's will to power and made it the creative source of value. If the reduction of consciousness to an epiphenomenon of the Will seems to point back to an organic understanding of culture against the decadence and nihilism of civilization, the emergence of life as a 'post-religious myth'[15] not only takes up the theme of the coming god but lays bare the radical historicism of the new mythology, whose figure becomes the eternal cycle of Dionysian creation and destruction.

In its thinking of original creativity, romantic historicism rings the changes on the relation between nature and history, the irrational and the rational, the conscious and the unconscious. This is summed up for Heidegger, as we have seen, by the opposition between spirit and life, *Geist und Leben*. This opposition, the primary code and topos of the philosophy of life, with all its familiar variants (natural/artificial, organic/mechanical, art/science, language/ reason, community/society, creativity/sterility), cannot escape its own contradiction. The revolt of 'life' against the sterile, empty forms of a late, decadent civilization and its reified 'world of conventions' – in other words: the romantic quest for the spontaneous roots of creativity – enacts a dialectic, whose 'law', according to Adorno, runs as follows: the more the rationality of irrational society advances, the deeper becomes regression, the flight from history back to nature and origin.[16] And yet, this dialectic of romanticism is not so distant from the dialectic of enlightenment traced by Adorno and Horkheimer. As Axel Honneth has argued with reference to Ludwig Klages's most important work, *Der Geist als Widersacher der Seele* (3 volumes, 1929–32), *Dialectic of Enlightenment* is itself indebted, more deeply than has been recognized, to the whole tradition of the philosophy of life and its critique of civilization. Adorno and Klages's critiques of modernity converge in a common anthropology and philosophy of history: the splitting of life between mind and its object appears as both cause and effect of the pathologies of modern society. Both critiques describe the self-instrumentalization of the self against the background of the philosophy of life and prescribe the turn to aesthetics as the path to the recovery of nature.[17]

The idea of creativity in the German tradition ends in cultural pessimism and a fatal and fatalistic dialectic of civilization (cf. Freud's reduction of history to the mythical struggle of Eros and Thanatos in *Civilization and its Discontents*), which fuelled the 'politics of despair' (Fritz Stern) in Wilhelminian Germany and the political fantasies of the 'Conservative Revolution' in the Weimar Republic.[18] It was Thomas Mann who warned in 1930 of the dangers of political regression and spoke of the connection between a romanticizing philosophy and National Socialism. This romantic vitalism drew its power and mass appeal from the revolt against reason and an irrational concept of life. It affirmed 'the life-giving forces of the unconscious, of the dynamic and darkly creative', and rejected life-destroying intellect in the name of a maternal-chthonic and holy underworld (with clear reference to Baeumler).[19] Indeed, who should know better than Thomas Mann, profoundly influenced as he was by Schopenhauer, Wagner and Nietzsche. During the First World War Mann had expounded in *Confessions of an Unpolitical German* his identification with an anti-western Germany and his romantic sympathy with death. From *Buddenbrooks* to *Doctor Faustus*, the recurrent theme of his work is that of the dialectic of sterility and creativity, the longing for revivifying regression, the 'breakthrough' to life and its civilizational consequences. In *Death in Venice* the writer Aschenbach experiences the barbaric and seductive music of Dionysus, the 'stranger god', in a 'frightful dream', which announces the disintegration and destruction of the whole moral order: 'its theatre seemed to be his own soul, and the events burst in from outside, violently overcoming the profound resistance of his spirit; passed through him and left him, left the whole cultural structure of a lifetime trampled on, ravaged, and destroyed'.

6 Newly Invented Myths: Wagner

If there is a figure central to romanticism, that figure is Wagner. The cult of Wagner, from Baudelaire to Mallarmé, from Nietzsche to George Bernard Shaw, responded to the longing, as Lacoue-Labarthe puts it, for a 'work of "great art" on the scale imputed to works of Greek art': 'here it was finally produced, and the secret of what Hegel had called the "religion of art" had been rediscovered. And de facto, what was founded was like a new religion.'[1] All that the romantics had projected in their new mythology appeared to be realized in Wagner's music dramas, which summed up the double thrust and double bind of romanticism's redemptive aesthetic mission. The Greek *Gesamtkunstwerk*, the work of art of nature, was to be born anew in modernity from the power of the modern symphony orchestra, without parallel in antiquity.[2]

The Wagner who points back to romanticism and its new mythology and at the same time forward to the theatrical aestheticization of politics in the Third Reich is indeed a central figure of romantic modernism. Through his work runs the fault-line of a Europe haunted by the twin phantasms of revolutionary redemption and *Götterdämmerung*. Wagner's revolutionary writings of 1849 resume and complete a vision of modernity reconciled to itself in the religion of humanity. The artistic realization of the coming god, the redemptive sacrificial death of Siegfried in the *Ring* cycle, buries, however, the birth of the new world in the downfall of the old world. But if we look more closely, we can see Wagner's fundamental ambivalence towards modern civilization. It is already contained in his whole concept of revolution: the Feuerbachian resurrection of human nature is equally inspired by a Bakuninian negation of history.

In the unsigned article 'The Revolution', which appeared in the Dresden

Volksblätter in April 1849 and is attributed to Wagner, the goddess of Revolution declares that she has come to destroy the whole insane order of things: 'Whatever is must pass away ... and I, the eternal destroyer, fulfil the law and create eternally youthful life.'[3] As the metaphor of creativity, revolution is scarcely distinguishable from the Nietzschean metaphor of creative/destructive life. The failure of revolution prepared the way for Wagner's reception of Schopenhauer and the transmutation of revolutionary destruction into the vision of the self-destruction of history. The centre of interest of the *Ring* shifts from the coming god to the dying god, to Wotan's unconsciously willed self-destruction as the crux of the drama.[4] Through Schopenhauer Wagner comes to grasp the unconscious theme of his work since *The Flying Dutchman*. As he writes to his imprisoned fellow revolutionary August Röckel in 1856: 'The most extraordinary thing in this connection I had to undergo at last with my Nibelung poem: I gave it shape at a time when I had, with my concepts alone, built up a Hellenistic-optimistic world the realization of which I held to be quite possible if only human beings desired it.' The aim of the Nibelung myth had been to expose the world of injustice, based on loveless egoism and the greed for power and money, which must crash to ruins and give way to a just world. Consciously the drama proclaimed that one phase of society – the bourgeois world of money, power and hypocrisy – is coming to its end. Intuitively, however, he had 'seen and recognized in its nothingness [*Nichtigkeit*] the nature of the world itself in all conceivable phases of its development instead of one alone'.[5]

Thus either side of the historically fateful divide of 1848/49, in the 'progression' from conscious to unconscious motives, Wagner reveals the ambivalence integral to the whole concept of *Naturgeschichte*. The historical-dialectical impetus of the new mythology – the synthesis of the ancients and the moderns, nature and history, origin and goal – collapses with the reversion of history to nature. Adorno reads the mythology of *The Ring* as unfolding the allegory of natural history.[6] If *The Ring* articulates in romantic-mythical disguise the dialectic of enlightenment, it points to the dialectic of romanticism as its inseparable other. Nietzsche and Heidegger's turn to the mythical powers of origin is built on the ruins not only of the dialectical philosophy of history but of western civilization as a whole. And here it is Wagner's revolutionary/re-volutionary construction of European history that serves Nietzsche – and through Nietzsche Heidegger – as the model for their eschatologies. Crucial to Wagner's interpretation of history is a myth that embraces the beginning and the end of history. This is the programme of *Opera and Drama* (1852), which continues the political revolution, and surpasses it, by placing music drama at the very centre of world history, and with it of course the lonely figure of the artist. In claiming to have found the creative solution to the riddle of nature and of history, Wagner endows himself with the collective genius of the people, that is to say, with the capacity to invent new myths.

Wagner republished *Art and Revolution* with a new introduction in 1872, the year in which Nietzsche's *Birth of Tragedy* appeared. The correspondences are striking. The more immediate, inspired by German victory over France and unification, is their common belief in the German spirit, Wagner's recognition of the destiny of the German race and Nietzsche's heralding of the German myth. The more fundamental correspondence is that given in the historical vision expressed by the motto to the original edition of 1849, inspired by Feuerbach's farewell to philosophy and quoted now by Wagner in his introduction: 'When art erst held her peace, state-wisdom and philosophy began: when now both statesman and philosopher have breathed their last, let the Artist's voice again be heard.'[7] Just as the downfall of tragedy, 'the free expression of a free community', presaged the dissolution of the Greek state, so now the farewell to philosophy, religion and the oppressive politics of the state announces the end of alienation: 'To *Philosophy* and not to Art', Wagner writes in 1849, 'belong the two thousand years which, since the decadence of Greek tragedy, have passed to our day. In vain did art send hither and thither her dazzling beams into the night of discontented thought.'[8] Despite the fact that Wagner's and Nietzsche's national enthusiasm soon cooled, the vision of the night of western history suspended between the once and future religion of art, proclaimed by Wagner after 1848, by Nietzsche after 1871, and by Heidegger after 1933, is equally a vision of the birth of a new humanity.

Wagner envisaged a universal not a national revolution in 1849. If the two thousand years from the shattering of the Greek religion, from 'the wreck of the Grecian Nature-State, and its resolution into the Political State', are to have any meaning and goal, it must lie in 'the gigantic march of evolution, from the fallen *natural Kinsmenship of natural community* to the *Universal fellowship of all mankind*.[9] In this evolutionary-revolutionary perspective, however, the universal and the organic cohere uneasily. All who resist and revolt against the utilitarianism and the criminal egoism of modern civilization, 'hideous oppressor of the true nature of men', are declared to constitute the Folk, the chosen people who will find the Promised Land.[10] The universal fellowship of communism is construed as the organic community, but how could it be otherwise if the task of history is to reunite the splintered fragments of 'the common Tragic Artwork' into the artwork of the future? In Wagner's aesthetic construction of history, Germany moves to the centre of the stage in the third and most important part of his revolutionary trilogy, *Opera and Drama* (1852). What makes Wagner's analysis interesting is not so much the familiar pattern of cultural destitution and its coming reversal as its aesthetic-genetic deduction. In his reading, Germany exemplifies the division of European civilization since the Renaissance, that is to say, the fault-line marked by the division between drama and opera. The whole thrust of *Opera and Drama* is directed to the redemptive meta-politics of the music drama as the task of the German nation. The recovery of the living power of myth, amid the 'spontaneous combustion' (Carlyle) of the old world,[11] announces the end of the state, prefigured for Wagner in the myth of Oedipus.

The music drama to come thus represents (once more) the goal of the reunion of nature and history, the marriage of the unconscious (music) and the conscious (the poetic word). From this perspective Wagner can reconstruct the *already completed* history and sociology of opera and drama, refracted through the prism of the quest for the revealed secret of creativity, which neither opera nor drama divided from each other could attain. Wagner traces their separation to the dual – popular and courtly – origin of European drama in the Renaissance, which modern drama could never overcome. Even if the separated halves of Greek tragedy point to the necessity of reintegration, Wagnerian music drama cannot be derived from the twin lines of opera and drama. Music drama's original imitation does not reside in a combination of the originality of Shakespearean historical drama with opera's classicizing imitations of Greek mythology. The completed history and failure of opera and drama alike document the negative, not the positive truth of music drama. The case for the condemnation of opera is straightforward: it is the unnatural product of an unnatural culture. It owes its origin not to natural genesis but to the conscious artistic intention of the imitation of the ancients, whose setting was the Italian courts of the Renaissance. Since it lacks all organic connection with the people, it must deform the natural essence of music, the spontaneous fusion of word and melody in popular song. Since it lacks inner organic life, it cannot advance beyond the arbitrary formal structure of aria, recitative and ballet, to which even Mozart had to submit. The aria, the artificial flower of opera, typifies the fundamental flaw of the whole genre: the means of expression (music) is made purpose, and the purpose of expression (the drama) made means.

Wagner spells out the sociological perspective evident in the inglorious end of opera: the birth of the culture industry from the spirit of commerce, in which the paying public completes the usurpation of the people, whose only role in the operatic spectacle is to appear as the crowd, the massed chorus singing in unison. Reaction rules supreme. Rossini is declared the Metternich of music, whose pandering to the corrupt tastes of a luxury class has revealed the secret of opera – attractive melodies divorced from dramatic intent, thereby bringing its history to an end. What follows is Hollywood *avant la lettre*: the cultivation of sensation, of 'effect without cause',[12] pursued by Berlioz and Meyerbeer. The technical perfection of the orchestra, realized by Berlioz, mobilizes 'industrial mechanics' in the service of 'dramatic' musical expression, while Meyerbeer, the rootless cosmopolitan impresario, the Jew without a mother language, substitutes a monstrous kaleidoscope of historicist idioms for dramatic development.

If the scene of the end of opera is Paris, the site of the impasse of modern drama is Germany. German drama is divided between the two poles of European drama: Shakespeare, the highest product of natural-popular drama, and his antithesis, the Racinean classical tragedy of the court and its operatic counterpart from Monteverdi to Gluck. Wagner opposes the inner, expressive form of natural drama to the outer, unnatural form of the imitation of the Roman imitation of Greek models, governed by a false understanding of Aristotle's *Poetics*. The Shakespearean stage by contrast offered a free medium for the unfolding of historical actions, unhampered by prescriptive rules. And yet, for all that Wagner stresses that music drama must follow the path opened by Shakespeare, he rejects not only the modern attempts to renew Shakespeare but the very foundation of his drama – the derivation of the dramatic action from history. Why this is so emerges from Wagner's analysis of modern, that is, German drama.

If modern drama is German, it is a belated not an original drama. Like Germany itself, the unnatural hybrid of European division, German drama is condemned to oscillate between the twin poles of Shakespeare and Racine. Goethe alone escaped from the dilemmas of modern drama by abandoning the stage for the untrammelled freedom of the dramatic poem, to give expression in *Faust* to what Wagner calls the true poetic element of the present and the dramatic theme of the future – the realization of thought in deed. The Faustian myth of modernity announces in anticipatory fashion the completion of the Shakespearean succession. When we recall that Beethoven long contemplated the composition of an opera based on Goethe's *Faust*, we can see that the artwork of the future proclaims itself the heir to Goethe's poetic drama and to Beethoven's symphonic music. Together they open the musical-dramatic space vacated by drama and opera.

To clear this space, however, requires a further step: the demonstration that modern drama cannot find its original source and adequate content in history. Here Wagner turns to Schiller.[13] Just as Goethe attempted to fuse classical form and organic content, so Schiller strove to impose dramatic form on a resistant historical material. Schiller's longing for the purity of classical form insulated from the prose of modern life remained a poetic ideal, whose lack of living content confirms the separation of the ideal and the real. Suspended between the heaven of classical form and the earth of practical reality, Schiller epitomizes the inescapable failure of modern drama and modern culture. This failure is summed up in Wagner's verdict: we do not have and cannot have a living drama. Does this mean that the novel, the medium of practical reality and revolutionary critique, can take the place of the drama? Wagner's answer is yes and no. Yes, in that, as the offspring of the scientific worldview and sociological analysis, the novel has penetrated and laid bare the secret of modern society – that politics is fate. No, in that, by completing the politicization of poetry, the novel falls victim to the dialectic of its form. By embracing the historical-political process of the present, the novel destroys itself as a work of art. That the novel can be seen as the continuation of the Shakespearean line of historical drama only confirms for Wagner that history cannot be the true subject matter of the drama. The prose of modern conditions defies the possibility of poetry.

The impasse is complete. Wagner has cut off all escape routes. There remains only the creative leap of total revolution, the meta-political leap beyond political fate. If politics is the secret of modern history, then poetry can return only with the end of the political state. On this side we have the prose of the novel, the medium of the *mechanism of history*, governed by oppressive external necessity. On the other side there beckons the poetry of the drama, the medium of the *organism of humanity*, governed by inner natural necessity.

If drama is to be born anew, it must be born from myth, from the myth that embraces the beginning and the end of political history. The myth, which at the beginning of history anticipates its own end, is the myth of Oedipus. Just as communism signified for Marx the answer to the riddle of history, so the Oedipus myth for Wagner answers the riddle of man, posed by the Sphinx. The answer, which we must realize through the emancipation of human nature, will bring unnatural history to an end. The whole (original) conception of *The Ring of the Nibelungen* thus corresponds to and answers Sophocles's *Antigone*, the key to Wagner's interpretation of the Oedipus myth, which in turn forms the centre of *Opera and Drama*: 'Holy Antigone! You I call! Let your banner wave under which we shall destroy and redeem!'[14]

The mythical music drama thus stands as the revealed truth of history. When Wagner states, 'we now know, and have gained the capacity to be the organic creative artist *with consciousness*',[15] he is formulating the message of *Antigone*: the destruction of the state will bring the unconscious of human nature to the self-realizing consciousness of society's natural essence, a consciousness collectively shared because it knows unconscious human spontaneity as its only truth and necessity. From the revealed truth of history springs the secret of creativity, *the conscious creation of the unconscious*, whose highest poetic achievement will be the invention of new myths, which the music drama alone can fulfil because through it we come to knowledge through feeling. Or as Adorno puts it: 'The only function of consciousness is to complete the circle of unconsciousness.'[16]

Wagner's myth 'contains the world's beginning and its end',[17] the myth which completes and closes the ring of history to give the myth of the end of myth: that is, the necessary downfall of the false gods of the state, the rule of politics, contracts, property, egoism and the greed for power. However, when we turn from *Opera and Drama* to *The Ring*, the closure of the ring of history leaves us with an open question: how are we to interpret the conclusion? This question is underlined by the four different endings to *Götterdämmerung* that precede the final version, whose ambiguity in turn compounds the problem of deciphering the future destiny of the world. Are we witnessing the end of *a* world or of *the* world, the end of one cycle of history or of all history?

Carl Dahlhaus for instance has no doubts as to the answer: 'The really authentic ending is obviously the [Feuerbach] version of 1852', since the Schopenhauer ending of 1856 denies the overall intention of the tetralogy.[18] Warren Darcy is just as convinced that the Schopenhauer ending can alone explain the inconsistencies of the cycle. He asks why Wagner abandons his hero and allows him to fail so utterly, left 'to play out a role whose *raison d'etre* had long since collapsed'. Why, in other words, does Wagner abandon the coming god of free love in favour of the tragedy of the dying god? Why does he identify the destruction of the gods with the destruction of the world, as his letter to Liszt of 11 February 1853 indicates even before the Schopenhauer experience of 1854? Because Wagner had come to see that Siegfried's actions repeat Wotan's fatal embrace of power, the renunciation of love and the entanglement in false treaties, because Wagner had come to see that the world is fundamentally evil.[19]

The whole controversy suggests that the problem of the ending is only apparently an open question, which in fact conceals the more fundamental problem inherent in Wagner's whole conception of the relation between history and myth, a relation that is precisely that of the ring, the closed circle. Once history is construed mythically, the end is necessarily contained in the beginning (the Fall, the curse of the Ring). That this prophetic structure can be filled with different intentions over the long period of the composition of *The Ring* does not alter the closure of the construction. It does tell us something, however, about the historical truth of Wagner's myth of history.

Wagner argues in *Opera and Drama* that we can only attain the truth of history when modern historical drama is replaced by the mythical music drama. Wagner would have found powerful confirmation in Schopenhauer's chapter 'On History' in *The World as Will and Representation* (II, ch. 38). Schopenhauer dismisses historiography's claim to be a science because history amounts to nothing more than the sorry spectacle of the eternal repetition of the same in different costumes but also because the historian can never penetrate to the essence of things. Only *art*, i.e. timeless myth as opposed to historical knowledge, can capture the true being of the world. In his essay on Wagner Adorno pays Wagner the negative compliment of agreeing with Schopenhauer. The historical truth of *The Ring* is the negation of history. Wagner marks the point at which insight into the blind fatality of the social order reverses into myth. The allegory of *The Ring* spells out the dialectic of man's will to domination that ends with man's subjection to nature. If the truth of myth lies in the reduction of history to nature, then the source of the ambivalence of Wagner's myth resides precisely in its mythic reading of history as nature, since history grasped as nature, that is, as natural history, can be with Feuerbach the redemptive truth of free and fearless love or with Schopenhauer the blind fatality of the hunger for power and possessions. The cyclic, natural-historical structure of *The Ring* can accommodate Wagner's original revolutionary intentions and his Schopenhauerian revision.

Rather than taking this revision as Wagner's last word, it is more appropriate to see the 'progression' from Feuerbach to Schopenhauer as revealing not only the inherent structural ambivalence of Wagner's myth of history but also beyond that the historical truth reflected in this ambivalence. Wagner is such a fascinating and representative figure because he embodies, across the fateful divide of the 1848/49 Revolution, all the contradictions of the romantic myth of the (long) nineteenth century. By turns anarchist, monarchist, nationalist, communist, driven by a hatred of the French, the Jews and capitalism, Wagner spans the spectrum of political positions in a Germany in search of an identity, caught between the romantic dream of the *Gesamtkunstwerk* and the gathering pace of industrialization, urbanization and modernization. The Wagner who points back to the new mythology of the romantics and forward to the aestheticization of politics in The Third

Reich, is indeed a central figure. Through his work runs the fault-line of the romantic myth of the nineteenth century: the twin phantoms of revolutionary-aesthetic redemption and *Götterdämmerung*, the Janus face of the myth of history in *The Ring*.

7 Myth and Enlightenment: Nietzsche

Wagner's programme of renaturalization was central to his revolutionary writings and to the original conception of *The Ring*. It was shipwrecked, however, as Nietzsche observed with Schadenfreude, by Wagner's encounter with Schopenhauer's anti-romantic metaphysics of nature.[1] Nietzsche's own Dionysian affirmation of the renaturalization of man drew its inspiration from Schopenhauer's philosophy and Wagner's music. *The Birth of Tragedy* is his version of the romantic new mythology, in which the lament over our lost mythical home serves as the counterfoil to the celebration of the return of Dionysus in Wagner's music. In his celebration of the coming god of a new aesthetic religion, Nietzsche rails like the romantics, against Hegel's verdict on the end of art, the possibility of great art in modernity. Unlike the romantics, however, Nietzsche breaks with the idea of a synthesis of antiquity and modernity to set myth and enlightenment, the tragic sense of life and the optimistic illusions of rationalism, in the sharpest, irreconcilable opposition in order to proclaim that the age of enlightenment has reached its limit and must give way to a new tragic culture.

From the romantics to Nietzsche we can observe a shared pattern of historical prophecy, which was activated and energized by the upheavals of the French Revolution, the 1848/49 Revolutions and the Franco-German war of 1870/71. The romantic myth of the nineteenth century looked to Greek culture, to the Greek *Gesamtkunstwerk*, as its point of departure and arrival and construed European history from the perspective of the loss of the mythical unity of culture and community and its coming restoration, whether as a 'mythology of reason', as Hegel, Hölderlin and Schelling hoped in the 1790s, or as the liberation from the slavery of the market and money (Wagner) and the decadence and nihilism of the modern world (Nietzsche).

In his 1886 appraisal of *The Birth of Tragedy*, 'Essay in Self-Criticism', Nietzsche asks whether this work of his youth is not itself 'German music' – the least Greek of all art forms – with its hatred of modernity and will to annihilation. If *The Birth of Tragedy* is indeed a romantic book, written in mystical ecstasy by the adept of an 'unknown god', this god remained Nietzsche's god to the last. The unknown god, who finally claimed possession of his disciple and prophet, is the coming god of romantic mythology. Nietzsche's Dionysus is the child of the marriage of German music and German philosophy: from the mystery of union between Schopenhauer's tragic philosophy and Wagner's Dionysian music arises the 'opus metaphysicum', *Tristan und Isolde* (*Birth of Tragedy*, chs. 19–20). The German *rebirth* of tragedy announces the mystical revelation of the coming god, knocking at the gates of the present and the future, a revelation, which at the same time lifts the veil of Maya to disclose the mystery of the Greek *birth* of tragedy. From mythical rebirth to mythical birth, Greece reborn in Germany communicates with the originality of a Greece in Germany's image across the two thousand years of western decadence since the death of tragedy and the death of antiquity. Germany has heard the music of the strange god heralding a new tragic culture, which will consecrate the eternal bond of love between Greece and Germany, for which the best spirits since Winckelmann have striven in vain (ch. 20). This was in vain, because, as Wagner had shown, opera and drama consumed themselves in the futile imitation of the ancients. Neither possessed the key to the mystery of origin: the god whose mask is Apollo.

Nietzsche's interpretation of the birth of Greek tragedy is not directed to philological reconstruction but to the prophetic invocation of the 'rebirth of German myth' (ch. 23), conceived amid the 'horrors and sublimities' of the Franco-Prussian War, as he writes in his dedication to Wagner. Nietzsche addresses Germany through the masks of Schopenhauer and Wagner, the gods of his youth who will fail him and with whom he must break, abandoning the philosophy of tragedy for the more compelling demands of a tragic philosophy in the name of the question, which he sees in retrospect as posed by *The Birth of Tragedy*: 'What would a music have to be like that would no longer be of romantic origin, like the German music – but *Dionysian*?'[2] This question defines not only Nietzsche's romantic origins but also their new Dionysian articulation. *The Birth of Tragedy*, this quintessential manifesto of national aestheticism, is indeed a romantic book but one whose reworking of the romantic inheritance, mediated through Schopenhauer and Wagner, makes it a second order romanticism, which unveils in its quest for the mystery of origin and creativity the onto-poetic historicism at the heart of the new mythology and by the same token the dialectic of romanticism inherent in the Dionysian music of myth.

The Birth of Tragedy proposes nothing less than the aesthetic redemption of the world, whose unifying focus is the mythopoietic power of tragedy, the uniquely privileged act of creation that is the bearer of Nietzsche's theodicy of the phenomenal world and of historical existence. The tragic work of art thus embraces the poles of nature and history. Its myth is eternal: Dionysus, the dismembered and suffering god of nature – and eschatological: the return of Dionysus, symbolized by the emblem of the title page, to which Nietzsche draws attention in his dedication to Wagner: Prometheus Unbound. The return of Dionysus marks the limits of the reign of enlightenment, the limits of the victory of light over darkness, of theoretical culture over mythical culture. The creative strife of light and darkness – the orgic and aorgic (Hölderlin), the new and the old gods (Hegel), world and earth (Heidegger) – also provides the matrix of Nietzsche's onto-poetics of nature and history. The *ricorso* of history from the birth (Aeschylus) to the rebirth (Wagner) of tragedy closes the circle of history and reopens the circle of origin: Prometheus set free by the Dionysian power of music. And here we are obliged to read retrospectively. Behind the strife of Dionysus and Apollo exemplified in Greek tragedy stand in first line Schopenhauer's metaphysical dualism of the world as Will and Representation and in second line his metaphysics of music, complemented by Wagner's reflexions on the relation between music and drama, orchestra and stage action.

Nietzsche's vision of the world and existence as an aesthetic phenomenon provides the key to his onto-poetics. It requires that we distinguish between the phenomenal world as the work of art of nature – that is to say, the work of the orginal artist-creator – and the second level of its representation in the work of art, which is accordingly grasped in a deeper sense than traditionally intended as the imitation of nature. To the homology between the two levels corresponds Nietzsche's aesthetic metaphysics of the world and his metaphysical aesthetics of art. That these two levels are ultimately one is what is revealed in tragedy, which is thereby elevated to the self-reflexion of the world process. Nietzsche's metaphysics of art thus rests on his metaphysics of the world but we could just as readily reverse the relation, since the two acts of creation manifest the one creative force of nature, comprehended in terms of Schopenhauer's answer to the riddle of the thing-in-itself: the distinction between *natura naturans*, the world as Will, prior to space, time and causality, and *natura naturata*, the world as representation and individuation of the Will. For Nietzsche, however, the phenomenal world is not only the representation but the realization in time and space of the Will's eternal longing for aesthetic redemption, premised on the metaphysical assumption that 'the truly existent primal unity, eternally suffering and contradictory, also needs the rapturous vision, the pleasurable illusion for its continuous redemption'.[3]

Thus, the sole spectator of the world as aesthetic phenomenon is its artist-god, and not his creatures imprisoned within the world illusion. As actors in the world theatre, we need and can find the aesthetic redemption of existence solely in the play within the play, since it is at the same time the play of the play. 'If the whole world as representation is only the visibility of the will, then art is the elucidation of this visibility, the camera obscura which shows the objects more purely, and enables us to survey and comprehend them better. It is the play within the play, the stage on the stage in *Hamlet*.'[4] Art's imitation of nature thus signifies the potentiation not the depotentiation of nature's primary process: the Will's longing for appearance attains a higher satisfaction in the second order dream vision of art (ch. 4), whose highest manifestation is tragedy, because it is here that we are raised to the level of spectators of the world theatre through our identification with the artist-god. Schelling's aesthetic absolute – the construction of the universe in the image of the work of art in his *Philosophy of Art* – finds its counterpart in Nietzsche's construction of the world as aesthetic spectacle, in which the redemption of the world and of existence fuse in the sublime moment of tragic catharsis, in which we sense our oneness with the world Will and the difference between essence and appearance, ground and existence, creator and spectators is cancelled. The moment of de-individuating identification transforms the empirical subject into the aesthetic subject. This moment is central to Nietzsche's aesthetics:

> Insofar as the subject is the artist, however, he has already been released from his individual will, and has become, as it were, the medium through which the one truly existent subject celebrates his release in appearance. ... The entire comedy of art is neither performed for our betterment or education nor are we the true authors of this art world. On the contrary, we may assume that we are merely images and artistic projections for the true author, and that we have our highest dignity in our significance as works of art – for it is only as an *aesthetic phenomenon* that existence and the world are eternally *justified*. ... Only insofar as the genius in the act of artistic creation coalesces with this primordial artist of the world, does he know anything of the eternal essence of art; for in this state he is, in a marvellous manner, like the weird image of the fairy tale which can turn its eyes at will and behold itself; he is at once subject and object, at once poet, actor, and spectator.[5]

We can now approach Nietzsche's aesthetics by turning to his starting point: the contribution to aesthetic theory to be gained from the recognition that 'the continuous development of art is bound up with the *Apollonian* and the *Dionysian* duality' (ch. 1). This apparently innocent contribution is of course polemical in the extreme: if the development of art is indeed tied to the eternal opposition and creative strife of these two principles, this development was completed and exhausted by the birth and death of Greek tragedy. Development can be grasped only in terms of the rebirth that brackets the intervening two thousand years of theoretical and Christian culture through a forceful conflation of the ancient and the modern. As we have already seen, the ancient – the birth of tragedy – is to be understood from the modern – the spirit of music.

Nietzsche's two principles, the Apollonian and the Dionysian, are introduced and elucidated with the aid of Schopenhauer. In these two 'artistic powers of nature' the world as Will and as Representation is translated into the mythical opposition of the god of light, plastic form and the principle of individuation, and the god of ecstasy and music, who breaks the spell of phenomenal illusion and semblance to reveal our unity with the innermost ground of the world. In turn, both the genesis and the structure of tragedy are mirrored in Schopenhauer's dream theory as Wagner interprets it in his Beethoven essay of 1870. Nietzsche's account of the genesis of tragedy (ch. 8) – an elaboration of Wagner's observation that drama projects itself from choral songs[6] – brings the duality of Dionysian *ecstasy* and Apollonian *dream* together in the one model of genesis and structure:

> In the light of this insight we must understand Greek tragedy as the Diony- sian chorus which ever anew discharges itself in an Apollonian world of images. Thus the choral parts with which tragedy is interlaced are, as it were, the womb that gave birth to the whole of the so-called dialogue, that is, the entire world of the stage, the real drama. In several successive dis- charges this primal ground of tragedy radiates the vision of the drama which is by all means a dream apparition and to that extent, epic in nature; but on the other hand, being an objectification of a Dionysian state, it represents not Apollonian redemption through mere appearance but, on the contrary, the shattering of the individual and his fusion with primal being.[7]

Nietzsche's account transforms the Dionysian/Apollonian polarity into a dynamic model of surface and depth. It is dynamic in its double movement of sublimation – the redemption of the Will in the dream vision of the stage action – and desublimation – the rending of the veil of Maya in a vision into the darkness and horrors of nature.

This simultaneity of Apollonian redemption and Dionysian knowledge, of surface and depth can best be grasped through Nietzsche's equation of the dramatic action with a dream vision, since the dream occupies a unique med- iating position between the darkness of the unconscious – the unrepresen- table Will – and the light of waking consciousness. As Wagner argues, following Schopenhauer, the dream faces in two directions. It is a second faculty of perception, both product *and* vision of the inner activity of life, which enables us to look inwards and to participate directly – through the suspension of the categories of space and time – in the essence of things.[8] This 'immediate self-image of the Will', the dream content of deepest sleep, can enter waking consciousness, however, only through a secondary process that translates the dream content into the allegorical dream that precedes awakening. In Freudian terminology: the drama is the Apollonian dream work through which the Dionysian primary process comes to representation. Wagner calls it a reversal of causality: the projection – Nietzsche: the dis- charge – of internal perception into an external image.[9] And the contrary movement, the vision into the heart of darkness, can be compared with the primal cry with which we wake in fright from the dream of deepest sleep. This primal cry gives voice and expression to the Will and is for Wagner the origin of the universal language of music.[10] The two faces or sides of the dream, the one turned to the unconscious, the other towards consciousness, thus find their objectivation in the union of music and drama. This structure is at the same time genesis: just as Nietzsche declares the chorus to be the womb of the drama so Wagner states that, as the idea of the world music already contains drama in itself, the inner laws of music constitute the unconscious a priori of drama.

Wagner's *Beethoven* essay reverses the argument of *Opera and Drama* in asserting the priority of music. The priority of the Dionysian over the Apollonian, of depth over surface, of the unconscious over consciousness makes Nietzsche's aesthetic of tragedy before and beneath the marriage of the two principles a Dionysian aesthetic, which is derived from Schopenhauer's metaphysics of music. Here too Wagner serves as the intermediary for Schopenhauer's insight that music has a different origin to the other arts since it is the unmediated expression of the Will and not the representation of phenomena. This insight, Nietzsche insists, constitutes the most important truth for all aesthetics. Indeed, the very basis of aesthetics lies in the recognition – and here Nietzsche refers to Wagner's *Beethoven* – that music cannot be judged according to the category of *beauty* (ch. 16). Nietzsche, however, omits Wagner's corollary – that music can be judged solely under the category of the *sublime* by virtue of its power to excite the highest ecstatic consciousness of boundlessness, and Wagner's statement that the effect of drama can only be sublime[11] – because Nietzsche's name for the sublime is the Dionysian. It is Dionysian music that engenders the sublime effect of tragedy:

> From the nature of art as it is usually conceived according to the single category of appearance and beauty, the tragic cannot honestly be deduced at all, it is only through the spirit of music that we can understand the joy involved in the annihilation of the individual. For it is only in particular examples of such annihilation that we see clearly the eternal phenomenon of Dionysian art, which gives expression to the will in its omnipotence, as it were, behind the *principium individuationis*, the eternal life beyond all phenomena, and despite all annihilation.[12]

Nietzsche's 'dream' model of tragedy also functions as his 'depth' model of culture and history. The beautiful Olympian dream world of Apollonian culture functions to protect life from the paralysing knowledge of the terrors of existence: 'In order to live the Greeks were compelled by deepest necessity to create these gods' (ch. 3), that is, to create an Olympian 'magic mountain' floating above the underworld of the subjugated titanic forces of nature, whose figure is Prometheus Bound. If the 'naive' realm of beautiful semblance and of Apollo, the god of healing and helping nature (ch. 7), presents in one the classical image of Greece and the romantic image of nature, Dionysus signifies the 'sentimental' longing for unity which sweeps away all the protective limits of civilization. The history of Greek culture accordingly appears as an alternation of forces that comes to resolution in the creative strife of Attic tragedy (ch. 4).

Nietzsche's twin deities are thus highly overdetermined: they must symbolize Schopenhauer's metaphysical dualism, the primary (ecstasy and dream) and the secondary (music and the plastic arts) artistic drives of nature, and the conflicting dialectic of nature and culture. In 'the beautiful which is but the beginning of the terrible' (Rilke) we recognize the Janus face of romantic nature and drive nature and behind it the perspective of Nietzschean vitalism: theoretical culture, the civilization of enlightenment, viewed under the 'optic of *life*'. The metaphor of life poses in the most fundamental and 'natural' form the question of romanticism: how are we to regain contact with the unconscious creative and instituting forces that generate and regenerate culture and history? This question of original history, of the birth and rebirth of tragedy, stands for Nietzsche under the sign of the return of the repressed. It signifies on the one hand the *ricorso* that leads us back from *logos* to mythos, and gives the eschatological structure of birth, death and rebirth of tragedy. On the other hand it serves, as we have seen, to conflate the old and the new in a conjuration of the archaic in the modern, of original history against modernity.

It is Nietzsche's historicism that explains how Dionysian music points beyond the birth of tragedy to the birth of tragic philosophy. The *ricorso* of history that joins origins and goal also unfolds a progression across the tripartite sequence of history that informs the three parts of *The Birth of Tragedy*. The sequence is artistic, Socratic and tragic culture. The first is governed by the eternal opposition of Apollo and Dionysus, the second by the historical opposition of Socrates and Dionysus, enlightenment and myth, and the third belongs to the coming god of a tragic culture and a tragic philosophy, Dionysus, the god, whose music possesses the power to unbind Prometheus (ch. 10), and to give birth once again to myth (ch. 16). Prometheus now takes the place of Apollo as the tragic mask of Dionysus.

The three cultures, artistic, Socratic and tragic, exhaust the possibilities of culture. They embody at the same time the three types of cultural historicism and correspondingly the three types of *Naturgeschichte*. Greece offers the paradigm of original organic culture as the collective work of art of nature, which manifests 'how necessary and close the fundamental connections are between art and the people, myth and custom, tragedy and the state'.[13] The 'natural' implication of organic historicism – that cultures develop and decline – is given a tragic twist by Nietzsche: Greek tragedy did not die peacefully; it committed suicide. The gravediggers were Euripides and his anti-musical, anti-tragic daemon, Socrates. What they represent is the destruction of the justification of the world and existence as an aesthetic phenomenon by the optimistic will to correct life, to justify the world and existence theoretically. Like Hegel, but with opposite intent, Nietzsche regards Socrates as a world-historical turning point, to whom is allotted the negative centre of *The Birth of Tragedy*. The death of tragedy, myth and music follows from the unnatural revolt of reason against instinct, consciousness against life, science against art, in short, the negation of the very being of Greek culture. This revolt casts its shadow over the whole history of Europe to the present – the ever-lengthening shadow of Socratic-Alexandrian culture and its historical-critical spirit alien to its life-giving powers of myth. Socratic culture thus appears as the unnatural other of organic culture. It signifies the second historicism of history divorced from nature, the historicism of dissatisfied modern culture with its monstrous craving for the exotic and its self-consuming hunger for knowledge, whose truth is 'the loss of myth, the loss of the mythical home, the mythical maternal womb'.[14]

This second, 'sentimental' historicism is divided, however, against itself. It is the source and matrix of Baeumler's two romanticisms, the female-religious, which clings to the origin, and the male-aesthetic, which dreams of rebirth from the maternal womb. Baeumler aligns Nietzsche with aesthetic romanticism but this continuity with the new mythology of the romantics, directed to a synthesis of ancient and modern, naive and sentimental – for which Nietzsche's symbol is Socrates the musician – can be grasped only in the light of a more profound discontinuity, that is, in the light of Nietzsche's second order romanticism, which knowingly embraces the contradiction between the two romanticisms in terms of a third, tragic historicism beyond the organic-aesthetic and the Socratic. This third historicism draws the consequences of the dialectic of enlightenment in a double sense.

In a first sense, Nietzsche argues that the hubris of Socratic culture will be its own undoing. The spirit of science, which rests on the faith in the explicability of nature and the universal healing power of knowledge, is forced to confront its own limits. Kant and Schopenhauer turned the weapons of critical reason against reason and struck a deadly blow against the optimism of Socratic culture, a blow from which theoretical man recoils, fearful of the consequences of his own logic. This logic has brought him to the point where the limits of knowledge *reverse* into the knowledge of the limits of the world of appearances, and the principle of individuation dissolves into the sublime, terrifying-ecstatic vision into the heart of things.

In a second sense, the dialectic, which drives enlightenment into the arms of tragic myth, contains its own dialectic – *the knowledge that the tragic myth is itself an illusion, a fiction.* This knowledge is a doubly tragic knowledge that is bearable only in the aesthetic guise of tragic myth. Nietzsche's second romanticism lives from the *will to tragic myth*, from the will to identify with the Will, which compels its creatures to live by means of its life-inducing fictions. These life-inducing stimuli comprise the three possibilities of culture: art's seductive veil of beauty, the Socratic delight in science, and the metaphysical consolation underpinning tragic culture that eternal, indestructible life flows beneath the flux of phenomena (ch. 18).

Nietzsche's second order romanticism corresponds to what we might call the impasse of a second order enlightenment. If the first enlightenment unmasked the metaphysical, religious and moral illusions of man, the second enlightenment must recognize the necessity of these illusions and is caught in its own dialectic: the recognition that reflexion is the enemy of life, that reflexion ends in nihilism, that its 'optimism' contains the 'germ of annihilation' of modern society (ch. 18). The unconscious life of original organic culture, destroyed by the first enlightenment (the death of tragedy), cannot be restored by a second enlightenment. Its tragic knowledge – the loss of myth and of our mythical home – is that of Socratic-Alexandrian historicism, which can be overcome only by the leap of faith. In Nietzsche's account of a self-cancelling enlightenment, which must return to myth, the dialectic of enlightenment is reduced to paradox,[15] in order that Nietzsche can embrace the paradox of 'tragic' myth, the post-enlightenment myth that knows itself to be an illusion necessary to life. The original contradiction of 'sentimental' historicism – the deadly antagonism of enlightenment and myth, reflexion and unconscious life – returns in its own self-cancelling 'anti-dialectical' form. The negation of the dialectic of enlightenment in the name of life produces its own negative dialectic: since 'life' and 'myth' are themselves concepts of reflexion, they represent not the overcoming of nihilism but the will to a higher nihilism beyond good and evil.

Nietzsche's aesthetic theodicy reduces history to natural history. It negates the very work and meaning of history. The Dionysian reunites us with nature beneath and prior to history; it reduces consciousness and the autonomy of thought to an epiphenomenon of the organism. As Heinz Röttges puts it: Nietzsche attempts to rescue the 'I' through the mimicking of the merely natural.[16] The formula for Nietzsche's theodicy is accordingly *amor fati*, the will to Will, which finds its redemption in identification with the creative-destructive artist-god, in the ecstatic submergence of the individual in 'life'. The return of the repressed brackets history and the work of history in order to recover the world as cosmos – a cosmos that is its own eternal self-justification. The aesthetic theodicy of *The Birth of Tragedy* can thus claim to transcend and comprehend the contradiction between original (or organic) historicism – the birth of tragedy – and secondary (or Alexandrian) historicism – the death of tragedy – in a third and higher historicism, the onto-poetics of world theatre.

The paradox of a self-negating enlightenment finds its only possible, i.e. aesthetic, resolution in the transformation of the eternal opposition of reflexion and life, enlightenment and myth into the double vision of tragedy:

> For now we understand what it means to wish to see tragedy and at the same time long to get beyond all seeing. ... The striving for the infinite, the wing-beat of longing that accompanies the highest delight in clearly perceived reality, reminds us that in both states we must recognize a Dionysian phenomenon: again and again it reveals to us the playful construction and destruction of the individual world as the overflow of a primordial delight. Thus the dark Heraclitus compares the world-building force to a playing child that places stones here and there and builds sand hills only to overthrow them again.[17]

Heraclitus's world game can only be an aesthetic vision. Translated back into the historical world, it leads to the doctrine of the eternal return of the same, the ultimate paradox of the aesthetic justification of a meaningless world process. Since this 'tragic' nihilism is indistinguishable from modern 'anti-tragic' nihilism, it demands not only the aesthetic protection of myth but the rebirth of myth: the *creatio ex nihilo* which will transform the nothingness of modern history into a sublime work of art, willing itself in its self-creation, creating itself in its self-willing.

8   Mytho-Logics

Horkheimer and Adorno construe the logic of modernity, indeed of the whole of human history, as a logic of the will to rational mastery and the domination of nature. Reason and the subject are defined by the equation of knowledge and power. This logic is to be understood as a dynamic imaginary that penetrates and assimilates the other logic of modernity, the counter movement of autonomy. Democratic self-determination is instrumentalized and perverted by the totalitarian will to power. The reduction of self-determination to self-preservation cuts off any possibility of the democratic rescue of enlightenment to leave only a rescue of myth – the remembrance of nature in the subject, the appeal to the mimetic dimensions of thought and art – as the other of the self-destruction of reason. But even here, as Adorno's excursus to *Dialectic of Enlightenment* – the *Philosophy of Modern Music* – demonstrates, the ongoing process of rationalization consumes art itself, just as conversely the culture industry functions as the ultimate parody of the aesthetic education of man. The rescue of myth, insofar as it must substitute for the rescue of enlightenment, can only follow the path of negativity. This separates it not only from an enlightenment that has become mythical but also from the fascist instrumentalization of myth. If, as Adorno writes at the end of *Philosophy of Modern Music*, the truth of art lies in its anticipation of a coming society, which is no longer grounded in power relations, its authenticity derives from the 'echo of the primordial, the remembrance of pre-history [*Vorwelt*]'.

As authentic art, true myth preserves the connection between pre- and post-history across the realm of fallen history, the realm of the domination of nature. Adorno's negative romanticism is not so distant from Wagner's myth of the beginning and the end of history. It is therefore not surprising that

Adorno arrives at his first formulation of the dialectic of the domination of nature in his 1938 interpretation of *The Ring of the Nibelungen*. Does *The Ring* bear witness to romanticism's deeper comprehension of the hubris of enlightenment or to the dangers of romantic regression? Just as the rescue of enlightenment founders on the devaluation of democracy, so the rescue of myth draws back from the mytho-logic of romanticism. For all that, myth represents the aesthetic counter paradigm to rational mastery, that is, to the enlightenment's denaturalization of man and society. The mytho-logic of renaturalization is a counter logic of modernity, directed not only against the modern project of the unlimited growth of knowledge, production and power, but also against the universal project of democracy. Romantic autonomy asserts the authenticity of particularism as opposed to the conflictual democratization of society. It promotes the idea of the aesthetic totality against the disenchantment of the world, the disintegration of community and the fragmentation of meaning. Particularism contrasts culture with civilization, ethnos with demos, the organic with the mechanical, the subject embedded in a world and language with the transcendental subject of cognition. The primordiality of being-in-the-world, which refuses the subject/object split of rationalism, ties romantic epistemology to the primacy of world disclosure and its code of the originary and the derivative, the authentic and the unnatural, the living and the dead.

Romantic historicism in both its organic and aesthetic forms constitutes a counter logic of modernity which is based on a radically new conception of nature as immanence, from which flows in turn a radically new conception of society, politics, religion, art and knowledge, which regrounds history in nature at the same time as it ungrounds the enlightenment's 'unhistorical' foundation of modernity in sovereign reason and the sovereign subject. Organic historicism comprehends particularism as the indwelling god, the innate genius of a people, an original unity of nature and spirit, which manifests itself in an unconscious collective creation. The understanding of all cultural phenomena in their historical conditioning and variety posits a natural-historical unconscious governing the genesis and development of a world, a cultural totality out of itself. It thus proposes an original answer to the *querelle des anciens et modernes* which accepts neither the progressive historicism of the moderns (with its code old/new) nor the authority and normative model of ancient rationalism. Originality, conceived as authenticity, replaces and displaces innovation and imitation, both equally inimical to the inner organic form of a culture, which must be shielded from the imitation of foreign influences – just as its unconscious natural development must be protected from the corroding ferment of critique. The radicality of organic historicism lies in its translation of transcendence into the immanent imaginary of particular cultural worlds, the internalization of the sacred Other into the unconscious creative working of a historical nature.

This translation makes cultural totalities the subjects of history and the spirit of a people the source of all creative powers. The consequences and the dialectic of this counter logic are readily apparent: the historicization of man reduces reason to history, e.g. the historically developed becomes the new normative basis of thought as opposed to the legacy of natural law and to rationalist law. The reduction of reason to history leads in turn to the reduction of history to the normative value of life in the philosophy of life. Vitalism is the irrational response to historicism's relativism and its nihilistic consequences. This logic of immanence, which reduces reason to life and history to the biological cycle of the growth and decay of cultures, becomes a deadly logic of modernity when particularism becomes nationalism and race is raised to an exclusive and absolute integrating value.

Organic historicism is governed by the analogy between art and nature. Aesthetic historicism by contrast is guided, in the words of Carlyle, by a 'natural supernaturalism', that is, by the quest for a 'New Mythus' through which the romantics will radically recast 'into terms appropriate to ... their own age, the Christian pattern of the fall, the redemption, and the emergence of a new earth'. It is a re-appropriation whose goal – 'to naturalize the supernatural and to humanize the divine' – is conceived immanently. The new mythology announces an aesthetic religion, with poets and philosophers as its prophets. The new gods will be born from the holy marriage of mind and nature. The 'blended might' of this marriage summons 'Genius, Power, Creation and Divinity itself' (Wordsworth).[1] We enter here – through the marriage of mind and nature – the circle of creation, the circle of a self-originating renewal and return authenticated by the work of art, the original manifestation and highest expression of the creativity of nature. Spinoza's 'deus sive natura' heralded the transformation of created nature into the creative nature of Schelling's philosophy of nature, the 'organic system' in which beginning and end meet.

In turning to nature as the regenerative source of meaning, aesthetic historicism arrives at a new conception of creativity, which involves a revolutionary (i.e. re-volutionary) reworking of the idea of origin. The dying God of transcendence is reborn as the coming god of immanence. The gods of the new mythology become the aesthetic figure of refoundation, through which the public, binding and unifying function of communal art is to be recovered and the *Kunstreligion* (Hegel) of Greece restored. This future past origin – this original imitation – lives from the specifically modern, 'sentimental' imaginary of a 'naive' original culture regained through conscious creation. If, for Schiller, we become nature again through reason, it is aesthetic reason alone that can complete the circle of creation and escape the vicious circle of the conjuration of return. The mythology of reason of *The Oldest Systematic Programme* accordingly is crowned by the highest idea of all, the idea of Beauty. In an early, suppressed preface to *Hyperion* Hölderlin envisages the new world to come under the aegis of youthful beauty: 'They will come, Nature, thy men. A rejuvenated people will make thee young again, too, and thou will be as its bride. ... There will be only one beauty; and man and Nature will unite in one all-embracing divinity.'[2]

The romantic *divinization* of nature responds to the Enlightenment's *domination* of nature. Each registers the transition from transcendence to imma-

nence, from the created to the self-creating world of modernity. In each case
the imperative of creation contains its own dialectic. The beautiful synthesis
of aesthetic religion depends on the analogy between art and nature. Its corollary, however, is the assimilation of the sublime to the beautiful and the sup-
pression of the negative sublime by Schelling and the Jena romantics, which
finds its conclusion in Hegel's recapitulation of aesthetics as the science of the
beautiful. The new mythology can preserve its utopian potential only under
the sign of revivifying beauty. In Kant's Third Critique the sublime is subordinated to an overarching harmonization. The 'sublime' implications of the
double aesthetics of modernity only become apparent with the reversal of
romantic nature into drive nature. This reversal dissolves the idealist synthesis, predicated on beauty, and collapses the utopian philosophy of history
into a tragic philosophy of history and a tragic anthropology. We can relate
this transformation of history back into nature to the double image of Greek
antiquity since the romantics that culminates in Nietzsche's *Birth of Tragedy*.

Nietzsche's Dionysian sublime is the very antithesis of Kant's moral
sublime. Where Kant asserts the moral autonomy and tragic freedom of the
subject, Nietzsche celebrates the sacrifice of individuation. *The Birth of
Tragedy* represents the ultimate logic of the aesthetic religion of the romantics. If the world can be justified only as an aesthetic phenomenon, it is a justification, in which the world appears as a dream vision – a beautiful illusion
– masking the horrors of the abyss. Nietzsche's double aesthetic, which assimilates the beautiful to the sublime, 'takes back' the new mythology in the
name of a tragic philosophy of natural history, conceived as the eternal disso-
nance between Will and Representation, noumenon and phenomenon.
History is redeemed solely but supremely by the tragic work of art. The
world is indeed, as Friedrich Schlegel observed, a work of art eternally giving
birth to itself. Nietzsche's sublime reveals, however, that aesthetic historicism,
cut loose from a dialectical philosophy of history – still the inspiration for
Wagner's *Art and Revolution* and *The Artwork of the Future* – necessarily
regresses to onto-poetic mythicization.

Nietzsche radically naturalizes the onto-poetic implications of the new
mythology at the same time as he takes back its synthesis of the ancients and
the moderns. The triadic schema of the romantic philosophy of history is
retained but only in order to proclaim the return of a mythic and tragic antiquity against a decadent modernity. Nietzsche sets myth against enlightenment, in a move that deconstructs not only enlightenment but also
romanticism. The mytho-logic of Nietzsche's second romanticism accepts
Schiller's self-reflexive argument that the naive is a construction of sentimental consciousness, that is, that the Olympian world of beautiful illusion is
a Dionysian projection, in order to affirm the primacy of the mythical sub-
stratum of history, the Dionysian Will behind man's life-enhancing mythologies. In his 'Self-Critique' of *The Birth of Tragedy* Nietzsche defines the
double dialectic opened up by his mytho-logic: 'to view science from the optic
of the artist, art however from the optic of life'. Just as art deconstructs and
ungrounds science, so life in turn deconstructs and ungrounds art, to leave

'life' as the will to fiction, the will to myth, in whose name Nietzsche lays bare the dialectic of enlightenment and the dialectic of romanticism. Demythologization and remythologization describe here a vicious circle, which Horkheimer and Adorno will perpetuate through their equation of enlightenment and myth.

Heidegger will outflank and outbid Nietzsche by treating his doctrine of the Will to Power as the ultimate expression of the nihilistic logic of modernity since the Greeks. The Will to Power completes the epoch of occidental history and thereby opens the way to the other, incipient beginning:

> Nietzsche, the thinker of the concept of the Will to Power, is the *last metaphysician* of the West. The era, whose culmination unfolds in his thought, the modern age, is an era of the end. That is to say: an era, in which sometime and somehow the historical decision arises, whether These Last Days mean simply the end of Western History or the new counterpoint of another beginning.[3]

Heidegger displaces the prophetic world-historical role of Nietzsche (and Wagner) by repeating it more originally, in order to lay claim to the ultimate eschatological key to the beginning and end of the History of the West, presented once more under the sign of return. The fatal figure of enlightenment – repetition (*Wiederholung*) – is to be overcome through the bringing back (*Wieder-holung*) of the origin. Heidegger's other beginning stands for the escape from the vicious circle of modernity (the *Gestell*) through the creative circle and its leap of origin: the origin, which is the *work* of art, figured in the work of *art*.

The Origin of the Work of Art returns the history of aesthetics, outlined in the Nietzsche lectures, to its pre-aesthetic beginning in 'the magnificent art of Greece' in order to go beyond the last two stages of this history: Wagner's will to the *Gesamtkunstwerk* as the religion of the national community, and Nietzsche's counter movement to Hegel which elevates art over religion, morality and philosophy. Wagner's aesthetics, based on music's sea of feeling, 'the plunge into frenzy and the disintegration into sheer feeling as redemptive', means that the theatre and the orchestra, not great poetry and art, have come to determine art. This 'growing barbarization' is reinforced by Nietzsche's reduction of aesthetics to a physiology of art.[4] Heidegger answers *The Birth of Tragedy* by casting Nietzsche as the inversion that completes the rule of Platonic aesthetics. But, as Heidegger's return to Hölderlin indicates, he in fact repeats the romantic myth of the nineteenth century to become the final expression of this 'most ambiguous century', which, as he writes, 'must be demarcated simultaneously from both ends, i.e. from the last third of the eighteenth century and the first third of the twentieth'[5] – in other words, from Herder and Goethe in the 1770s to the Nazi revolution in 1933. Although Heidegger situates himself beyond the nineteenth century, his other beginning – Hölderlin's Greek-German symbiosis against a Wagnerian Third Reich[6] – in fact recapitulates the romantic imaginary of the retreat and return of the gods and its threefold of organic, aesthetic and onto-poetic historicism.

Heidegger's *Origin of the Work of Art* presents the most concentrated and at the same time the most comprehensive statement of the romantic idea of origin: the origin which transforms our familiar relations to the world and to the earth and defines more originally event, advent, creation, form and truth in the light of the openness of Being prior to all subjectivity. All art is essentially poetry, that is to say, myth: 'the saying of world and earth, the saying of the arena of their strife and thus of the place of all nearness and remoteness of the gods'. Heidegger's return to Hölderlin returns philosophy to poetry. It brings the conception of Being as Time back to its once and future origin: Being and the Word, the undivided unity of mythos and *logos*. Poetry advances to the highest instituting power that founds the historical Being of a people: to live poetically is to dwell historically *in the origin*. The work of art is thus accorded the highest dignity. It is 'das seiende Sein', which discloses the Being of beings.[7] It is, in Schelling's terms, the illumination (*Lichtung*) and transfiguration (*Verklärung*) of the darkness of the ground. Schelling's originary circle of the (theogonic) world process is translated into Heidegger's happening of truth in the work of art. Heidegger incorporates Schelling's eternal strife of darkness and light into the 'primordial strife' of earth and world: the 'work' of art consists in the 'setting up of a world and the setting forth of earth'.[8] The unity of world and earth is brought to presence in the work of art. This is the act that, in transforming nature (*phusis*) into history, founds the historical being of a people. Onto-poetic origin is conceived by Heidegger as a *creation ex nihilo* in the sense that truth can never come from 'the sheer "not" of beings'. On the contrary the truth of the work of art deposes and nihilates ordinary being in order to anticipate – in the 'leap out of the unmediated' of poetic projection – the 'withheld determination of historical *Dasein*'.[9] As bestowing, grounding, beginning, origin means 'to bring something into being from out of its essential source in a founding leap'. The essence of art as origin lies in the 'distinctive way in which truth comes into being, that is, becomes historical'.[10] And the essence of this essence, Heidegger tells us, is that the work of art is itself the god: the statue of the god in the temple 'lets the god himself be present and thus is the god himself'.[11]

Heidegger reworks the double aesthetic of modernity by replacing Nietzsche's fusion of the Apollonian and the Dionysian by the strife of world and earth. From the tension of the ontological difference between the instituting and the instituted, sublime ground and beautiful figure, arises as with Nietzsche the onto-poetic conception of the *world* as phenomenon, which in turn informs the onto-poetic conception of *history* as the site of the manifestation and retreat of its abyssal ground. For Heidegger the whole cycle of history is contained in the beginning. The leap of origin, 'in which everything to come is already leaped over',[12] becomes all important, since it is only from the origins that historical decline – the departure from the essential sphere of the beginning – can be experienced and thought. The primacy of the ontological, established in *Being and Time*, where it is stated that everything that arises from the ontological field partakes of 'degeneration' (§ 67), is transferred to history. Seen in the light of origin and its fading (the departure of the god from the temple), the original history of peoples and cultures reveals the history of Being as it emerges and withdraws. The mytho-logic of *origin* (the union of mythos and *logos*) is thus tied to the mytho-logic of *decline* (the history of the West as the nihilistic forgetting of Being) without confronting, however, its own 'sentimental' contradiction, its own mytho-logical circle. At stake is the question, whether great art, despite Hegel's verdict, is still possible in modernity. Is art still capable of the political task of founding the community, of bestowing shape and direction to the city? The political community as the supreme *work* of art – politics transfigured in art – is central to the romantic counter paradigm of modernity. The romantic vision of a sublime and beautiful politics is underpinned by what Horkheimer and Adorno identify as the very principle of myth – immanence.

Heidegger's circle of origin – 'to bring something into being from out of its essential source in a founding leap' – can offer escape from the night of enlightenment only so long as it remains the 'sentimental' myth of the loss of myth. The loss of community is the truly *original* myth of modernity, from which arises the romantic counter imaginary of sacred immanence – manifested in the subject, genius, nature, love, community, nation, myth, aesthetic religion – in response to the withdrawal of the divine. If, for Horkheimer and Adorno, the rescue of enlightenment lies in the reflective rescue of myth, it signifies a path of indirection and suspense that is short-circuited by the romantic phantasm of immediacy, the return of the origin in the community. The collapse of royal power in the French Revolution – the collapse, that is, of the theological politics of absolutism – leads to the chaotic eruption of quasi-natural events. The abyss, revealed by the return of the social to its origins, opens up, according to Richir, the space of the political sublime from which emerges the 'people' – not as the transparent community but as infinite and in-definite plurality caught up in a gigantic theatre in search of the meaning of events. The 'people' as the new foundation will destroy the power of the theological-political, vested in the despot. The political sublime signifies the dissolution of all given institutions, in which the anarchy of liberty, equality and fraternity becomes the horizon of the utopian community. It is utopian in that the experience of the sublime means the institution of man into his suprasensible symbolic destiny. The symbolic community of humanity cannot be identified, however, with empirical political society because the idea of the instituting symbolic and of the utopian community must remain *unpresentable*. Richir identifies the transcendental illusion of modern politics with the dream of overcoming the gulf separating nature and freedom, the empirical and the idea. It is this illusion of the *unmediated* institution of society, which drives the Terror's phantasm of 'the one undivided virtuous people'. Precisely the will to realize the utopian community reinstitutes the power of the despot and death and prefigures the totalitarian movements of our century. Instead of the revolutionary politicization of the aesthetic, the aestheticization of politics seeks to represent the unpresentable through the short circuit of the transcendental.[13]

Nancy's analysis of the loss of community in modernity traces a comparable 'sublime' mytho-logic. Rousseau, Schlegel, Hegel, Bakunin, Marx and Wagner conceive modernity as the loss of community in response to the death of God. The idea of community anticipates the coming god who will redeem alienated society through the reunion of man with the divine. This dream of a new poetic-religious foundation of modernity has a new humanity arising from a new myth, while simultaneously aware of the loss of the power of this myth.[14] The idea of natural history and the new mythology thus articulate *the founding imaginary of romanticism*: myth, divided in and against itself, corresponds to the split between nature and history and to their coming reunion. The self-imagining of nature as humanity and of humanity as nature forms the utopian horizon of the naturalization of history and the historicization of nature.

If romanticism is the invention of the scene of the founding myth, it is confronted from the beginning by its original contradiction. For Nancy the very idea of newly invented myths is not only dangerous but also futile, and must implode as fiction, leaving as its nihilistic truth the will to myth, which is necessarily and essentially totalitarian, both as regards the form and the content of myth. As form, myth is tautegoric (Schelling): mythic speech says nothing but itself, its will to myth is therefore nothing but the will to will. As content, myth is bound up with its self-engendering effectivity, that is, with the setting-into-work of a self-celebrating and self-consuming immanence: 'This is why political or collective enterprises dominated by a will to absolute immanence have as their truth the truth of death. Immanence, communal fusion, contains no other logic than that of the suicide of the community.'[15]

Nancy and Richir spell out in the sharpest fashion the political dangers inherent in modernity's transcendental illusion of foundation. To construct, however, a dialectic of romanticism or of enlightenment from the perspective of the totalitarian conclusions of the long nineteenth century would be to replicate the mytho-logics of Adorno's and Heidegger's philosophical discourse of modernity, that is, to postulate a fatal historical determinism, which must itself write a totalitarian conclusion to history. Both are guilty of conflating modernity with a logic supposedly immanent to (natural) history. Let us say rather that the transcendental illusion of modernity is tied up with what we may call the transcendental paradox of enlightenment and romanticism, and that if we are to posit a logic, it can only be in their own terms, that is to say, in terms of their respective founding paradoxes. The paradox of enlightenment is the freedom that is its own presupposition, to which corresponds the project of the denaturalization of man; the paradox of romanticism is the origin that is its own presupposition, to which corresponds the project of the renaturalization of man. Paradigm and counter paradigm, these rival logics of the domination and the divinization of nature contain their own dialectic. Enlightenment autonomy is always threatened by the immanent contradiction of denaturalization: the reversal of freedom into unfreedom (the perpetuation of the blindness of nature); romantic incarnation is always threatened by the immanent contradiction of renaturalization: the reversal of the spiritualization of nature into the naturalization of spirit, of creative into destructive nature. Each bears witness to the failed internal dialogue of modernity.

Part Two
Modernism and Civilization

Introduction: Artifice and History

The course that led from Kant's Third Critique to Heidegger's *The Origin of the Work of Art* was a lethal one. It ended in the ruination, even damnation, of the German nation. Its poisonous effects are still with us. More than a half century after the end of the Second World War, aesthetic nationalisms and regressive mythologies continue to attract adherents in large numbers. Whether these fatal ideologies are clothed in organic or poetic historicism – and no matter whether they trade on promises of organic totality, community, national aesthetic creation or language as a primordial home of peoples outside of modernity – the results are damaging in the extreme.

What is the antidote to this poison? Enlightenment? In part, yes. Science, progressive history, money, markets, industrialism, urbanization, rationality, procedures, legal reform and differentiation are not bad things. Indeed, they are often very valuable. But they are not perfect things, either. Most importantly, they are not self-sustaining things. Utility, mechanism, rationalization, accounting and all of the rest of the figures of enlightenment have a habit of devouring themselves if they have no counterweight to restrain their excesses or to fill them with the ballast of meaning.[1] It is this tendency of enlightenment to feed on itself and become dispirited that, in the first place, opened the door to the romantic plunge into the abyss.

Romanticism offered the aesthetic redemption of modernity. The romantics gave priority to sensibility over functionality, particularity over universality, interiority over externality, mystery over lucidity, the unconscious over the conscious, expression over construction, literature over technology, myth over science. Romanticism equated enlightenment with mechanism, soulless instrumentalism, and the domination of nature. It counter-posed its belief in monadic immanence to enlightenment causality, organic totality to systemic

79

differentiation, and natural harmony to the liberal-democratic conflict of opinions. Enlightenment was accused of causing violence against nature and human nature. Against the violence of enlightenment, the unity of earth and people, historical and biological nature was defiantly mobilized. In this vision, social vice would yield to natural goodness, self-determination would replace mechanical causality, society would give way to community, creativity would supplant sterility, and an enchanted reign of abundance would regenerate a disenchanted world.

The romantic redemption of modernity supposed the negation of enlightenment. However, the great moments of modern history in fact were never negations of enlightenment. On the contrary, they have always mixed enlightenment together with a countervailing 'humanism'. What this reflects is that successful forms of modernity are carriers of both enlightenment and a counterweight to the excesses of enlightenment. This counterweight is a force of balance not a dialectic of negation.

One way of thinking about this complement to enlightenment is to think of it as a kind of 'classicism'. It may seem paradoxical, but successful modernity is always underpinned by classical themes. By this we most definitely do not mean Dionysian knowledge, the cult of Sophoclean tragedy, or the immanent divinity of Greek myths. 'Classicism' as the engine of modernism is not a longing to repeat the unrepeatable beginning, or a wish to treat the past as the horizon of future possibility. It doesn't treat history as progression without progress, or as a fall from the grace of the origin, or as a union with harmonious nature. It doesn't appeal to the polis as a total work of art. The 'modern classical' is not a synonym for origin or birth. It does not mean digging back into the unconscious or the childhood of humankind. It doesn't idealize a beginning that gives birth to itself, or worship the immanent divinity of a holistic community.

Classicism as the engine of modernism – that is to say, classicism as rationalism – means re-birth in the sense of renaissance. All successful modernities – like those of Renaissance Italy, the Dutch Golden Age, the American Revolution and Victorian Britain – encouraged a strong relationship with the classical past without confusing this past with mythic origins. Jacob Burckhardt understood this far better than Nietzsche did. In *The Civilization of the Renaissance in Italy* and in *The Greeks and Greek Civilization*, Burckhardt showed great understanding of the power of societies to reinvent themselves under the rubric of civilization. Civilization is a power of renovation. Each particular civilizing era draws deeply from continuities with moments of the past that have a strong claim to the status of a classic period. At the same time, the force of civilization employs the past to form and reform society. Under the flag of civilization, societies are able to mediate change and continuity, progress and permanence. Indeed, in great civilizing periods, change is a cause of continuity, and continuity is a cause of change.

So then what is civilization? What defines these luminous periods that engender progress and permanence simultaneously? What characterizes a modern period that becomes classical, or a classical period that inspires modernity? The answer is not art – even though these are the periods of great advances in the arts. The answer rather is the city. Burckhardt's Greek civilization is the civilization of Athens. His Italian Renaissance is the civilization of the Italian city-states. Pieter Geyl's or Johan Huizinga's Dutch seventeenth century is a powerhouse of modernity and a workshop for reinventing classical humanism. Its driving force is Amsterdam and other Dutch cities. The same applies to America. As Hannah Arendt was to conclude – in a gesture that was quite contrary to her teacher Heidegger – the Americans gave rise to the most dynamic type of modernity not by desiring to return to a neo-mythic Greek origin but rather by adapting the Roman iteration of Greek civilization.[2] America was the modern imitation of the Roman imitation of the Greeks – as was England, in its own peculiar way. In Victorian Britain, the Promethean forces of industrialism and capitalism that Marx surveyed were in full force. Yet London and Liverpool were schools for Hellenism. This was not the Hellenism of orgiastic self-creation and underworldly powers, but the Greece of Epicureans and Cynics and Stoics, a Greece mediated by Roman and Christian history, and by British interest in ideas of Commonwealth.[3]

In all of these cases, the modern and the classical were not at odds, as in the German ideology. In the British case, classicism was as much a driver of industry, parliamentary democracy and imperial confederation as were utilitarianism and liberalism. Indeed, in all the foremost modern societies and economies, the forces of the classical past and the modern future synchronize. This synchronicity produces great dynamism and great form in tandem. Another word for this coalition of forces is civilization. The acme of civilization is the great metropolitan and cosmopolitan city where the classical and the modern merge.

In the civilizing process, the idea of the city acts as a bridge between the ancients and the moderns. The city is the regulative idea that unites modern and classical in a productive interplay of form and content, means and ends. The city, should we need reminding, is not just art. It is not just aesthetics. Its art coexists with industry, utility and rationalization. Thus, the most representative art of the city is architecture. It is representative because, of all of the arts, architecture is never purely aesthetical. It is practical and political, social and utilitarian, as well as aesthetic. It exemplifies most clearly the bridging power of the city – its superlative capacity to conjugate modern and ancient, present and past, utilitarian and ideal. The city in this sense is the practical objectivation of civilization.

The intimate relationship of the modern and the classical is nowhere better illustrated than on the same ground that produced the German ideology. In the early twentieth century, we see not only the intensification of romantic and poetic historicisms – most notably from Spengler to Heidegger – but also the rise of a remarkable modernism that was resistant to these currents. This modernism, with its exquisite sense of form and formalism, owed much to classical rationalism. The sources of it were various. They included Presocratic rationalism and the Pythagorean-Platonic sense of geometric reason, as well as Hellenistic, Roman, Christian, Renaissance and modern pagan enlightenment adaptations of classical rationalism.[4]

This current was never able to objectivate itself politically. For the most part it had loose social democratic sympathies – though at least one of its great figures, Leo Strauss, was instrumental in developing a very influential American neo-conservative kind of political modernism.[5] Still, broadly speaking, the key figures of this current of 'classical rationalism meets modernism' had vaguely left-of-centre affiliations. Their number included the architects Mies van der Rohe and Adolf Loos, and the philosophers Ludwig Wittgenstein and Hannah Arendt. In some sense, although we do not discuss him here, Karl Popper's treatment of Athens as the model of the first 'open society' is a parallel effort to merge classical rationalism and twentieth-century modernism.[6] Popper was a Viennese social democrat.

In Central Europe in the 1920s or 1930s, none of these figures was to have the kind of political, or even artistic, influence that they were to have later in the 1950s and 1960s in America or England. The dominant political currents in Central Europe in the interwar period, on the left and the right, were expressionist. Expressionist politics were aesthetic. This aestheticization produced totalitarian, fascist, radical national, ethno-national, pan-national and 'movement' politics characterized by violent struggle and mystical longings for community and redemptive mythologies. Modernism that had a strong classical rationalist undertow was objectivist, not expressionist, in its mentality. It was deeply interested in form, reason, mathematics, structure, order, shape and figure. The kind of social democracy that it identified with was that of Berlin or Vienna. This was the social democracy of the city. When the progenitors of classical rationalist modernism found themselves in exile from totalitarianism, the identification with the city continued, and even radically deepened. Arendt and Strauss became the great twentieth-century exponents of the political philosophy of the city, and also figures who were indelibly associated with New York and Chicago. In a parallel manner, Mies van der Rohe and the students of Loos applied a classicizing rationalism to the reshaping of the architecture of the American city.

None of these figures could do anything to prevent the catastrophe that befell interwar Central Europe. Their sense of cosmopolitan modernism though found a strong resonance in postwar America. They re-inspired, and re-confirmed, the instinct of America to blend the classical and the modern. Nobody would say that this is always, or even often, successful. No one would say that America is not afflicted by soulless enlightenment or by regressive romanticism. But suffering such afflictions is the modern condition. What matters is not that such discontents exist but that also there exists a cosmopolitan rationalism drawing on antiquity and modernity which carries on a critique of both enlightenment and romantic modernisms. Karl Popper was drawn to the fact that postwar Britain still had some of the liberal quality of this cosmopolitan rationalism, which Arendt, Strauss and Mies van der Rohe likewise discovered in America. The history of twentieth-century European rationalist modernism is also part of the history of American, or Atlantic, modernism. It is as much contiguous with the history of the unromantic and architectonic modernism of Americans like Louis Sullivan or Charles Ives as it is with any of the sentimental nationalist modernisms, let alone the method-obsessed enlightened modernisms, that abounded on either side of the Atlantic.

Our critique of enlightenment and romanticism is a critique of modernism. It is not anti-modern in the sense that romanticism is; but it eschews soulless modernism. At the centre of our critique of modernism lies the idea of a cosmopolitan rationalism. This is the rationalism of the world city. This rationalism is an affirmation of civilization in the following sense. Civilization is the subtle, humanizing and artful process by which human beings turn themselves into dwellers in the world city. Civilization is the work of the designing mind of the denizen of the world city. In the crucible of civilization, we find myth and science, gardens and machines, sensibility and calculation subordinated to the forms and figures of a 'made nature' and its geometrical and polyrhythmical structures.

It is to this artificing nature – this forming, fabricating, systemic nature – we now turn in the following chapters, as we explore the design of the nineteenth-century and twentieth-century aesthetic state and those countervailing figures in twentieth-century modernism that turned against such a conception. We observe how a classical modernism sought a way out of the swamp of Central European historicisms and romanticisms.

The very existence of anti-expressive, classical rationalist modernism confirms that, side-by-side with the historicist nature of romantic origins and drive powers, another nature exists. This is the nature of the urbs, and its civilization of the world city. This nature holds at arm's length the claims of myth and mass, garden and machine. In planned and unplanned ways, it coordinates the simultaneous motions and temporalities (past, present and future) of the city.[7] It shapes space through the architectonic play of light and shadow, and the forms and volumes of the figurative imagination. This is a nature that is neither mechanistic nor organic but functions as a model and matrix of connective reason. It is a designing nature. It joins, splices and intersects times, spaces, systems, modules, rationalities, points, lines and planes.

Civilization is an artifice. It is constructive. It does not rely on archaism, mythology, regression, unconscious forces, prophecy, coming gods or dying gods, acts of destructive creation or of spontaneous creation. Rather, it models itself on science, mathematics and geometry. It delights in the constraints of formal structures. The power of its music derives from compositional structure, not from myth or drama. It creates consciously and deliberately rather than unconsciously and ecstatically.

The works of civilization – the works of the cosmopolitan world city – are works *conceived in continuity with a continuously reinvented past*. For the classical rationalist modernists of the twentieth century, this meant the modern imitation of the Pagan Enlightenment's imitation of the Renaissance imitation of the Roman imitation of the Greek classics. In this sense, that which is 'classical' is timeless. It is not origin or source; it is reason, structure and form that is endlessly reinvented, extended and applied in different times and places. Form, structure and reason are not simply methods. Cosmopolitan reason is not just 'following rules', or methodical engineering. It is not a formula, law or technique. It does not suppose that what is new is good, and what is old is bad. It is progressive but without deifying progress.

The civilization of the world city pays little attention to redemption. It is not bound to the redemptive gods of a mythical original time that it feels compelled to worship. It invests little faith in a millenarian future run by beneficent experts and engineers who will save humanity. Its imagination is a projection of reason, its beauty is mathematical, its dramas are public, its attention is concentrated, its politics is cosmopolitan, and its bias is urban. Its worldly focus means that suffering is not redeemed by the beautiful illusions of the artist. Rather it is offset by the capacity of human beings to order and structure themselves, their relations and their world. Art, at the best, is a model for this. Suffering cannot be eliminated, but it can be obviated by the power of human beings to introduce lucid and rational forms. These forms do what enlightenment on its own often has great difficulty doing. They impart meaning to human life. They also give pleasure.

The pleasures of the civilization of the cosmopolitan city are not those of terrible-sublime catharsis or orgiastic ecstasy but the pleasures of architectonic beauty. These are pleasures of rhythmical structure not of romantic genesis. As we explore in the following chapters, it was this – the debate between structure and genesis – that was such a key debate in the nineteenth and twentieth centuries. This debate posed a question that had grave practical implications: what is most important – form and structure or genesis and source? The principal defender of genesis was Heidegger. He offered both a philosophical account of Greece as genesis and a poetic account of the earth as source. Heidegger saw the state as a work of art. The Italian Renaissance philosopher might have agreed with this description. But what Heidegger meant by the state as a work of art and what a Renaissance philosopher meant by the idea were two completely different things. In the latter case, beauty (and all its various synonyms) was a guiding idea of the state and its citizens. In the former case, art was the primordial, archaic beginning – the divine origin – that legitimated the state. This notion was not peculiar to Heidegger. Many nineteenth-century Europeans, who had already begun to lose faith in civilization, had already turned to variations of this idea of the divine origin.

The form or genesis, structure or source debate sounds innocent enough. But its consequences were far from innocent. The notion of a state with a divine origin legitimated horrible acts. But it should not be supposed that the notion of the aesthetic state went without critics. What we point out in subsequent chapters is the honourable and important role that twentieth-century modernism played in contesting genesis and source ideologies. Most particularly, we consider the lasting role that Mies van der Rohe and Ludwig Wittgenstein play in reconceptualizing the formal nature of civilization's creations. In their eyes – and in this they are representative of the best of twentieth-century modernism – the depths of civilization's creations are geo-metrical and plastic, not archaic or psychological or somatic. They are neither redemptive nor underworldly.

Civilization's art is constructive, not aesthetic. It draws from the universal-ities of reason and arrangement, not from the idiomatics of language or culture. In its great moments, it ransacks, incorporates and discards its own past for compositional elements.[8] Its art, ethics, science and politics are a poietics. As a poietics, its works are unexpressive and unromantic. Its works are like the works of Charles Ives and Elliot Carter, which replicate in sound the unsentimental New York that formed their art. These works, like the cos-mopolitan world city, are forged from a synoecism of rhythms, metres, colours, timbres, shadings and melodies.[9] This synoecism echoes civilization's nature. It is an interlocking of sub-systems and volumes, spheres and planes, forms and spaces, fictions and geometries. It is the nature of polis, cosmopolis and metropolis; it is the nature of complex systems, mediated societies and polyrhythmic lives.

9 The Gate

The promise of the romantic age was the *future past*. This was the promise that the past was the inimitable source of new beginnings, the original spring of creation. This past (the future past) was fundamentally different in kind from the past (the continuous past) invoked by the age of Enlightenment when it laid claim to the mantle of Roman antiquity. The 'Pagan Enlightenment'[1] drew sustenance from the Roman imitation of the Greeks, and all subsequent mimesis of that mimesis through centuries of renaissance, classicism, republicanism, humanism and rationalism. This was not the past – the past of new beginnings – as romanticism understood it. This was not a past in which history had been naturalized.

Natural history was organic – the history of cycles of birth, growth, decay and death. This past was not continuous. There was no thread – no line of mimesis or reinvention – that allowed what was ancient to be remade as modern.[2] There was no circle of classicism and modernism. This circle defined the figure of civilization. Like a wheel rolling on a road, the circle of civilization moved forward by circling back, the modernity of civilization (in this case, Greco-Roman-Latin-Pagan-Enlightenment civilization) being constantly stimulated and invigorated by the ceaseless reinvention of its own past. In contrast, romantic birth and death were ruptures in the continuity of the past. Romanticism's past was adventist. The natural history of humankind was the history of the birth and death of cultures. Where civilization was enduring, cultures came and went. The nature of birth was unconscious, primordial, sudden, terrifying and ecstatic (in a word – sublime). Death (romantic death) was suicidal, catastrophic and absolute. In contrast, civilization was the product of artifice – a made thing, an unnatural product, a material thing – augmented and reworked over long centuries.

Acceptance of the idea of a natural history of humankind (the history of the birth and decay of cultures) brought with it conundrums. It encouraged curiosity about the vast multitude of human cultures. But it also gnawed at the claims of any of those cultures to hold the allegiance and attention of the curious. As a consequence, cultures were transmuted into styles. Style possessed collective force only as (passing) fashion. Otherwise style was a matter of idiosyncratic taste. In this atmosphere, even civilization's most visible marker – architecture – became a simulacrum of multiple, disconnected pasts. All of civilization's conjugating metaphors and models were spurned. Thus, even those born to a culture might embrace the death of that culture. In the romantic age, birth and death were to become the 'true' content of culture. The fascination with origination and destruction, creation and oblivion overshadowed any interest in the forms and structures of civilization.

Culture oscillated between the fascinating-beguiling poles of poetic-mythological genesis and self-destruction, revolution and war, abyssal origin and frightful genocide, sublime institution and spontaneous conflagration, mysterious revelation and burial in the earth – i.e. between 'life' and 'death'.

Growth belonged in the interstices between Promethean creation and release in death, ecstatic advent and dreams of oblivion, enigmatic emergence and sacrificial suicide. Under the influence of romanticism, the normalized (non-rapturous, non-ecstatic) work of institutionalized culture became the work of collecting specimens (examples of the extinct species of the natural history of humankind) for display in museums and galleries. This in part served as a perpetual reminder of the irreducible idiosyncrasy of culture, its fundamental non-transitivity across time or space. At the same time, by placing the extinct representatives of the life processes of now dead cultures side-by-side, the museum or gallery, it was hoped, would aid in the search for the romantic Holy Grail – the imitable inimitable. The imitable inimitable was that which turned organic romanticism – the natural history of human cultures – into aesthetic romanticism. The imitable inimitable was the original moment of cultural creation that could be emulated but not repeated, or repeated but not emulated. It was an enigma that could be understood without causing the loss of its aura of mystery. It was the mystery of an original moment, seemingly dead, that could ignite the life cycle of a culture, and begin its ascending descent from spontaneous-mysterious emergence through to its fascinating-terrible death. The museum and the gallery were conceived as the institutional correlative of this aesthetic romanticism. It was the 'house' of specimens of the imitable inimitable. It collected examples – many obscure examples – of spontaneous creation, providing a record of the natural history of sublime creation and uncaused causation. Such collections included specimens of 'miraculous' industrial, scientific and technological innovation, and nature's own history (not least the natural history of biological species). These seemed to demonstrate that not only was the knowledge of nature contingent (and forever evolving) but also that nature itself, for all of its apparent regularities, was subject to spontaneous evolution.[3]

When the work of accumulating specimens from the natural history of humankind got underway, no common meaning (syntax) could be attributed to what was collected. Yet this work was justified by the belief that, somewhere in the museum, the key to the *future past* – the moment of unrepeatable emulation – could be deduced from the accumulated evidence of the episodes of humankind's natural history. For the naive, the spectacle of the seeming richness of this natural history was enough to justify the work of the museum and the gallery. But the more sceptically minded understood that this natural history told the story not of richness but of creative-destructive conflagration, and it was this terrible beginning-end that was the operative *future past* of the romantic age.

The explosion of galleries and museums and library collections in the nineteenth century was quite remarkable. It was also a fraught time. The labour of collection of cultural objects caused Europeans in particular great epistemological anxiety. For if it was true that human society displayed as much natural diversity as the biosphere did, then what was just and moral and good? The 'enlightened pagans' of eighteenth-century Europe had been able to answer such questions with conviction. Human beings possessed a faculty of discernment or judgement that gave good guidance to those who had the chance to refine and exercise their 'taste'. But, with the rise of the belief in a natural history of humankind, Europe, from the late eighteenth century, subjected itself increasingly to the *critique of taste*. Once the epitome of the consensual judgement of the educated, 'taste' became a synonym for idiosyncrasy and ipseity. The decisive turning point in the history of the concept of 'taste' was Immanuel Kant's *Critique of Judgement* (1790). The appearance of that treatise definitively signalled the coming of a new European spirit: *the aesthetic*.

Kant stood halfway between the rationalism of the eighteenth century and the romanticism of the nineteenth century. The contradictions built into the 'critique of taste' are well illustrated by Kant's readiness to defend the *universality* of taste but at the same time deny taste *objectivity*. Individuals could judge the beauty of artworks, cuisine, clothing and so on, and could expect others to agree with those judgements, yet, Kant insisted, there was no objective criterion – no common thing, no *res publica* – upon which such judgements could be based. A Florentine of the Cinquecento could appeal to the beauty of the city as a guide to making such judgements. But, for the denizens of Kant's hometown of Königsberg, the sense of there being a common world to hand, upon which critical judgements could rest, was already disappearing.[4]

In the absence of objectivity, the universality of taste – or concurrence in judgement – was only possible under very peculiar conditions. One such condition was *eclecticism*. The idiomatic taste of a German burgher for Chinoiserie or for Italianate colour schemes – a taste that his neighbour might have found repugnant – could nonetheless be claimed to be universal on the grounds that it was part of an eclectic mix. The unsympathetic neighbour could assent to the ambient mixture, while dissenting from some of its constituent parts. As the objective worldliness that had once constituted European city life started to dissipate, under the influence of Romanticism, Europeans began to crave for a previously unheard of *bricolage* of bits and pieces. These were variously assembled from Europe's own multilayered past, far-flung colonial possessions and its trading and diplomatic contacts. The European will to an organizing, shaping power – the power of plastic reason and beautiful form – which had been a defining characteristic of its civilization, was swiftly reduced to a *will to collect*. This was the will of the museum curator.

One of those who grasped this disarming fact was Nietzsche, who warned that the consequence of the newfound 'historical sense' of Europeans was to turn their past, and other people's pasts, into a giant rummage sale. Declaring that 'the taste and tongue for everything was an ignoble sense',[5] Nietzsche tartly observed that his age was an 'age of costumes', and its intellectual edifice, History, the storeroom of those costumes. 'We parade ourselves as romantic or classical or Christian or "national"'. Styles were adopted, then cast off rapidly. No style lasted. Punctuating the style-masquerade were moments of despair when Europeans felt that 'nothing suits us'.[6] To combat this bleakness, the 'hybrid European' simply put on another costume. 'Again and again another piece of the past and of foreignness is tried out, tried on, taken off, packed away, above all *studied.*' This was the genius of the age. This was *the first studious age of costumes*. The denizens of this age, nineteenth-century Europeans, were the grand parodists of world history.

Virtually alone among his intellectual contemporaries, Nietzsche saw not only the absurdity but also the dangers of history as the *history of styles*. 'For when the past of every form of life and mode of life, of culture that formerly lay close beside or on top of one another streams into us "modern souls" thanks to this mingling, our instincts run back in all directions, we ourselves are a kind of chaos.'[7] Nietzsche, though, was hardly blameless in all of this. His own faux-prophetic style conveyed the sense that he was always waiting for the 'artist-god that is coming' – even long after he had left behind the suppositions of *The Birth of Tragedy*. The costume dramas of the Europeans, of course, appeared ludicrous in the light of such prophetic hopes. But, even measured against the more sober aspirations of Greek-Roman-Latin civilization, they were still ludicrous. The haphazard trying on of romantic, classical, Christian and national costumes was the sign of an unfathomable chaos in the European soul.

If there ever was a warning to Europeans of the consequences of this chaos, it was the Balkans. Viewed from afar, the eclectic Balkan mix – of Orthodox and Serb, Muslim and Albanian, Catholic and Croat – was a tableau of many-sided idiolects and cultures, which appealed to the culture archiving and style browsing impulses of romanticized Europeans. Barely ten years after Nietzsche had addressed his salutary warning to his contemporaries, the Balkans – once the symbolic midpoint between the old Viennese and Constantinopolitan cosmopolises – descended into the bull-pit of national terrorism. Not only did European powers not prevent the cultural expression of national resentment and genocidal idiolects, they tolerated and encouraged it. They did so in the 1890s, before the First World War, before the Second

World War, and once again in the 1990s. Over a disastrous century, the Balkans – right on Europe's doorstep – proved time and again that historicized taste was incapable of creating beautiful compositions or humane order.

The loss of the ordering power – the civilizing power of plastic reason and beautiful form – affected not just the Balkan margins but the European heartland as well. Indeed, most graphically in the 1930s and 1940s, the inner sanctum of Europe became 'Balkanized' in a manner that eerily paralleled the vertiginous descent of its outlands into the deadly abyss. The Balkans was the liminal foreshadowing and mournful echo of European decadence. It anticipated Nazi pan-nationalism and totalitarianism, and Vichy toleration of the same. Like a Rome no longer able to give definition to its margins, Europe's loss of centre was first volcanically registered on its periphery.

The Roman historian Tacitus, long before, had seen in the most open-eyed manner the consequence when the centre no longer held. Narrating the events of 69 CE – when two Gallic tribes consorted with German tribes against Roman rule – Tacitus has the Roman commander Quintus Petilbus Cerialis address the Gauls with this warning:

> You are surely not going to tell me that you expect a milder regime when Tutor and Classicus are your rulers, or that less taxation than now will be required to provide the armies to defend you from the Germans and the Britons? For if the Romans are expelled – which heaven forbid! – what else will result but worldwide war in which each nation's hand will be turned against its neighbour.[8]

Centuries later, Rome's inability to enforce Pax Romana fulfilled the historian's bleakest anticipations. Nonetheless, the idea of Pax Romana survived even the Germanic invasions during the Roman twilight, and persisted in various guises – from Catholic universalism through the Holy Roman Empire to the Congress of Vienna. From the Greeks, Rome had inherited the notion that *phusis* (nature) was a force superior to the *nomoi* of tribes ('nations'). In Roman translation, this was taken to mean that the most diverse nations could live together peacefully so long as they accepted the *aegis* of a natural 'law' that gave effect to itself not through rules or norms but through reasoning, forming and judging. Even a Europe fragmented into feudal domains, petty kingdoms, mercantile city-states and absolute monarchies persisted with this ordering image, and thus spared itself the depravations of 'worldwide war'. Only in the nineteenth century was *phusis* finally, assuredly spurned, and in doing so the tribalism of nations was reborn. *The revenge of nature was 'worldwide war'.*

If nationalist hatreds in Sarajevo triggered the First World War, Europe's own more subtle slide into imperial rivalries and 'a kind of chaos' paved the way for it. Nothing expressed this vortex more visibly than the nineteenth-century appetite for 'style'. Premier cities of Europe had once marked their coming of age with an eloquent mastery of form. Now their slow decay was measured by the accumulation of signs. Notably Vienna – only recently the

exacting city of Mozart – was overcome with an indiscriminate ornamenta-
lizing fetish. The interiors of the houses of the Viennese bourgeoisie were
decked out in a checkerboard pastiche of art styles – bits and pieces of
Empire, Cinquecento, Gothic, Rococo and Ottoman. This was a society in
which 'good taste' had risen to the rank of first among values.[9] Central European exteriors were similarly historicized. In Wilhelmine Germany, architects worked indifferently in gothic and classic styles; picturesque designs of
mixed architectural origins abutted Baroque façades.[10] The consequences of
this rampant aestheticism were not reserved to matters of visual appearance.
Historicism degraded the invisible framework of Europe, making it suscep-
tible in the longer term to ethno-national and pan-national entropy. Through
the makeshift ornamental portal created by the rule of aesthetics, racialism
and 'national socialism' made their entry. As a wholesale plunder of the past
proceeded apace, the power of *phusis* (nature), the civilizational shaping force
of Europe, collapsed.

Europe had traditionally provided two accounts of *phusis*. The first reached
its apogee with the civilization of the Romans. Roman accounts of natural
law relied on the innovations of Greek cosmology and philosophy. When its
might was eventually exhausted, Rome became the foundation of a Latin civilization in the West and a Greek-Roman-Byzantine civilization in the East.
The first great creations of Latinate Europe were the Romanesque architecture and other three-dimensional arts of Provençal and Lombard cities.[11]
Subsequently, this Latin and Western civilization was reconfigured north of
the Alps – in the Gothic mode of medieval Christianity. Christian (Thomist)
accounts of natural law relied in no small measure on preexisting pagan
accounts. All of the strands of Latin civilization had a cosmological countenance and a sense of intellectual power and intellectual virtue that circled
high above the *nomoi* (the rules and customs) of tribal and village life, and
above the rulebooks, moralism and sin baiting of everyday church life. European modernity brought a weakening of the universalism of *phusis*. Paving
the way for this atrophy, the Protestant Reformation caused a fundamental
rupture with the Latin *universitas*. The global empire building of Europeans
disguised this for a period. But, by the close of the nineteenth century, the
waning of the classical idea of nature was apparent. The clearest sign of this
weakening was the rise of nationalism that strove to replace European dynas-
ties, multi-national empires and city-states with nation-states or by ill-defined,
genocidal pan-nationalist empires.

Classical nature had promised a union of all 'Europeans' – perhaps even
ultimately all human beings. City, empire and church were universal institutions that attracted individuals irrespective of origins. All participated in a
universal nature. All belonged to a common (Greco-Roman-Latin-Pagan-
Enlightenment) civilization. This civilization was defined by its city-building.
Its literature, its philosophy – its *logos* – drew its inspiration from the visible
form (*eidos*) of the city and its elements. This form was timeless: it persisted
in the face of the passage from one age to another, and the contingencies of
wars, economic cycles and cultural fashion.

The continuities of this civilization were achieved by the artful adaptation of the form of the city. This process of adaptation had the paradoxical effect of meeting the demands of passing time but simultaneously rising above the times. Aldo Rossi took seriously the metaphysical character of the city that European civilization created when he observed of it that there was 'a more or less clearly articulated bond ... established between the stages of things throughout history'. Whatever the differences between historical periods, 'it was possible to verify a certain constancy of themes', and it was this constancy that assured 'a relative unity' to the urban expression of Europe.[12] Such permanencies were evident in the way in which monumental architecture and the layout and plans of cities were adapted in order to bridge the chasms of history. Rossi's examples are telling: at Nîmes the Roman amphitheatre is transformed by the conquering Visigoths into a fortress that became a little city of two thousand inhabitants around which the medieval city grew.[13] In a similar manner the Roman Emperor Diocletian's Palace at Split became a city.[14] Theatre and city, palace and city, building and urbs – one was an analogy of the other. Civilization (literally the procession of the city) persisted through epochal change by analogy. The greatest changes (from classical architecture to Gothic architecture) coexisted with the greatest continuities (the siting of cathedrals in old Roman administrative centres). Perhaps the most significant of all of the continuities between the Roman and the medieval eras was the love of building, and the conviction that civilization was transmitted to other places through the *via media* of architecture.[15]

The core of Greco-Roman-Latin civilization is material. It perpetuates itself through impression on matter – a type, a figure, a rhythmic character impressed on the physical world. *Phusis* is the sum total of all such impressions. *Phusis* 'changes' in the sense that types, figures and rhythmic characters are *adapted by analogy*. The made is re-made analogically. Layers of the made pile up on one another, like lines of music in medieval polyphony. Such *polypoiēsis* is the representation of the act of creation. This view of creation is quite unlike the romantic view of creation as the spontaneous act of the artist god who is the uncaused cause of creation. It is no accident that the Roman deity of 'beginnings' was the double-faced god, Janus. The name Janus was derived from the word for gate, *ianua*, and from its ambidextrous connotation of simultaneous exit and entry. Janus was the god of doorways, passages and bridges. On the coins of the Roman republic, Janus was portrayed as a head facing both ways. This sense of 'both ways' (forward *and* backward, up *and* down) was an intuition of creation – creation as the polymetrical concatenation of entry and exit, a passage or bridge between entities and forces, an ambidextrous juggling of lines, figures and movements. Nothing makes clearer the association of creation with the polymetrics of entry-exit than the fact that Julius Caesar, when he reorganized the Roman calendar, named the first month of the year (January) after Janus.

Creation is 'two faced' – the transfigured figure of entry-exit, or in the medieval Latin setting, the lower and upper voices of the motet, the figure of the plainchant transfigured by the parallel voices, with the *cantus firmus* of the

chant acting as a scaffolding about which the multi-levelled motet is constructed. Such Janus-faced beginnings are very different in spirit from the acts
of 'originality' that romanticized moderns came to equate with the idea of
creation. Modern 'originality' was a unique point rather than the multiple
lines of counterpoint. Historicism looked on history as series of unique
starting points.

The romantic, and later historicist, views contrast sharply with the Janus-
like self-conception of European civilization. The Janus-like Europe passed
through many phases, each drawing on a fertile vein of polyphonic remaking
(civilization's 'renaissances'). Typical of this, Machiavelli's *Discourses* – a
meditation on the city of Florence – daringly recast the Roman history of
Livy both as an affirmation of continuity with the classical and as a start-
lingly precocious product of its own time of Renaissance. It became an
analogy for Machiavelli to diagnose the troubles of Florence. Many moderns
gave up this dual capacity for continuity and distinctiveness – and the accompanying true lie of material analogy – for the sake of truthfulness and the
authenticity of self-invention. The first device for portraying self-invention
was the seventeenth-century idea of the Social Contract. At its heart, this idea
was marvellously simple: viz. society was created on the basis of honest,
transparent and reciprocal promises. Likeness, similitude, mimesis, adaptation
and models – all of these lost currency as Europe rushed to embrace contrac-
tarian truth. Analogical-mimetic reference to a locus classicus was replaced
by a search for a credible account of unique origins.

It seemed, for a time, that the appeal to theories of Natural Right (and the
foundational myth of the Social Contract) might provide a coherent account
of social origins. But, by the middle of the nineteenth century, it was evident
that the theory of Social Contract was a circular account of modern bourgeois society – the society of contractors. It was not clear how it might be
applied to explain the genesis of ancient or feudal or patrimonial states.
Appearing in the midst of the crisis of contract theories, the science of history
offered an alternative account of social formation. The historical sciences of
the nineteenth century *supposed that discrete, unique (self-contained) socio-
historical entities – rather than continuing, synthetic (analogical) civilizational
formations – were the proper object of inquiry*, an attitude elegantly summar-
ized by Wilhelm Dilthey: '*Ages are structurally different from each other.*'[16]
Even more frankly: 'It is a dream of Hegel's that the ages present stages in
the development of reason.' Historicism was a rude awakening from that
dream. Instead of porosity and interweaving, different ages presented (to each
other) a closed framework of meanings. Each frame formed 'the horizon of
the age'. Through it, 'the meaning of every part in the system of the age is
determined'.[17] Each frame was closed by virtue of '*the centering of ages and
epochs on themselves*'.[18] It is true – Dilthey acknowledged (in a manner remi-
niscent of Marx) – that 'every age refers back to a preceding one, for the
forces developed in the latter continue to be active in it'.[19] But this 'reference
back' is merely a reminder of the insufficiency of each self-contained age –
each epoch (including what was for Dilthey the contemporary epoch of

'national liberation') 'bears in itself the limits, tensions, sufferings which prepare for the next stage'. The past – the historians' realm – is the story of 'limits, tensions, sufferings' of epochs, rather than the narrative of a continuously reconfigured civilization.

This is quite unlike how the classical historians understood their inquiries. For Thucydides, Polybius, Machiavelli and Guicciardini, the subject matter of their studies was *politics* – 'the interaction between states', 'cunning politics and warfare'.[20] After the eighteenth century, the preoccupation of the historian moved *'beyond political history to culture'*.[21] The 'political historian' (Machiavelli) assumed that the past (Rome) was a guide to the present (Florence). In contrast, the historian who turned to 'culture' supposed the past to be a series of alien worlds.[22] Each world can be understood but only in terms of the closed framework of that world. The historian of cultures 'understands' the past by portraying how specific actions are linked to the whole (the homogeneous meaning-horizon) of a discrete epoch, *rather than to the whole of a civilizational path*.[23] By grasping the spiritualized common medium that a society has created for itself (the objective mind we call 'Rome', for example), we can understand the behaviour of those who were part of that world (the Roman soldier, farmer, etc.). But that world has no active relationship to those who are the members of other, subsequent worlds. Every historical phenomenon, Dilthey supposed, is finite.[24] Finitude meant that, with the collapse of Rome, no one would again be 'Roman'. Florentines, eighteenth-century French, English and Americans, and many others besides, had at one time or other seen themselves (sometimes with momentous political consequences) as 'Roman'. These aspirations beyond historical finitude could only be regarded as cases of false consciousness.

Neither the romantic nor the Nietzschean exemption of the Greek 'origin' from historicist relativism affected this at all. The Greece of gods and tragedies was an absolute. It was the unique point that was the paradoxical model of imitable uniqueness. Its uniqueness lay in its aesthetic power, specifically in the mythology of the powers of its artist-like gods. This was not a subject for renaissance. Rather it was a provocation for moderns to create their own unique point, or wait in prophetic hope for the coming of new archaic creator gods. Historicists and anti-historicists alike found it impossible to imagine themselves in the position of Machiavelli for whom evening was a time of communion with the best representatives of Europe's civilization. In a letter to his friend Vettori, Machiavelli tells how, banished from Florence, and after the daily grind of rural exile, he would return to his lodging to re-create himself.

> [I] enter the study, and at the door I take off the day's clothing, covered with mud and dust, and put on garments regal and courtly, and reclothed appropriately, I enter the ancient courts of ancient men, where, received by them with affection, I feed on that food which only is mine and which I was born for, where I am not ashamed to speak with them and to ask them the reason for their actions; and they in their kindness answer me; and for

four hours of time I do not feel boredom; I forget every trouble, I do not dread poverty; I am not frightened by death; entirely I give myself over to them.[25]

Such a form of union-conversation eluded the nineteenth-century 'hybrid Europeans' and their Nietzschean critics alike.

The children of the historicist age, even when mesmerized by philological, archaeological and historical interrogations of the past, paradoxically could not 'give themselves over entirely' to the attentions of 'ancient men' for a time each day. History of the modern kind created an insuperable *barrier to the past*. Or rather, more exactly, it made of 'the ancient' something that was *in the past*, rather than as it had been for Machiavelli something *out of time*. There was no longer any common thing (*res publica*), nor any timeless form (*eidos*), nor any immortal conversation uniting past and present. The best that the historicist could do was to create a medley of far-flung symbols, forms, decorative flourishes and curiosities, and put them into exhibitions, museums, domestic interiors and façades. Even then, there was little sense that Nietzsche's studious European had anything like the natural ambidexterity of a Roman or Constantinopolitan.

For all of the collecting of the world's art and bric-a-brac, the 'hybrid European' was a provincial figure. While this provincial talked about the hermeneutic 'understanding' of the 'unique cultures' of 'other nations', this 'understanding' was an anaemic faculty. This was not least because Europeans of the nineteenth and twentieth centuries, in spite of their sojourning in foreign parts and their mania for collecting the baggage of world cultures, were in the end principally preoccupied with their own (national) origins. Each foreign artifact in a national museum was an assurance of the universal validity of the collector nations' own ipseity. The curatorial nation could justify the claim of universal but unique significance for its own schools of national painting, theatre, and literature – no matter how much they might pale in comparison with Aeschylean Athens or Brunelleschi's Florence or Mozart's Vienna – if the nation displayed the idioms of other nations in its museums. This was an attempt to master Kant's paradox of taste. The only way that national idiosyncrasy (frequently second-rate) could have universal validity was for the idiomatic to take its place in the universe of idioms in the national museum.[26]

While the nineteenth century was a period of extravagant church building, it was the art museum that was the true shrine of the age. In the act of erecting national monuments, theatres and the like, the denizens of the nineteenth century began to conceive of the emergent nation-state as a work of art – and the museum as its sacred hearth. The museum was the temple of the national religion of aesthetic creation. The most radical anticipation of this was Napoleon I's dream of turning Paris into a museum.[27] This vision of the 'city as museum' resonates in the growing propensity to treat the museum as the symbolic heart of the nineteenth and twentieth-century city – just as the temple, basilica and cathedral had previously served as the monumental keystone of the European and classical urbs.

The rise of the museum as an axiomatic symbol was preceded in the eighteenth century by the opening of courtly art collections to public view. These had included the royal collections in Paris (1750) and Vienna (1792), the works held by the Elector of Bavaria (1783), and the Medici collection that had been bequeathed to the city of Florence (1789).[28] The British Museum was created as a public institution in 1759. Such public viewing initially relied on the adaptation of existing buildings – such as the Grande Galerie of the Louvre or Britain's Montagu House. As the rule of aesthetics entrenched itself, it was the Germans who led the way in creating purpose-designed galleries for the public display of art collections. The impetus for this was the creation of quasi-national kingdoms in German-speaking territories. The invention of the purpose-specific gallery helped state builders answer a conundrum. They needed the authority of the past to achieve their task – tradition was a powerful legitimating device for the state. Yet the emerging nation states were unprecedented, and thus could not rely on appeals to the past, however the past was conceived – whether it was conceived in a 'dynastic-traditional' or 'pagan enlightenment' sense. Curation – the technique of institutional collection – both mobilized the past and anaesthetized it. It turned civilizational continuity into cultural archaeology, ensuring the nation-state both a legitimating connection with the past and (at the same time) immunity from the past.

The most decisive moment in the creation of the modern (national) art museum arrived with the partnership of Ludwig I of Bavaria and the architect Leo von Klenze. In 1812, Ludwig managed to acquire the pedimental sculpture unearthed during the excavations at Aegina carried on by C.R. Cockerell and Karl Freiherr Haller von Hallerstein. Ludwig resolved on a plan to build a museum specifically for the display of sculpture, and commissioned Klenze. Klenze offered him three designs: in Grecian, Roman and Renaissance styles. Klenze's Grecian temple-form design won Ludwig's approval, and so was born Munich's Glyptothek (1815–30). This was followed in quick succession by Berlin's Altes Museum (1823–30) designed by Karl Friedrich Schinkel around the Hellenistic motif of the long colonnade. Such historicizing classical 'revival' forms were the rule for nineteenth-century museums, accompanied inevitably by debates about what was the 'appropriate' style for specific commissions. Klenze used a Cinquecento style when he designed the (paintings-only) Alte Pinakothek (1826–36) for the Bavarian state, while he dressed-up St Petersburg's Hermitage Museum in a hybrid Greco-Roman style.

Such revivalism was typical of 'the age of costumes'. The borrowing of architectural styles was part and parcel of the collector mentality that impressed itself on the European spirit. America was not far behind Europe in its fascination with collecting. In the second half of the nineteenth century, Americans began to catch up with Europe: with the opening of the Metropolitan Museum in New York City (1870) and the Boston Museum of Fine Arts (1870), followed by art museums in Philadelphia (1875) and Chicago (1879). On an even more auspicious scale, the full-fledged Napoleonic vision of the 'museum city' began to be realized in Washington when the Smithsonian museum was established on L'Enfant's Mall, the symbolic coronary artery of the District of Columbia. Eventually the Mall came to be lined with the Smithsonian buildings, unambiguously identifying the American state with the curatorial spirit. Embracing the rule of aesthetics, the nation-state legitimated itself by becoming the 'collector state'. The European state pioneered this aesthetic form of legitimation by funding 'great collections'. In America, where nation-state building was considerably weaker,[29] forms of societal self-representation and validation clustered around the 'private-public' philanthropic endowment of cultural institutions – with a similar effect. Aesthetic legitimations began to replace the pagan enlightenment legitimations of early American republicanism.

The consequence of this was for the older notion of 'civilization' (connoting civic actions or public works) to become transmuted into the collecting of 'culture'. The infamous removal of the Parthenon marbles (1801–3) by Lord Elgin from Ottoman-administered Athens is a case in point. To this day, the refusal of the British government and the British Museum to return the pedimental marbles is a symptom of how much the 'identity' of the nation-state became bound-up with the 'great collections' of 'national cultural institutions'. At the same time, protest at the appropriation of cultural treasures by other nations could also provide an inverted vehicle for the assertion of national 'identity'. (Thus, Greek claims on the Parthenon marbles proved as much a form of national self-definition as British insistence on the prerogatives of the collector state.) This stands in sharp contrast to previous 'civilizing' regimes in which the material creation of the civitas (circuses, squares, temples, promenades, precincts, streets and avenues) was preeminent, and in which the sacred was not represented by an aesthetic collection but a Janus-like gateway, bridge or passage between the mundane and the extraordinary, linking the utterable and the silent. The Janus gate was possible where *the city itself was an analogous whole*. After the watershed of the early nineteenth century, when the classical idea of the city as an analogous totality declined in influence, library, museum and gallery – with their collections of discrete, in many cases stolen, objects – acquired a central religious-symbolic role, especially in official eyes. Indeed, in what otherwise was a vociferously discursive modernity, it was the 'cultural institution' that became the 'all-hallowed' gathering place where the rule of silence was applied, and a certain sacred awe made itself present.

The end of the intuition of the city as an analogous whole, and the correlative rise of the rule of the aesthetic, brought into doubt whether there was or indeed could be any objective criterion of beauty. A Roman, an Alexandrian, a Constantinopolitan and a Florentine all knew that beauty existed because *they could simply point to it*. Beauty was demonstrable with the silent gesture of the outstretched hand. Beauty was 'there' in the city. The city was the material incarnation of beauty. Things were beautiful because they fitted into the polymetrics, resonant harmonies, interlocking scales and subtle proportions of the city. The part was an analogy of the whole. The modern 'museum-city' on the other hand is made up of contingent, idiosyncratic objects. In this it takes its cue from the organization of the museum. A Rembrandt painting pulled out of the context of Amsterdam, a Canaletto out of the context of Venice, are stripped of their connection to an encompassing architectonic world. As the opening of collections to the public made exposure to such decontextualised objects a commonplace experience, it became necessary then to justify the 'value' of these works. Hence, the development of aesthetic ideologies, philosophical aesthetics, art criticism and museum catalogues. But, having begun along this path, the problem that presented itself, and that Immanuel Kant immediately observed was: how does one speak in a universal voice about the idiomatic?

The organizers of 'great collections', sponsored by states or patrons, sought to answer this question by accumulating cultural idioms with the aim of exhaustively documenting historical periods or epochs (and, later on, anthropologically defined societies). When *cata-logia replaced ana-logia*, and 'the collection' replaced 'the city' as an imaginary locus of meaning, there was a loss of constructive power. As anyone who has ever walked through a great museum of art will recognize, the only thing that joins idioms together is contiguity, and the enduring lesson of the European age of historicism is that contiguity does not suffice to relate idiomatic cultures in anything more than a temporary and accidental manner. Cultures (the *nomoi* of customs, attitudes and styles) have an irreducible ipseity. It is only the power of civilization (nature, *phusis*) that rises above idioms. Without such civilizing *coniunctio*, there is only barbarism. The hermeneutic fusion of horizons (the best instinct of the curatorial nation) is illusory. Idioms do not reciprocally translate.

The failure to translate has horrible political and social consequences. In the absence of some greater underlying force of conjointment, neighbours who have lived side by side for generations can and will kill each other when cultural tensions reach splitting point. This is *the modern lesson of the Balkans*. All appeals to the 'museum principle' of 'understanding' do little or nothing to obviate this. The *ancient lesson of Athens, Rome, Alexandria and Constantinople* is that only the old 'city principle' of 'the beautiful-good' is capable of successfully joining idioms.[30]

This is not to suppose that the classic city (in any of its incarnations) was ever a crucible of blissful harmonies. Tensions beset it, like any other human constellation. The contestations of power and law, family and state, belief and counter-belief tore at the ligaments of the city. Nonetheless, while such divisions were accompanied by sufferings and suspicions, each social class or status group had a stake in the beautiful form of the city. Each had to accommodate the other – not as social contractors do (with an eye to *self-preservation* and *self-interest*) but for the sake (*telos, peras*) of the civitas. Each had to learn the rhythms of the other, not in the name of 'understanding', but for the sake of the analogous whole, the common thing, the immortal *eidos* of the cosmopolis. The cosmopolis is the city that is subject to the natural order (*kosmos*) of reason, form and rhythm. The denizens of such a city have to *internalize many time signatures*, and learn to overlay and coordinate them. This requires a *Janus-like ambidexterity*, a bilateral capacity for simultaneous entry and exit, looking forward and back, and moving in vocal register up and down. It demands an ability to sustain a complex interplay of opposites.

10 Civilization and Aestheticism: Schinkel

The difference between the civilizing state and the aesthetic state is summed up in the difference between their respective attitudes to the past. The civilizing state looks to the past for exemplary models of reason. Reason in history is embodied in historical forms and structures that possess qualities of harmony, proportion, rhythm, equilibrium and the like. The aesthetic state looks at history to find the privileged origin – the archaic source of greatness that either could be reiterated in the present or else represents the beginning of the organic and authentic development of a present-day society or, finally, is the origin of the natural history of humankind.

The tensions between the civilizing state and the aesthetic state are well illustrated by the career of Karl Friedrich Schinkel (1781–1841). Schinkel was the great architect of post-Napoleonic Berlin. In his earliest pronouncements on architecture, Schinkel offered the view that the meaning of a building lay in its *taxis*, its 'made order'. In a letter of 1818, he put it this way:

> The beauty of a building does not lie primarily in the ornament employed but rather first and foremost in the choice of relationships, which arise initially in the divisions and organization of the plan, which then determines the profiles and the façades.[1]

It is difficult to think of a more succinct definition of classical architecture: *the beauty of building lies first and foremost in the choice of relationships*. This idea of architecture parallels classical Greek rationalism, and its interest in mathematical relations, and in the accompanying sense that invisible geometrical relations (first made legible in the act of planning) were more real than the picturesque appearance of decorative ornaments and mouldings. The plan was the first step in making 'mathematical' relationships (in particular relationships of harmóny and proportion) visible. Writing to his wife in October 1817, after having seen the Parthenon marbles in London, Schinkel remarked:

> To say that art derives from the imitation of nature is very incorrect. It is more correct to say that it derives from mathematics as the basic harmony of form and eurhythmics; it must penetrate through nature to this [form].[2]

The classical Greeks, though, made no such radical distinction between nature and numbers. For them, mathematics was a representation of *phusis*, and *phusis* was the embodiment of a set of relations that provided order in the cosmos. A building was a realization of that order and a representation of it – achieved via the harmonies and eurhythmics of built structures.

While Schinkel denied that architecture imitated nature, what he had in mind was an idea of nature that was quite different from the Greek *phusis*. By his day, the concept of nature had been thoroughly romanticized and aestheticized. Aestheticized nature was much like the academic picturesque nature beloved by painters. It was atmospheric. The rise of romantic nature paralleled the decline of the architecture of relationships. Even neo-classicism was infused with a romantic spirit. In France, with the rise of the Ecole des Beaux-Arts as the cornerstone of architectural education, architecture became subjected to the 'arts of drawing'.[3] The notion of the architect as romantic illustrator even subsumed the geometrically sensitive architecture of a Boullée and a Ledoux. Boullée and Ledoux's work, ostensibly a form of neo-classicism, was in fact a species of the romantic sublime, in which mathematical relations had become ciphers for romantic mystery.

In a sense, *all* modern architecture, including Schinkel's, became indebted to the idea of architecture as a painterly and atmospheric art. The architecture of perspectives and renderings, as an almost painterly sub-genre, squeezed aside the architecture of relationships. As Schinkel progressed through his career, the idea of an 'architecture of relationships' was overshadowed successively by architectures of 1. the privileged origin, 2. organic historicism, 3. autopoiesis and 4. elevation.

The architecture of trabeation: the privileged origin

Schinkel created his earliest masterpieces – the Schauspielhaus (1818–21) and the Altes Museum (1822–30) – in the context of the post-Napoleonic rebuilding of Berlin. In this phase, stripped pilaster supports, horizontal entablatures and freestanding columns dominate his building art. These serve to represent the system of trabeated ('post and beam') construction. This idea of foregrounding trabeation had been brought to architectural self-consciousness with the publication of James Stuart and Nicholas Revett's *Antiquities of*

Athens (1762). This was then echoed in the attention that Schinkel in the early 1820s pays to the mimesis of post and beam construction. This reflects a contemporary romantic fascination with the Greek mind. Irrespective of the patina of neo-classicism in Schinkel's work, what this meant was a fascination with the quasi-archaic origins of the Greek mind, not with its rationalist notions of nature and order.

The care that Schinkel takes with interlocking of large and small scales in the building designs of this period suggests continuing affinities with his earlier 1818 desire for an architecture of relationships. But this rationalism is over-determined by the allusions to trabeation. These evoke the not-fully-rational vernacular artisanal world of archaic Greece. This was not a world of heroes and gods, but it was not the world of Ionian science either.

Organic historicism

In the next phase of Schinkel's career, the preoccupation with the regulative idea of construction continues but in an increasingly romantic and historicist manner.

In this phase, architecture is portrayed as the continuation – by humankind – of the constructive activity of nature. On the surface of things, this conception of architecture is not far removed from classical Greek rationalism. In the classical view, nature (*phusis*) is an ordering of forces that the architect seeks to represent. But, by Schinkel's time, this definition of nature had fallen out of favour. (Shaftesbury was the last philosopher to employ it creatively.) Instead, nature had become not an ordering (a cosmos) but a primitive beginning. Marc-Antoine Laugier popularized one version of this romantic nature.[4] For him, architecture was an imitation of the work of Natural Man. This work was the uncaused cause of the human artifice. All true architecture was a return to the primitive hut, the *sui generis* archaic beginning of building.

There is no doubt that the strong representation of trabeation in the classical Greek temple, just as in Schinkel's early 1820s cultural temples, nods its head to humankind's archaic hut-building impulses. But nonetheless this is still overlaid with knowingness and an attitude of proto-rationalism. As Schinkel moves away from such rationalism, he however also sidesteps Laugier's theory – for a more sophisticated and elaborately historicized romanticism. In Schinkel's version, the primitive construction (the hut) is only the first instance of the continuation by humankind of the constructive activity of nature. Thus architecture does not imitate the hut (= nature) but instead represents the evolution of nature that begins with the hut but which then develops episodically. Architecture tells the story of the natural history of construction.

This conception of architecture as natural history came to the fore in a series of royal estate buildings that Schinkel designed, notably the Lusthaus (pleasure pavilion) near Potsdam in 1825. These designs are essays on the origin of architecture. The origin of architecture is the seed of a natural form that develops into a more complex organism. (This idea of romantic nature was made common coin by two of Schinkel's contemporaries – Goethe and Alexander von Humboldt.) In this spirit of romantic natural history, Schinkel's Casino at Schloss Glienicke (1824–5) emerges out of the landscape via a series of transitions that take the visitor from the river, along the shore, through long pergolas at either side of the site's pavilion, and finally into the building's interior. This is a metaphorical journey from primordial nature through the primitive wooden shelter represented by the pergola to the enclosed building of stone. This passage represents *a natural history of architecture*.

The Court Gardener's House (Charlottenhof, Sanssouci Park, Potsdam, 1829–33) continues this essay on the origins of architecture. The entry to the house involves a graduated transition from the surrounding landscape. The person who retraces this developmental sequence first encounters a primitive ('Pelasgian') perimeter wall marked by a random 'pattern' of rustication and the vernacular Italic of vine-covered trellises mounted on coarse rectangular piers. This scene is succeeded by regular masonry and trellises mounted on baseless Doric columns with simple capitals. Architectural details are refined as the visitor moves closer to the main building, entering a teahouse in the guise of a porticoed temple. The proportions and capitals of the teahouse piers are still closer in resemblance to classic architectural orders. Finally, behind the teahouse temple, there are two Doric aedicules – a culminating moment in which the architectural detailing reaches a mature form.

The architecture of autopoiesis

From the romantic natural history of architecture, Schinkel subsequently turned to an exploration of the *generative laws of building*. The trigger for this exploration was his 1826 trip to France and England. During this visit, he studied with great sympathy the technique of modern industrial building being pioneered by English factory builders. From this moment, he abruptly moved from a fascination with the formative history of architecture to an interest in the self-formation (autopoiēsis) of the single building. Underlying the latter preoccupation was the notion that *the form of a building is most appropriately derived from the nature of its construction*.

Construction, in this view, is no longer the key to unlocking the natural history of humankind, or a cipher for the natural history of architecture. It is instead a key to understanding the nature of built form. Built form (ideally) is an elaboration of its own structure. 'In architecture', Schinkel declared, 'everything must be true, any masking, concealing of structure is an error.'[5] In Schinkel's Bauakademie (1831–6), the internal frame of brick piers and vaults were mimicked on the exterior brick walls. Alternating squares and elongated rectangles – shapes created by polychromatic brick work – on the projecting piers of the external wall surface imitated the alternation of floors

and rooms, and their changing scale. Vaulted brick window pediments mirrored the brick vaults of the interior construction.

In the terracotta decoration of the building, though, Schinkel returned to
historicist preoccupations, with the terracotta panels depicting the history of
the art of building.

The architecture of elevation and abyss

In the final phase of his career, Schinkel turned to the idea of building 'up
high'. In this 'architecture of elevation', Schinkel stays at least nominally
within a classical register. In 1834, Schinkel proposed the construction of a
palace for the King of Greece on the acropolis at Athens. Schinkel's scheme
combined the architecture of the Roman villa, Greek stoa, Byzantine poly-
chromy and the open timber ceiling of an English medieval building.

Schinkel's turn to panoramic heights, initiated by his acropolitical experiment, was confirmed by his very last architectural scheme (extant in engrav-
ings and drawings only) of a palace for the Tsarina of Russia – a sister of the
Crown Prince of Prussia. This palace-pavilion was to have been built on the
edge of a dramatic precipice overlooking the Crimean Sea, the very image
affirming the watery frontage and coastal orientation of classical Greek civilization while at the same time evoking the mountainous abyss of an archaic
'Balkan' modernity. Schinkel's last architectural gesture emphasizes the defiance of gravity by building 'up high'. Defiance of gravity is an essential
aspect of classical grace.[6] It is what was later to give the aura of grace even to
the modern skyscraper, a building type unprecedented in antiquity. That
which is elegant and graceful lifts itself from the earth. Yet, in so doing, if it
is lifted in a certain manner that invites vertigo, the defiance of gravity can
also suggest a plunge into the depths of the abyss.[7]

Schinkel's final work hints at the abyss from which the new gods of
romantic mythology will arise, in a storm of divine fury. These are the
coming gods of creative destruction. They emerge in mythic fashion from
somatic depths that can be only be seen from edifices high in the sky – edifices
like Neuschwanstein (1869), the castle built by Wagner's patron, King
Ludwig II, who was obsessed with mountains and Wagner's operas. One
cannot but help think of Hitler's mountain retreat at Berchtesgaden in this
connection.[8] Height has two meanings: one is the lightness and gravity defiance of classical grace; the other is the sacred-magic mountain – the Balkan/
mountain – from which the climber looks down into the demonic-creative
abyss. The Balkans as a symbol of political decadence is a middle term
between Ludwig's Neuschwanstein and Hitler's Berchtesgaden.

Crimea, in the outlands of Europe, was part of the same liminal zone as the
Balkans. Once controlled by the Ottoman Empire, these were territories that
dynastic empires and great European powers cajoled, manipulated and fought
over. Had any of them been successful in their grander designs, the history of
the twentieth century might have been a different story. But, as it was,

Europe could never master this liminal zone that stretched from the Black Sea to the borders of the Austro-Hungarian Empire. Its failure of mastery was devastating. It led to one of the worst wars in human history, the First World War – the definitive war of senseless slaughter. This war also demonstrated the inconclusiveness of Europe's own internal political order. It brought to an end the 'old Europe' of city, empire and church. But what replaced this order was – and in many respects still is – of an uncertain nature. Civitas was replaced with Nation, Empire with Pan-nationalism and Civilization with Culture. The emancipation of culture from the tutelage of transnational (imperial) institutions at the time was regarded as a prime achievement of the dawning age of liberalism. But the effect, more often than not, was and has remained murderous particularity.

Cities, empires and churches all waged wars. But emancipation of national cultures paved the way for *total war* – viz. the attempt of one culture to *eliminate* the other. European cities, empires and churches had been in varying degrees universalistic umbrellas, amenable to persons of 'diverse origins' so long as they accepted the centrality of the (merchant, imperial or heavenly) city. When the nation replaced the city, this polymetrical coding disappeared. One could no longer be 'Syrian *and* Roman', so to speak. If this led to a 'flowering', even to a 'manufacturing', of cultures in the nineteenth century, it also led at the same time to the nationalization, or *Balkanization*, of cultures. Even in the best-case scenario of liberal nationalism, where adherents admitted that a particular culture (*their* culture) only had a limited validity (circumscribed by time and place), when nations clashed (over waterways, trade routes and territorial boundaries), invariably these geographically circumscribed claims to validity were turned into antinomic cultural statements that could only be resolved by the defeat or humiliation of one or other of the parties.

Pan-nationalists, whose imaginations were inflamed by the idea that a given language or culture possessed a 'genius', recognized such antinomies from the very start. With the *reductio ad absurdum* insight of the fanatic, they knew that culture in the age of the nation was ultimately a matter of a *cultural war to the death*. The condition of the Balkans both anticipated and triggered the national vendettas that tore Europe apart in the Great War of 1914–18.

This was a war from which Europe never recovered.

11 Truth in Building: Mies van der Rohe

After the civilizational trauma of the First World War, Europeans faced the question: was it possible *to disengage from the rule of aesthetics*?

The power and attraction of Modernism as a movement was due, in no small measure, to its promise of restoring to Europe a 'matter of fact' objectivity lost in the haze of aestheticism. In the early 1920s, in postwar Berlin, the search for an alternative to the rule of aesthetics was pursued with an almost inhuman intensity. War, defeat, the collapse of Imperial Germany, the failure of the Luxembourgian Revolution, and the rise of the endlessly compromised Weimar Republic provided an atmosphere in which it seemed plausible that a new, unromantic, constructivist figure of creation might emerge from the rubble and chaos of lacerated Europe. While this was to largely prove an illusion, it was not a patently absurd illusion.

One of the greatest markers of Greek-Roman-Latin civilization had always been architecture. As much as any art and more than most, architecture had felt the depravations of nineteenth-century romanticism and historicism. In response, architecture was buoyed by the exploration of geometric, plastic, constructivist and architectonic conceptions of artistic order that occurred among artists in the period 1900–30: in the works of Picasso, Braque, Mondrian, Lissitzky, Rodchenko, Le Corbusier and the like. This modernist movement knew that it was separating itself from romanticism and historicism. But the way it chose to do this was often very confused and confusing. In some respects the geometric spirit of the 'pagan enlightenment' – the interest in form that had passed from Pythagoras and Plato to Palladio and Shaftesbury – returned in the works of modernist masters like Mondrian. At other times, geometries were expressions of a functionalist enlightenment overly fascinated by machines. All the same, a type of Platonism was registered in many of the critical modernist works of the early twentieth century. Even then, the egoism of the destructive-creative urge of the romantic artist-god or artist-genius was not absent from this cohort. However, such tendencies were at least counterbalanced by a respect for the impersonal character of plastic reason and geometric power.

The crosscurrents between the excesses of aesthetic creation and the power of forms, Romanticism and Platonism, aesthetic religion and constructivist order are spectacularly etched into the work of the great modernist architect Mies van der Rohe (1886–1969). His career in Berlin in the 1920s and 1930s exemplifies the difficulties of European attempts to come to terms with aestheticized culture and politics. Mies proved in the end to be the most Platonic of modernists, yet, like many of his peers, his rejection of romanticism was bound up with a fascination for technological enlightenment.

Mies issued one of the toughest declarations of independence from the rule of aesthetics. In 1923, he announced – on behalf of his contemporaries – that 'our specific concern is to liberate building activity from aesthetic specialists. And make building again what it has always been. Building.'[1] Great building henceforth was to be judged by the criterion of *honesty*.[2] The aesthetic specialists – masters of 'juggling historical allusions' – created buildings that were 'dishonest, stupid, and insulting'.[3] In their place, Mies demanded 'for the buildings of our time: absolute truthfulness and rejection of all formal cheating'. But how could this be achieved?

Mies answered this question with a kind of historicism – in his case a steely historicism aimed squarely at the historical jugglers of nineteenth-century arts and letters. The commonplace of all such 'historical understanding' was the notion that socio-historical ages are structurally different from each other. Because of this, Mies argued, the *recycling* of architectural forms of past epochs could not make for great architecture *today*. Great building, which was also *truthful building*, belonged to its own time. *The truthful building was an impersonal expression of the will of an epoch*:

It is not the architectural achievement of earlier times that makes their buildings appear so significant to us, but the circumstance that the antique temples, the Roman basilicas, and also the cathedrals of the Middle Ages were not the work of individual personalities but the creations of entire epochs. Who asks, when viewing such buildings, for names, and what would the accidental personality of their builders mean? These buildings are by their very nature totally impersonal. They are pure representatives of the will of the epoch.[4]

This, Mies remarked, is their significance. Only thus do they become the 'symbols of their time'.[5]

Artful, which is also to say truthful, building arises neither out of the immortal city nor out of the romantic 'fountainhead' of the architect but *'out of its own epoch'.* Artful building addresses the vital tasks of human need and meaning 'with the means of its own time'. It is stamped with the impersonal spirit of a historical epoch. *History* denies the claims of the civitas. The city had once been the impersonal crucible of architectonics. But, when Mies spoke of Rome, he did not mean the immortal city but a period in time – 'Roman times'. *Impersonality*, on the other hand, denied the claims of romanticism. A great building is not an individual creation. It is not the *signature product* of the romantic architect-hero. Rather it is the *spiritual product* of its epoch, and as such the great building 'today' cannot be a replica of great buildings of past epochs. There is an absolute barrier that intercedes between past and present. An architect who attempts to use the contents and forms of earlier building periods is engaged in a futile endeavour, Mies warns. 'Even the strongest artistic talent will fail. We find again and again that excellent building masters fail because their work does not serve the will of the epoch. In the final analysis, they remain dilettantes despite their great talent.'[6]

These views, first set forth in 1924, served Mies throughout his life. In one of his last philosophical pronouncements, in 1960, he was still pressing the case that the 'best examples' of the architecture of a civilization express 'the innermost structure of its epoch'.[7] Such architecture stands in contact with the most significant elements of civilization. It is this architecture that is truthful or authentic. 'Only a relationship that touches on the innermost nature of an epoch is authentic. I call this relationship a truth relationship. Truth in the sense of Thomas Aquinas: as *adaequatio intellectus et rei*, as congruence of thought and thing.'[8]

The question that haunted Mies to the end was whether any modern architecture could express the innermost structure of the contemporary ('modern') epoch? Mies first attempted to answer this question in the 1920s when he surveyed the history of civilization, and the role of the building arts in it. The categorical framework for this survey was provided by a mixture of Diltheyan 'life philosophy' and Marxian historicism.[9] Crucial for Mies was the Diltheyan bifurcation of the 'life' of human beings into *purposeful social organization* and *cultural patterns*. In Dilthey's view, the 'meaning' of 'life' can be 'understood' as the simultaneous 'expression' of purpose and of pattern. All 'life' is a set of signs – the 'outer' expression (purposeful acts and judgements) in the material world of something 'inner' (the mind). Such signs are best 'understood' by relating them to the widest possible context – first of all to the 'plans' of individual lives, then to the 'systems' of purpose (economy, education, law, politics, science and building), and finally to the patterns of a 'culture'. The hopes and fears of individuals rest on their relationship to purposive systems such as law. These systems regulate human wills externally. But behind all such systems are the structures of 'the spirit' – the 'objective mind' of each socio-historical culture. There is no Roman law, for example, without the spirit of Roman law. Spirit is not concerned with outward, purposively conditioned facts and occurrences (i.e. with the realm of the senses) but with 'values', with objectivated mental creations that provide life with its connections, forms and patterns. Human purposes (goal-

rational actions) are meaningful insofar as they are embedded in a spiritualized pattern of life.

According to Dilthey, the relationship of purposes to patterns is not subject
to the judgement true or false, but to the judgement *truthful or untruthful*.
Dissimulation, lies or deception can break the relation between expression
and the mental content that is expressed. This applies to the relationship
between building (system) and architecture (pattern) as much as anything
else. Mies argued that all major epochs of building could be characterized
from the standpoints of 'life condition' and 'culture'[10] – with the exception of
those epochs whose building art arose directly out of the landscape, such as
in the case of societies composed of single-farm settlements and cluster vil-
lages. In the latter case, building types 'do not follow a set pattern but arise
spontaneously.' They are

> completely intertwined with the ground out of which they arose; they and
> they alone are in truth native. They grew out of the primal material of the
> landscape. No one invented them, but they grew in the true sense of the
> word out of the needs of the inhabitants, and they reflect the rhythm and
> character of the landscape in which they are embedded. These features are
> typical for all farmhouses regardless of where on earth they may be
> found.[11]

City life, on the other hand, is conditioned by patterns. This may be prefigured in the centring of village life around the common – 'a free, rational
order' – but it is cities, not 'communities', that *draw their spirit from the patterns of deliberate composition.*[12] This in particular applies to those European
city types based on guilds, trade or courtly life. In such cases, the building art
is 'the spatially apprehended will of the epoch'.[13]

From the beginning to the end of his public career, Mies insisted that, while
building was a purposive system, and while the architect had (with maximum
realism) to take this into account, *the art of building arose out of spiritual
things*: it was the spatial execution of spiritual decisions.[14] Thus, while it was
the case that 'only where the building art leans on the material forces of a
period can it bring about the spatial execution of its spiritual decisions',[15] at
the same time, connection with the spiritual structure of the times is essential
for great architecture:[16] 'the building art is not merely a technical problem
nor a problem of organization or economy. The building art is in reality
always the spatial execution of spiritual decisions.'[17] These views of the 1920s
were repeated essentially unchanged in his 1938 Inaugural Address at the Illinois Institute of Technology. In that American setting, Mies argued that true
architectural education is concerned not only with practical goals but also
with values.

> By our goals we are bound to the specific structure of our epoch. Our
> values, on other hand, are rooted in the spiritual nature of man. Our prac-
> tical aims determine the character of our civilization. Our values determine

the height of our culture. Different as practical aims are, arising out of different planes, they are nevertheless closely connected. For to what else should our values be related if not to our aims in life? And where should these goals get their meaning if not through values? Both realms together are fundamental to human existence. Our aims assure us of our material life, our values make possible our spiritual existence. If it is true of all human activity where even the slightest question of value is involved, then it must be more true in the field of architecture.[18]

Mies concluded that in its simplest form architecture is entirely rooted in practical considerations, but that it can reach up through 'all degrees of value' to the 'highest realm of spiritual existence, into the realm of the sensuously apprehensible, and into the sphere of pure art'. [19]

The peculiar problem of architecture in the modern age was the contradiction between purposiveness and spirit. Its spirit seemed out of step with its technical and economic achievements. In principle, Mies believed, a 'culture' arises out of the economic givens, conditions and structures of a time.[20] When 'the living conditions of a particular people' change, this leads to a change of 'formal expression' (culture). However, such changes are not immediate. Indeed, they are slowly, even painfully wrought.

The change of the ideological superstructure takes place often very much later and much slower than the change in the societal ground. The exterior shell of things, the crystallization of life processes, remains standing even then and exerts its influence long after its kernel has been hollowed out. Even where one no longer comprehends their meaning, one still adheres to the forms.

Mies was not just making an academic point. He was judging the contemporary condition, where he believed that the 'expression of vital forces' had deteriorated into 'senseless banality'. 'We ourselves are witnesses to such a tragedy. The sins committed in this respect today exceed the imagination.' The material foundation of modern building had changed epochally but the spiritual superstructure remained anchored in the past. Mies accepted that, in time, culture would catch up with system:

[The] situation in which we find ourselves today is in no way comparable to that of earlier epochs. It is totally new and it will know how to express this in an equally new building form. I have already pointed out earlier that economic changes in a society are by no means instantly and automatically followed by changes in ideology, but take a much longer time to develop. It should therefore not surprise us that despite fundamental changes in the structure of our existence, the exterior form of our life has not yet been able to create its new expression. This transformation will take place only gradually, by and by.

Nevertheless, Mies concluded, despite these tendencies, the 'urgency of life' would increasingly articulate itself and push away 'the old, long-obsolete forms'.

Part of the explanation for the delay was that contemporaries failed to grasp that the structure of the modern period was fundamentally different from earlier epochs. Its (nascent) *spirit* was different. This was a secular, not a religious, age. Its *material* conditions were different. This was an age of technical innovations, of new inventions – an *industrial* age. Yet Mies believed that his contemporaries had refused 'to draw consequences for the building arts from the changes in living conditions'. So long as this 'tragic' disjunction persisted, there could be no truthful buildings. How might then the architect go about becoming 'the instrument of the will of the epoch'? How might the architect learn to *serve* the age? Certainly not by living in the past. Anyone who rested their building practice on a 'love of historical things' had a 'total lack of historical understanding'. Mies's historicism confirmed the existence of an insuperable barrier between past and present. But, equally, the assertion of individual will could not achieve a truthful building either.[21] Yes, reasoned Mies, it was a characteristic of the modern age that there was a great detachment of the individual from community. The modern individual asserted a right to advance personal talents and develop personal forces. This development was the basis for a distinctively modern spiritual freedom – the will to think autonomously and search independently. In this conception, the individual will freely sets its own aims and wrestles with the powers of nature.

The course of Mies's reasoning, however, quickly segues from this liberal Kantian picture of modern humankind to a (more realistic) Diltheyian and almost Marxian picture. Whatever powers modern individuals may have to set their own 'life plans', these powers are subsumed within purposive systems. The goal-rational individual asserts the self's autonomous powers against the communal nomos, against the earth, against landscape, etc. – against the claims of geocentric idiomacy. But to do this, modern humankind needs an ally in the purposive system of technology and in the purposive systems of organizations.

> Will freely sets its aims, places them in the service of use, and wrests performance from conquered nature. Nothing seems impossible anymore. Thus begins the reign of technology. Everything succumbs to its impact. It detaches man from his restrictions, makes him freer and becomes his great helper, breaks down the isolation of geographical locations and bridges the largest distances.[22]

The result of this is that the world shrinks more and more, becomes surveyable, and is 'investigated down to its remotest recesses'.[23]

The conquest of localized, geocentric *nomoi* – the customs and rules of communal societies – is aided and abetted by large-scale systems and organizations. The consequence, perhaps unintended, of the revolt of modern individual will against the constraints of nomoi is the creation of autonomous (autopoietic) systems. 'Technology follows its own laws and is not man-related. Economy becomes self-serving and calls forth new needs. Autonomous tendencies in all these forces assert themselves.'[24] The central question for Mies was: can we master the will of this technological epoch? 'Our time is not an external course on which we run. It has been given to us as a task that we have to master ... . We have to become master of the unleashed forces and build them into a new order.' But such mastery also, in the same breath, meant *serving the epoch*. 'We see its immense power and its will.... We have to affirm it, even if its forces still appear menacing to us.' How then – given all this – could the 'master builder' *serve and master* the modern epoch?

Mies's earliest solution (1924) rested on the insight that the greatest buildings of prior ages were *impersonal*.[25] As we have already heard him put it: nobody who views the ancient temples, the Roman basilicas or the medieval cathedrals asks for the name of their builders. The greatest architecture – irrespective of the age – possesses an *anonymous, silent power*. It is part of a *collective creation*. Mies thought this to be a truism of all historical epochs. He resisted the proposition, though, that there was a type of polyphonic impersonality that cut across historical epochs, fusing the temporalities of historical periods into the motet or fugue of the great city or cosmopolis. This idea of trans-historicality underpins Aldo Rossi's declaration that great architecture is 'the architecture of the city'.[26] What Rossi (1931–97) meant by this was that great architecture adapts itself to, and extends, the extant forms and figures not of a historical epoch but of the *transhistorical city*. It is an architecture not of 'values' nor of 'the spirit of the age'. Rather it is an *architecture of memory*. This is not an architecture of the past in the sense of one preoccupied with the copying of past forms. Nor is it the architecture of the museum city (the architecture of collection). Rather the architecture of the city orders the multiple temporalities of the past, present and future into a polymetrical structure. The structure is the *enduring, anonymous collective power* of the city.

Mies's insistence on impersonality, like that of Rossi, is entirely correct. In matters of 'the spirit', the individual signature counts for little. Greatness is anonymous, and in determining what is great in modern architecture, 'questions of a general nature are of central interest'. In this respect, 'the individual becomes less and less important; his fate no longer interests us. The decisive achievements in all fields are objective in nature and their originators are for the most part unknown.'[27] This view contradicted all romantic notions of the artist-as-hero. 'Genius' in architecture had in modern times produced a lot of self-advertising buildings that lacked the anonymous 'spiritual' power of great cathedrals, basilicas or temples. So where in the modern epoch could we find such 'spiritual' power? Where could moderns turn? In Mies's judgement, they could turn to works whose originators are for the most part unknown.

It is here that the great anonymous trait of our time comes into view. Our engineering buildings are typical examples. Gigantic dams, large industrial complexes, and important bridges arise with great natural ease without their builders becoming known.[28]

Just as the master builders of the past took their bearings from unknown artisans and engineers, so Mies recommended the same for modern architects. He advised that they pay attention to the pragmatic systems of purposive rationality (the building or engineering organizations) that produce works of steely beauty from whose patterns the architect can learn. Goal-rational techniques provided crucial clues to a modern spirituality. In order for modern architects to create truthful buildings, they must *first* be prepared to accept that the system of building had fundamentally changed. They must extract pattern from a radically new system of technics.

> If one compares the ponderous weight of Roman aqueducts with the spider-thin power system of a contemporary crane, or bulky vault constructions with the dashing weightlessness of new ferroconcrete structures, then one gets an inkling how our form and expression differ from those of earlier times.[29]

Yet the exact relationship of purpose and pattern in modern times caused Mies a lot of conceptual trouble.

In Mies's earliest, optimistic moments (*c.* 1924) – in an atmosphere of Modernist exuberance – he simply declared that the purpose of a building was also its meaning, and that utilitarian structures would become instruments of the epoch by 'fulfilling their purposes'.[30] The thing that distinguished the modern epoch was a change of purpose and – what followed from this – the whole apparatus of the building system (means, materials and technique).[31] Mies's chief concern was to get the building trades to accept this change, and to give up their old (handicraft) methods.

> I hold that industrialization of building constitutes the core problem of our time. If we are successful in carrying out this industrialization, then the social, economic, technical, and even artistic questions all solve themselves.[32]

At the heart of this programmatic industrialization was the acceptance of new materials.

> The industrialization of the building trades is a matter of materials. This is why the demand for new building materials is the first prerequisite. Technology must and will succeed in finding a building material that can be produced technologically, that can be processed industrially, that is firm, weather-resistant, and sound and temperature insulating. It will have to be a lightweight material, the processing of which not only permits but actually demands industrialization. The industrial production of all parts can only be carried out systematically by factory processes, and the work on

the building site will then be exclusively of an assembly type, bringing about an incredible reduction of building costs.[33]

Programmatic industrialization equated systematic rationalization with an eye to economizing.

Mies in the same year was already defending himself against charges that modern materials were inferior. 'The objection has been raised that the glass wall does not adequately insulate against exterior temperatures.'[34] Unsurprisingly, he insisted that such fears were exaggerated. 'Buildings with large glass fronts already exist and it has not come to my attention that the large glass planes are considered disadvantageous.'[35] Yet, in the course of the 1920s, he would come increasingly to see that the battle cry of 'rationalization and typification' and 'calls for economizing' were only limited solutions to pragmatic-systemic problems, such as housing shortages.[36] By the end of the 1920s, he had come to see that the art of building – insofar as it was the spatial execution of spiritual decisions – had to find a way of *ordering* the systemic forces of economy and technology. Left unchained, these Promethean autopoietic systems were creating (amidst modern life) a kind of chaos.

Chaos is always a sign of anarchy. Anarchy is always a movement without order. Movement without central direction. Chaos occurred before. When the order of antiquity degenerated into late antiquity. But out of this chaos a new order arose, the order of the Middle Ages.[37]

By the end of the 1920s Mies had come to sense that his own epoch, and its technical-economic systems, had failed to establish a 'pattern' – a spiritual superstructure – commensurate with the Promethean drive powers of its means of production. The question left unanswered for Mies was how such an ordering could be achieved in the epoch's own terms, so that its building would be a truthful, and thus also a great spiritual representation of its own times.

12   The House of the Gods: Heidegger

Schinkel's dream of building high up on a cliff facing the sea anticipated the fascination with 'the akrotic' – the towering hill – that came to mark a Europe fatally shaken by the Great War of 1914–18. This war took Europe to the fatal edge. As in other societies in similar circumstances – for example Athens after the Peloponnesian War – rebuilding was a priority. *From the rubble, the Phoenix rises.* Yet in what image could traumatized Europe rebuild?

Historicism had problematized Europe's relationship to its own past. No longer could temple-form, basilica or cathedral serve to memorialize the war dead nor could these building types serve as a consoling reminder of the great works, renaissance power and spiritual continuities of Greco-Roman-Latin-Pagan-Enlightenment history. Thus war-traumatized Europeans sought out other, more archaic, memories – memories of something that preceded the temple-form. After the caesura of the Great War, even some of the most sophisticated Europeans sought consolation in a profound archaism.[1] The attraction was not merely, or even principally, to the traditional (village) *Gemeinschaft* of preindustrial Europe, but, much more radically, to a 'geotheism' – a quasi-deification of 'native' lands. This theism fell below the classical threshold of European civilization.

If the self-inflicted catastrophe of the First World War stimulated feelings for the archaic, these were sensibilities that had been growing in western societies since the mid-nineteenth century. By the time of the *fin de siècle*, the retreat to a kind of geotheism and an immanent 'Balkanization' – in the sense of 'mountainization'[2] – of Europe had brought with it an accelerating break-up of the artificing consciousness and *kosmopoiēsis*[3] that had been synonymous with the civilization of Europe since 'the Greek breakthrough' during the eighth to fifth centuries BCE.[4]

115

Prior to that 'breakthrough', human self-awareness had been profoundly geocentric. The focus of archaic religiosity had been the sacred mountain. Nature's mountains surrounded the human abode, and human creation was thought of as a receptacle for these divine, sheltering powers.[5] Such geotheism was typical of large-scale pre-Hellenic societies. Whether it was Mesopotamian ziggurats, the pyramids of Precolumbian Teotihuacán or those of Egypt, the imaginary signifiers of those societies mimicked the shape of mountains. The 'Greek breakthrough' was signalled by the emergence of the temple-form. The temple was a mimesis, but not of natural forms (the mountain, the cave). It was a mimesis of a human artifice (the house); on a higher level, it was a mimesis of 'the struggle of forces' at work *in* nature, in the relationship between humankind and nature, and within humankind. The temple displayed house-like qualities; its mathematically proportionate structures were representations of the countervailing forces of nature familiar to Ionian physics; the arrangement of its peripteral colonnades of columns mimicked the muscular formation of sea-borne rowers defying the power of the sea, or else the phalanx of Greek hoplites standing firm against the enemy.

The image of the sacred of the ancient Greeks had very human characteristics, and the temple correspondingly stood out in counter-position to the landscape. This did not mean that Greek building was hostile to the landscape. Anyone who has been to Delphi, the greatest of all of the Greek sacred sites, will testify that it is not. Delphi nestles without a hint of tension in the thighs of the mountains. Yet the temples of Delphi also stand upright, independent of the protective embrace of the mountains, and are in no way imitative of, or overpowered by, their surrounds. The Greeks built 'up high' – on acropolises, on hill sites adjacent to their harbour cities. But they did so in a way that underscored a soaring lightness that took them away from the earth.

Along with the Roman basilica, the Greek temple was the pre-eminent model of European civilization until the end of the nineteenth century. Its tectonic arrangement of horizontal and vertical, like the Roman double-coding of entry-exit, or the medieval Latin multi-layering of high and low registers, provided an enduring image of the union of opposites, the fundamental polyphonic structure of social order. Thereafter, a decisive rupture occurs. The way forward to this rupture was prepared by the romantic deification of the landscape, and the poetic habilitation of the (alpine, lake and forest) wildernesses of Europe.

It was in America – and not Europe – that the most telling experiments with geocentrism occurred in the nineteenth century. In many ways less mature than Europe, America in some ways leapt ahead of her – anticipating by decades the 'retreat to the earth' that would resound in the European mind in the cataclysmic interwar years of the twentieth century. America's own cataclysm, its Civil War (1861–5), provided a decisive impetus to the search for a reassuring 'grounding' – a return to the archaic source of the earth. In part geocentric ideologies of land and earth moved to the gravitational centre of American life after the Civil War because of the sheer scale of that war, and in part because Lincoln's Republican Party finally brought

Alexander Hamilton's nationalist vision of America – a minority view among America's founding generation – to triumph over its anti-Federalist opponents in the Civil War. In this manner, Lincoln and his party accelerated (though never fully achieved) the shift of America from a classical republican polity to a modern nation state. In the decades after the Civil War, America was preoccupied with continental expansion.

Geocentricism served the ends of both national grounding and spiritual restitution after bloody conflict. This ideology is explicit in the work of the American architect Henry Hobson Richardson (1838–86). His post-Civil War 'Romanesque' style – with its monumental stone buildings, heavy round arches, rough cuttings and sense of massiveness – conveys a powerful sense of earth-bound defensiveness against the world. Although dubbed Romanesque, Richardson's signature style is not strictly anything in particular – it drew on early Christian and Syrian sources, Italian Byzantine architecture, Romanesque monasteries and cathedrals, on Gothic Revival and so on.[6] In that aspect, it was a conventional kind of nineteenth-century historicizing bricolage. More significantly, it managed to distinguish itself with a visage of stone-like monumentality that owed more to an archaic Mycenaean or Egyptian building than to any form of Greco-Roman-Latin architecture. In this later aspect, Richardson's work was an index of the shift of Atlantic consciousness toward the primordial.

In a lighter vein, the same kind of post-Civil War eclecticism – but in this case bereft of Richardson's geocentric metaphysics – is to be found in nineteenth-century American picturesque architecture, notably the American Queen Anne, Shingle, Eastlake and Stick styles. This picturesque architecture was distinguished by a mixing of ornamental details and motifs from a variety of historical periods. As in Europe, the American nineteenth century opened up a Pandora's Box of indiscriminate narratives. Domes, mansards, cornices, brickwork patternings, pilasters, turrets, pinnacles, urns, balconies and balustrades were borrowed from Baroque France, Renaissance Italy, Gothic Flanders and Elizabethan England, and haphazardly mixed together.[7] The profusion of architectural motifs caused such details to become empty visual effects, i.e. *signs*.[8] The fact that these details were plundered from a variety of different, mostly unrelated, historical sources had the effect of creating either buildings that referred to no past in particular or buildings whose past was some kind of indefinite time.[9]

By making the past indefinite, the nation was freed from its hold. It was freed from the renaissance power and architectonic order of Greco-Roman-Latin history. The picturesque was a statement of *free invention* ungoverned by any consistency or reason across time. This freedom from consistency or reason pleased the historicist mentality. The sheer variety of the picturesque was seen as sufficient without the need for any enduring element or theme to tie the plundered assortment of details together into an ordered (cosmo-poiëtic) whole. What the eighteenth century had called reason or nature – viz. *the ordered arrangement of things* – was in crisis. Nature was romanticized, and became in the course of the nineteenth century redefined biologisti-

cally as a field of 'growth'. The picturesque was a visual representation of
this. With its variegated asymmetries, it conveyed a sense of restless biomorphic growth. Still, the picturesque, while a mimesis of biomorphic nature,
stood apart from the earth, and it is in this light that the radicalism of H. H.
Richardson stands out. His gesture towards the Greco-Roman-Latin lineage,
viz. his invocation of the 'Romanesque', belied an overriding fascination with
the idea of the 'ground-norm' – the notion that 'earth' not 'artifice' provided
the basic justification of the validity of social arrangements.

A further step in the direction of geocentricity – the disappearance of the
house or building *into* the earth – was taken in America at the turn of the
century by Frank Lloyd Wright (1869–1959) who conceived of buildings that
grew out of the landscape. Wright's conception mimicked not only the self-
propagating formative power of romantic nature, but also the very forms of
the earth itself. Wright took as his model not the vertical rise of the Pre-
Columbian mountain but the flat landscape of the Midwestern prairie. 'We of
the Middle West', wrote Wright, 'are living on the prairie. The prairie has a
beauty of its own and we should recognize and accentuate this natural
beauty, its quiet level. Hence, gently sloping roofs, low proportions, quiet sky
lines, suppressed heavy-set chimneys and sheltering overhangs, low terraces
and out-reaching walls sequestering private gardens.'[10] Wright's Prairie
Houses – the classic of the genre being the Robie House in Chicago (1908) –
brilliantly adapted geocentricity to modern American conditions. This
Wrightian vision, though, had no precedent. While Wright had no hesitation
in presenting himself as a romantic 'genius' unneedful of models, other Americans lacked such overweening self-confidence, and the search for precedents
led them into the embrace of an infinitely older geocentric spirit, the Pre-
Columbian.

An explicit imitation of Pre-Columbian forms, the Pueblo Style, was conceived by A.C. Schweinfurth in California in the 1890s, and, subsequently,
relaunched (in 1905) by W. George Tight, the university president-cum-
architect of the University of New Mexico at Albuquerque, whose protean
vision of a university-pueblo was to become the starting-point for the distinctive regional architecture of the Southwest United States. In both the Midwestern Prairie and the Southwestern Pueblo architectures, a mimesis of –
presented as a return to – the forms of earth plays a major role, and is a
token of a deep disenchantment with the city. In America, the work of
Wright and Tight was coterminous with the Progressive Era, an age also
characterized by its uncomfortableness with the city. Progressives in America
imagined the city as a place of corruption; a place that was overcrowded,
alienated, and diseased. The empty plains stretching from Illinois to Arizona
promised redemption from the 'evils' of the city.

The discomfort of Americans with the urbs is frequently explained as the
legacy of Thomas Jefferson who excoriated the city as a moral sore on the
body politic. While Jefferson's animus influenced the American mentality,
Americans were not alone in their repudiation of the city or in their search
for images of 'grounding'. The same search for 'the ground' erupted in early

twentieth-century European consciousness. Just as bloody civil conflict steered Americans towards the consolations of the earth, the catastrophe of the Great War of 1914–18 accelerated Europe's own embrace of geotheism. After 1918, Europeans turned to exalt the therapeutic, spiritual and redemptive qualities of 'the magic mountain'. In the climate of the times, reconciliation with the mountainous 'Balkan nature' was regarded as a powerful tonic for cataclysmic social distress. The romance of 'Balkan nature', in certain crucial aspects, was a continuation of the current of late eighteenth-century romanticism that had habilitated the mountain as an object of aesthetic pleasure and as a *via media* both for escape from 'social demands' and retreat from the kinetic energy of the city. But fascination with the imagery of 'grounding' was not a purely romantic preoccupation. It is rather indicative of a generalized European desire to find an earth-like 'foundation' on which society could then be constructed – a 'foundation' that somehow escaped the impress of human artifice.

Even Kant – the exemplar of enlightened Europe – invoked the ambiguous image of the 'ground-work' of universal morality, sliding between the images of the constructive work of the builder and the earth in which a building's foundations are encased. A parallel elision between earth and artifice is apparent in the art movements of interwar Germany. The Weimar era in Germany opened with Bruno Taut's vision of *Alpine Architecture* (1919), an expressionist sketchbook that featured peaks of mountains remade in glass, and alpine lakes filled with crystalline forms. The grounding of the earth and the liberation of the peak, the artifice of the glassmaker and natural indomitability of the mountain are all alluded to in this image. In 1922, Mies van der Rohe turned this expressionist epiphany into a Plan for a Glass Skyscraper that was a contradictory manifesto for a new epoch – its cliff-like towering quality evocative of the pre-Hellenic worship of mountainous power, while its see-through glass membrane was a de-materializing gesture that suggested flight from the earth toward an epiphanic dissolve of white light. In this moment, European architecture suddenly leapt ahead of its American rival. While in the 1920s and 1930s, American architects found themselves recapitulating – in the ziggurat designs of Art Deco skyscrapers – Pre-Columbian mountain imaginary, with its steep verticality and rectilinear shapes,[11] the Central European modernist imaginary managed to combine both the mystical dissolve of light and the towering solidity of the sheer cliff-face. The traces of humanism (the striving for spirited elevation and soaring flight), enlightenment (a building whose interior was visible from the outside), Christianity (in the figure of the person who looks upwards and outwards towards the light) and of the archaic (the cliff-like edifice), appear simultaneously in Mies's Glass Skyscraper.

The expressionist city par excellence was Berlin. The Berlin that Mies knew in the 1920s was a richly articulated *demi-monde* and a cosmopolis filled with exiles of all kinds. It was a stranger city, a *xenopolis*, one remarkable for its artistic power, yet also notable for its political isolation and civic emptiness. Radicalisms of various kinds flourished in the city. Mies – on the surface a relatively apolitical figure – encoded these radicalisms in his designs. His 'glasshouses', where everything was visible from the outside, were designed on the assumption of there being few possessions (either on display or stored away) inside. Only a minimum of furniture or objets d'art was permissible (and even the positioning of these was carefully prescribed). This minimalism extended even to objects out of sight. The architect intentionally provided relatively little storage space. This was the antithesis of the Pre-Hellenic and patrimonial idea of building-as-storage. It invoked an ascetic notion of socialism. Yet for all its evident challenge to the collector mentality of the nineteenth-century bourgeoisie, such a form of socialism did not belong to the world of the civitas. Its secret desire was for *a communism without the commune*. A recurring theme throughout the Weimar era is socialism defined in terms of the house – a socialism that answers 'the housing question'. Thus the socialism of the times was not a municipal type, a Berlin socialism, a communism of the commune, but rather a 'housing socialism' given practical effect by the preoccupation of Weimar architects and administrators with the matter of worker housing. (Mies himself participated in one of the best-known worker housing schemes – the Weissenhof project in Berlin) The preoccupation with the question of housing – with the *domus* rather than the *civitas* – indicated a fundamental lack of interest on the part of the Weimar Republic in the architecture of the city.

Under conditions where civic aspiration, and hence the possibility of civic greatness, no longer beckoned, what could provide the animating spirit of the architect so that architecture might rise above the functional or the banal? One answer was *nature*. This was not the universal nature of the civitas (the cosmographic nature in which all things – physical, biological, topographical, human and divine – have a nature, and in which the civitas is a point of connection between the sub-systems of nature). Rather it was the idiomatic nature of land, mountain, forest and stream. This answer, encouraged by the legacy of nineteenth-century romanticism, prompted the architect to turn from the image of the polymetrical renaissance city and dream instead of assimilating the 'built environment' to the 'natural environment'. We see the ambition to reconcile building and idiomatic nature already in the work of Schinkel when he designs features like the pergolas of the casino of Schloss Glienicke (Potsdam, 1824–5) as a zone of transition between building and landscape.

When architectural modernism made its dramatic appearance in Germany in the 1920s, the historicizing aspect of Schinkel (be it his classical or gothic stylings) was repudiated. But the neo-romantic categorical imperative that buildings be interdependent with nature was radically reaffirmed in modernist designs. For Mies, breaking down the boundaries between inside and outside, building and nature was an article of faith. He used the most modernist of materials – *glass* – to achieve precisely this: the minimizing of the distinction between inside (artifact) and outside (nature). Mies conceived of expansive glass walls as a membrane between the built and the natural. This idea found its first mature expression in Mies's Tugendhat House (Brno, 1928–30), and, after thought-experiments like the Plan for the Three Courts Project (1934) in the less welcoming atmosphere of post-Weimar Germany, the idea was to reach its stunning apogee in Mies's American period design, the Farnsworth House (1946–51).

As its owners later attested, the glassed-in rectangular box that Mies set in the countryside of Plano, Illinois, was a barely livable abode.[12] Its glass membrane offered little modulation of the extremes of summer and winter temperature. However, it is doubtful whether the Farnsworth House was actually designed as a human abode at all, but rather as a temple. This house was the culmination of Weimar architecture, the epitome of the romantic reconciliation with nature, and an antidote to the Weimar era's own spiritual chaos. In short, it was an answer to Mies's own search for a new order.

Nietzsche's pronouncement of the 'death of God' provoked artists and thinkers, like Mies, who had grown up in 'Old Europe', to search for an alternative sense of the sacerdotal. The most far-reaching philosophical attempt to postulate a 'new god' was made, as we've discussed, by Heidegger. Mies's own 'house of the gods' fulfilled Heidegger's late romantic image of the temple as the work of clearing – the opening-up of open air, open space – a made-thing that opens to light, clears, reveals and in so doing *makes space* for the protective grace of the new old gods.[13] The Farnsworth House, though, is more radical in its conception of the temple than even Heidegger allowed. Whereas, for Heidegger, 'the building encloses the figure of the god, and in this concealment lets it stand out into the holy precinct through the open portico',[14] in Mies's conception of the temple, *there is no concealment*. Sheathed in glass, the interior of the Miesian temple-house is completely visible from the outside.

For both Heidegger and Mies, truth was a matter of revelation. *That which is revealed is truth*. Both were raised as Catholics; yet, both had little time for the institution (the 'positive religion') of the Catholic Church. The apostate Heidegger turned to a romanticized Hellenism and an aestheticized spirituality, while Mies was drawn to Platonizing philosophies of an Augustinian and Thomist kind.[15] Both Heidegger and Mies served tangentially in the Great War. Like all of their generation who did, including Wittgenstein, they witnessed the pulverizing of the illusions that the age of historicism had created. There was no way after the Great War that anyone could plausibly construct a philosophy or a form of life around the notion of 'understanding'.[16] Thus building became, for them, a kind of *Bildung* of a promised society and a resting-place for truth enervated by the age of historicism. Building (properly speaking) was not the building of temples of 'understanding' for a curatorial (museum) society. Rather it was the making of something that was *capable of shaping-forming a society*.

The difference, though, between the modernist Mies and the conservative revolutionary Heidegger was as deep going as the similarities. If Mies represents the free flight of Europe, Heidegger represents its desire for grounding. Mies's instinct was to keep the building off the ground. He built, in an edifying religious fashion, toward the sky, while Heidegger looked downwards, towards the enclosing shelter of the earth.

For Heidegger, making, *poiēsis*, is revelatory. It lets that which reveals itself ('presences') come forth into 'unconcealment'. The revelation of truth contained in the act of *poiēsis* is not transcendent but immanent. The most fundamental kind of *poiēsis*, namely *phusis*, is the arising, the coming-forth of something out of itself.[17] Thus truth is not the revelation of a transcendent God, or even the objectivation of a Neoplatonic demiurge, rather it is the very 'happening' of *poiēsis*.[18] The work of art (the temple) *portrays* (or represents) *nothing*.[19] Its significance rather is its *work*. The temple-work of creating boundaries or forms reveals a world. It opens a centre where whatever it is that stands within that centre can be (can stand revealed).[20] The figure (the sculpture) of the god stands at the centre of the temple. It is the *enclosure* of the figure (the sculpture) of the god and the analogous *delimitation* of a sacred precinct – the setting of its boundaries – that 'opens a world'.[21] *The temple-work is the source of all of the templates of nature.* The temple-work has a steadfastness – standing there, it holds its ground against the raging storm, and thereby makes the pattern of the storm manifest in its violence. Likewise, the gleaming of the temple's stone brings to light the light of day and the darkness of night. The temple's firm towering makes visible the invisible space of air. The steadfastness of the temple reveals the surge of the surf; its repose brings out the raging of the sea.[22] The temple-work is what makes all of the things found in the natural landscape – trees and grass, eagle and bull, snake and cricket – 'first enter into their distinctive shapes and thus come to appear as what they are'.[23] The temple, in its standing there, first gives to things their look and to men their outlook on things.[24]

Heidegger's account of *poiēsis* is a romantic translation of the axiom of Greco-Roman-Latin civilization, viz. that it is *the human artifice* (*the building*) *that gives form-shape to the human constellation*. Temple, agora, forum and church were the central signifiers of this civilizational path. (Even God's domain was a civitas.) For the human constellation, Heidegger substitutes nature. The building is the defining force of romantic nature (trees, storms). Yet, whatever the displacements at play here, Heidegger does give full due to the *work* of building. Indeed, in his most radical moments, he declares that it is *the work that lets the god be present*, and thus *is the god himself*. In this Heidegger consorts with the 'Old European' civilization builders, only then to deny this consorting – with an equally daring gesture – by declaring that the temple-work *not only opens a world*, at the same time it *sets this world back on the earth*. Thus, truth (*alētheia*, revealing) is grounded. By virtue of this grounding, truth is harboured, preserved, watched over, protected, kept safe through concealment. ('The clearing in which beings stand is in itself at the same time concealment.')[25] Truth is protected by a native soil. The *phusis* of creation is not universal. There is no residue of the universal cosmography of the ancient Greeks in Heidegger's treatment of *poiēsis*. Rather, in his rendering, the temple-work is rendered inactive *if it is dislodged from its native ground*.

Accordingly, the will of nineteenth-century collectors to rehouse the sacred sculpture of Greek temples in the art-temples (museums) of European capitals was a vain gesture to recapitulate the world-opening of the Greeks. 'The Aegina sculptures in the Munich collection ... are, as the works they are, torn out of their native sphere. However high their quality and power of impression, however good their state of preservation, however certain their interpretation, placing them in a collection has withdrawn them from their own world.'[26] Even when we 'make an effort to cancel or avoid such displacement of works – when, for instance, we visit the temple in Paestum at its own site or the Bamberg cathedral in its own square – the world of the work that stands there has perished'.[27] Consequently the collector and traveller in the age of historicism were engaged in futile activities. What modern Europe, or in Heidegger's more provincial, nativist conception, Germany, lacked were *its own works*. Copying, collecting, visiting the works of other times and places was illusory if one expected this to revitalize the *Gestaltung* of German-speaking Central Europe. For 'the work belongs, as work, uniquely with the realm that is opened up by itself'.[28] The world is only ever the world of a 'historical people'.[29] The Greek temple therefore was fixed in place. Tied, so to speak, to the rocky ground on which it was built.

This view – that there are as many incommensurable work-world horizons as there are 'historical peoples' – in the end was not so far removed from the historicism of Dilthey who insisted that human activity is always woven into wider social-historical contexts. Each historical unit (nation, age, period) is self-contained.[30] Each epoch constitutes a closed horizon, and each socio-historical unit is *centred on itself*. If work-*poiēsis* brought forward the world of an epoch, it was closed to appropriation by another epoch. It was closed to renaissance.

For Heidegger then, the temple-work shaped the Greek world. It did this by *revealing* the qualities, the being, of stone, wood, metal and so on:

> The rock comes to bear and rest and so first becomes rock; metals come to glitter and shimmer, colors to glow, tones to sing, the word to speak. All of this comes forth as the work sets itself back into the massiveness and heaviness of stone, into the firmness and pliancy of wood, into the hardness and luster of metal, into the lightening and darkening of color, into the clang of tone, and the naming power of the word.

The made-thing, the work-temple, the handiwork of the artisan gave shape-form to everything in the Greek *phusis*. But this *phusis* was not universal (even if the Greeks believed otherwise). It was not universal, Heidegger contended, because of that *into which the work sets itself*, viz. *the earth*, is not universal.

In setting itself back into the earth, the building reveals the earth (as it did wood, metal, colour, and so on) – and yet the ground on which the temple is built reveals itself in a very peculiar manner. For the earth shows itself *only when it remains undisclosed and unexplained*.[31] We can take a rock from the ground and break it open, reasons Heidegger, but this will not disclose anything about the rock. The rock 'does not display in its fragments anything inward that has been disclosed.'[32] The earth only reveals itself when it is perceived as that *by nature which shrinks from every disclosure and constantly keeps itself closed.*[33] In other words, *unconcealment* (*truth*) *rests on concealment*. Concealment is not untruth (lie, fiction). It is mystery, seclusion and withdrawal. The opening of the world rests upon the seclusion of the earth – or, more specifically, on the 'native ground' of a 'historical people'. Thus, while the world is the immanent unveiling, the self-disclosing openness 'of the broad paths of the single and essential decisions in the destiny of an historical people',[34] in the end, the world 'grounds itself on the earth'.[35] While the world cannot endure anything closed, the earth 'as sheltering and concealing, tends always to draw the world unto itself and keep it there'.[36]

Heidegger's statement is the philosophical epitome of a powerful, if controverted, current of twentieth-century interwar belief that preferred the allure of the earth (geocentricity) to the *poiēsis* of the world. The geocentric politics that came to dominate both the left and right wings of the political spectrum in the 1930s had a disposition starkly at odds with the cosmopolitical orientation that distinguished the Greek-Roman-Latin-Pagan-Enlightenment shaping of European civic life. A Central European culture – that emerged outside of the orbit of this shaping – began to set the tone for European life. In the heated context of the interwar period, geocentric politics stimulated all kinds of nativist, regionalist, pan-nationalist and isolationist trends.

While the high modernism of the 1920s and 1930s stressed the *Open*, the period's countervailing geocentric political movements[37] emphasized the idea of the *Closure* of the earth. In architecture, this was translated as a desire to 'return to the vernacular'. In 'regional' (nativist) architecture, the struggle of the vernacular carpenter with nature was charmingly represented. Exposed beams or lintels, roughcast render and so on, alluded to the rough power and earthy cunning of vernacular life. But such representations were *ultimately subordinated to a quest for home truths, for a return to origins*. It is perfectly true that geocentric political movements also found expression in the last gasp of architectural classicism, notably in the megalomaniac 'classicism' of Nazi pan-nationalism and Stalinist national empire building. But this was so alarmingly fraudulent that it had virtually no staying power beyond its instigators' reigns of terror. In contrast, cults of folk vernacular authenticity – whether promoted by American romantics, German national conservatives, or modernists in search of honesty – continued to influence successive generations long after the interwar era.

The idealized, 'close to the earth' work of the vernacular builder was equated with a 'völkisch' honesty. This was a *poiēsis* – a making or a work – set into the earth. It was a *reconciliation of disclosure and closure*. An architecture that attempted the same was motivated by a desire to recapitulate the 'honesty' of the artisan or the 'purity' of the folk-builder who was 'of the earth'. This was an architecture that distanced itself from the artificing – and in that sense, the lying or untruthful – sophistication of classical architecture. This was an architecture that relished the connotation of being 'indigenous' – of being specific to a native land, and *part of a landscape*. The ideal building was autochthonous. It had the appearance of *having sprung by itself from the land*.[38] If a building developed 'genetically' – if its structure had an organic relationship with the 'native' land – then the artifice of the building (its 'lie') could be mastered.

The search for 'truth-concealment' in building had first appeared in an architecturally self-conscious way at the turn of the twentieth century. The adobe experiments of Schweinfurth and Tight, the Californian bungalows of Greene and Greene, the Plains-like lines of Frank Lloyd Wright all combined a geocentric grammar with honest materials and aspirations to regional authenticity. What seemed – after the explosive appearance of European modernism in the 1920s – like a dead movement suddenly found life again, and came back with a vengeance in the 1930s. The mercurial resurrection of Frank Lloyd Wright's career culminated with the most perfect domestic expression of geocentric architecture, his 1937 Fallingwater, a building constructed around a stone hearth and over the cascading water of a Pennsylvania woodland stream. Yet, for all of its closeness to the earth, this was still a modern geocentricity – the artful cantilevering of its design set the extremities of the building hovering in the air, wing-like above the earth.

The dialectic of openness and closure haunted the twentieth-century mind. Even the chameleon architect-advocate turned architect, Philip Johnson, who had introduced America to the masters of European modernism in his 1932 Museum of Modern Art exhibition, and had championed Mies as the greatest of them, was (momentarily) caught up in an archaizing Zeitgeist, making a wholly fantastic pilgrimage in 1935 to be at the side of Louisiana's folk-populist demagogue governor, Huey Long, who had carved a very successful career for himself out of denouncing the 'big city'.[39] If the quixotic comedy of Johnson's political misadventure makes us smile wryly – Johnson's overtures were forcefully rebuffed by Long – it was an escapade that was far from idiosyncratic for the times. It betrayed the powerful spell cast by the idea of a geocentric nomos over the most sophisticated minds, even ones, like Johnson, who strongly identified with the institution of the public museum and with the imaginary of the museum city that had seemed destined to replace the cosmopolis in the modern age.

Geocentric politics inevitably had its more polished and its cruder proponents. The former were distinguished by their avoidance of the wholesale rejection of an opening to the world. Heidegger mounted probably the subtlest advocacy of a geocentric politics that did not have one-dimensional closure as its ambition. He proposed instead a precarious dialectic in which the opposition of earth and world gives rise to a mutually affirming struggle. These opposites 'raise' each other into the self-assertion of their natures, but in the struggle each opponent carries the other beyond itself, eventually into the intimacy of simple belonging to one another. 'The earth cannot dispense with the open of the world if it itself is to appear … a resolute foundation.'[40] It is precisely this *resolute foundation* that Mies van der Rohe rejected. His temple, the Farnsworth House, is notable for the fact that it hovers above the earth. It is mounted on steel stilts four feet above the ground. The platform-terrace that abuts the house likewise is pointedly separated from the earth. The Farnsworth House is paradigmatic in its rejection of the idea of the dwelling set back into the earth.[41] Indeed, in all respects, it is an insistent manifesto on behalf of the Open.

13   The Iron Cage: Wittgenstein

From beginning to end, Mies's designs were essays in Openness. His 1922 Plan for a Glass Skyscraper envisaged a soaring tower of transparency.[1] Completely sheathed in glass, the inside of the skyscraper was designed to be visible to the outside, while the view of the outside from the inside was unobstructed by any load-bearing walls. Like the liminal zone between inside and outside, the layout of the interior was similarly subject to the principle of Openness. Conceived of as an open plan, the space of the office was left radically undefined – as if a continuous void. Specificities of *place* were transformed into abstract *space*. By creating wall-less interior zones, open space promised unobstructed movement and communication. At the same time such open space served as a kind of *universal* space. Because it was undefined by strong (masonry) boundaries, it was adaptable to an infinite range of future uses. Mies applied these same principles to his domestic villas of the 1920s and 1930s. In his unexecuted Brick Country House (1924), interior walls were turned into free-standing curtains or screens. These screens neither enclosed rooms nor barely even suggested room-like areas. They constituted no real termination, or enclosure, or points of rest in the house. Rather they encouraged the perception (and perhaps also the fact) of endlessly flowing movement through the house. *Space was turned into an endless series of transition zones.*[2]

Even in the 1930s amidst the chaos of the disintegrating Weimar Republic and the rise to power of the Nazis, Mies was never tempted by the allure of the protective embrace of the earth. Instead, in the designs for his Court Houses, he conceived a classic, almost Epicurean, strategy to escape the maelstrom of the outside: a house built around an interior court – an Italian Renaissance or Roman figure – with its face turned away from the violent streets, and yet open to the sky.

Mies never forsook the ideas of unimpeded movement through open (universal) space and the mutual opening up of interior and exterior to each other through the medium of glass. But, in his exile in the United States (from 1938), he redefined his architecture as a kind of classicism. This development starts at the moment of his exile in the United States (when he begins designing the Illinois Institute of Technology campus). It acquires mature form in his Lake Shore Apartments (1948–51) in Chicago, and reaches a pinnacle with his design of the Seagram Building (1954–8) in New York City.

In America, Mies embraced a kind of modern classicism – *a steely classicism*. In Paris in the 1920s, Le Corbusier already had conceived of a stripped-back architectural modernism based on Platonic geometry.[3] The essence of art, accordingly, was circles, triangles and squares – and their stereometrical (solid) equivalents: spheres, pyramids and cubes. Echoes of this pared-back vision of the classical appear in Mies's American work. Mies strives to reduce the gap between surface appearance and geometrical form to an absolute minimum. This effort culminates in the Seagram Building, a work of chaste geometries and immaculate proportions – a Neoplatonic solid in the midst of the modern metropolis.

Le Corbusier was not the only figure in the 1920s to attempt a geometrizing reconciliation of the classical and the modern. Something disturbing in the nature of the Great War impelled quite a number of artists and philosophers to find a sanctuary in the concentrated essentials of form. Le Corbusier's fascination with Greek ideas of proportionality and geometry are well known. Less well known is Ludwig Wittgenstein's contemporaneous experiment with built proportionality. Wittgenstein's (1926–8) design of his sister's house on the Kundmanngasse in Vienna was the second in a trilogy of great works that include his *Tractatus Logico-Philosophicus* (1922) and his *Philosophical Investigations* (1953). Written on the battlefields, Wittgenstein's *Tractatus* was an oblique but unfailingly powerful response to the weak thought of aestheticized Europe. In its turn, Wittgenstein's architecture mirrors the conclusion of the *Tractatus* – that *meaning is something to be shown, not spoken of*. Architecture possessed the capacity *to show the 'meaning' of 'things'* – something that discourse, not least philosophical discourse (which Wittgenstein the philosopher remained ambivalent about throughout his life) could never achieve. In turning to architecture, Wittgenstein turned to the tacit assumption of Greco-Roman-Latin civilization that meaning arose in the first instance out of artifice and *eidos*, not discourse or *logos*. The meaning of things arose not from words, rules and laws but from forms, structures and rhythms.

Wittgenstein's architecture stood at a self-conscious distance from the historicism of nineteenth-century Vienna. In searching to find a built form that was something more than 'costume architecture', Wittgenstein took his cue from his fellow Viennese, Adolf Loos (1870–1933), who had sought to strip away all historical signs ('ornamentation') from the surface of buildings. Loos believed that this strategy was essentially classical, and more particularly *Roman*, in nature.[4] How seriously can we take Loos's self-comparison with the Romans? Certainly, like the Romans, Loos was preoccupied with interiors. Whereas the Greeks thought of a building as a sculpture (a plastic solid) observable from the street,[5] the Romans thought of a building as a container in which one spent time. The Greek building thus remained an (elongated) cube onto which was loaded a solid triangular prism (the gabled roof). From inside, what was visible was a single cubic volume of basically unvarying dimensions. For all of the Apollonian mythology of the Greeks, the emphasis was on stereometrical solidity, not on the dematerializing filtering of light into the built artifice. The Romans transfigured the Greek classical idea of the building – firstly by defining it as space (*templum*) rather than figure (sculpture). Onto a cubic or cylindrical base the Romans added the spherical dome (e.g. the Pantheon) or the spherical apse (e.g. the Basilica of Santa Sabina) – structural supplements into which de-materializing light could flood. Mies adapted Plotinus's late Roman metaphysical image of the streaming in of light. This was unsurprising given Mies's great interest in Platonic-Catholic philosophy. In contrast, Loos's interest was in the Roman space idea. Loos's variation on the space theme was to pile cube on cube. His particular innovation was to arrange these cubic forms in asymmetrical interlocking patterns.

With characteristic rigour, Wittgenstein – who was an acquaintance of Loos and a close friend of Loos's student Paul Engelmann – turned Loos's Roman idea inside out. Loos, following the Romans, focuses his energies on interiors. In Wittgenstein's hands, Loos's schema of intersecting cubic volumes has its greatest impact on the exterior of the building.[6] Wittgenstein saw building not as the containment of space but as the creation of a sculptural object. Wittgenstein *made something Greek out of Loos's Roman experiments*. The building once again took shape as a sculptural solid. However, this was a highly abstracted sculpture – a set of interlocking Platonic solids. Gone (seemingly) is any reference to the play of structural forces – no post-and-beam references, no ornamented allusions to structure of the kind that Schinkel had mastered. In the Kundmanngasse villa, the material power of architectural detailing – the shape of building elements (columns, pilasters, architraves and pillars) – gives way to a glacial flatness. One of architecture's chief methods for representing the play of material power is the use of contour patterns.[7] By means of the counter-position of convex and concave, recessed and bulging, indented and protruding, inclined and flat, curved and straight, lines and shapes can be made to represent the architectonic act of *the shaping of matter*. Wittgenstein's architecture employs only the barest minimum of such contour patterns. Instead, Wittgenstein relied on the logical power of mathematical proportionality to achieve his architectural ends. The Kundmanngasse house is a meticulous study in proportionality, though one seemingly crafted after the musical adeptness of the Wittgenstein siblings rather than after the more formal mathematics of, say, a Palladian classicism. The progression of rooms in the Wittgenstein villa – from less formal to more formal – replicates a musical progression, and mimics the proportional relationship of notes in the musical scale.[8]

Without the play of concave and convex, the architect risks sacrificing the three-dimensional depth-material aspect of existence to its two-dimensional planar-surface aspect. Loos had intended this risk to be obviated by the use of the 'spatial plan'.[9] While the planar surface of a building was stripped of contour patterns, the whole of the interior of a building was meant to be conceived three-dimensionally. Loos thought of *interior space* as a composition of intersecting cubic *volumes*. The interpenetration of larger and smaller, higher and lower volumes produced the depth effect that previously had been achieved by the contouring of planar surfaces or the singling out of the contours of the structural members (beams and columns) of buildings. Wittgenstein's innovation was to apply Loos's 'spatial plan' idea as a way of shaping the exterior plastic form of a building. In order to do this Wittgenstein had to depart from the classical precept of symmetry. He lowered the far left bay on the *front* façade of his sister's villa in order to emphasize the lower height of the interconnecting cubic volume at the *side* of the villa. The effect was to sharpen the drama of the 'spatial' interlocking of volumes, and the sense of their depth (i.e. the *third dimension* of foreground and recession). Wittgenstein also set the building's portals slightly out of symmetrical alignment both with the villa's windows and with each other. He also refused to give these entrance-ways symmetrical counter-weights in the design.[10]

The cumulative effect of these architectural tactics was to sacrifice symmetry, hitherto an indispensable facet of classical architecture, in order to achieve stereometrical depth. This should not be taken to be a deliberate anti-classical gesture, as evidenced by the fact that the employment of volumetric asymmetry subsequently impacted on even ostensibly 'traditional' twentieth-century classicists, and those who otherwise continued to use contour and post-and-beam patterning. The asymmetrical intersection of cubic volumes is a notable feature, for example, of Leon Krier's *House at Seaside* (1985).

The retreat from symmetry is understandable. When historical bricolage became the frame of architecture in place of *phusis*, symmetry lost its architectonic significance, and became instead a nostalgic sign of an unattainable past. The much more interesting questions of architectural representation of the forces of nature and creation were, accordingly, lost from sight. To the extent that classicism became an 'academic' form in the nineteenth century, the idea of architecture as a representation of nature (*phusis*) disappeared. One no longer built a (classical) building in the image of 'the clash of forces' of nature but rather as a (self-defeating) recapitulation of some unreiterable historical horizon. Symmetry had once been the representation of the *telos* of equilibrium to which the 'struggle of forces' in *phusis* gravitated. In the historicist age, symmetry became an easily recognizable *sign* of the classical, and thus a front-line and almost necessary casualty of the modernists' repudiation of the building 'decorated in signs'.

The question, though, remained: how could the architect, who did away with contour and post-and-beam patterning, represent architectonically the clash of forces in physical and social structures? A lack of interest in the representation of structure (even where an architect showed sensitivity to the classical mathematics of proportionality) suggests a lack of interest in representing the struggle of material forces of a universal nature. The flat surface of the modern building erased reference to acts of *kosmopoiēsis* and the shaping of matter. When the surface of a wall became a thin (uncontoured) membrane,[11] the effect was to strip away all analogy to the play of physical forces. The tendency was for the three-dimensional drama of *phusis* to be transformed into the two-dimensional canvas of a pure surface.

There is a *prima facie* case to be made that the volumetric experiments of early twentieth-century modernism led in an *atectonic* direction. That is to say, instead of becoming again a master of structure, the stripping of walls bare made the modern architect the guardian of the tabula rasa, the always open possibility of white (blank) space. Measured against the visual expectations established by post-and-beam iconography, there is little in Wittgenstein's villa that acts as a mimesis of structural forces. However, there is another way of thinking about this matter – one that begins not with a consideration of the three-dimensional depth of architectural detailing but with the interplay of abstract volumes. The intersection of volumes can be understood as an *alternative* way of representing the clash of tensile forces.[12] The building art that supposes this is a kind of *leveraged architecture* – i.e. one based on the classic mechanics of the lever, and the asymmetrical balance of forces.

Archimedes of Syracuse (d. 212 BCE) worked out the theory of asymmetrical balance. In his treatise *On the Equilibrium of Plane Figures*, he postulated that *equal weights at equal distances balance. If unequal weights operate at equal distances, the larger weighs down the smaller.* In a more general formulation of the implications of this, Archimedes identifies the point at which equal or unequal weights balance. *Two magnitudes, whether commensurable or incommensurable, balance at distances reciprocally proportional to the magnitudes.* Thus where a lever, or a set of scales, has different weights acting on it, equilibrium is achieved when the relation or ratio between weights is the inverse of the relation or ratio between the distances from those weights to the point of support.

Wittgenstein, in a manner of speaking, is a legatee of Archimedes.[13] The cubic volumes of the Kundmanngasse villa are the visual analogues of such weights. The centre of gravity (the fulcrum) of an imaginary lever that holds them in balance is the point marked by the light fittings atop the asymmetrically placed entranceway of the front (south-east) elevation of the building. This fulcrum point is positioned proportionally closer to the 'heavier' side of the building. An imaginary lever holds variously weighted parts of the building in equilibrium. Much of this arrangement, we can be sure, Wittgenstein worked out intuitively. But his was an intuition built on schooling as an engineer. Just as Archimedes's axioms were the geometry of an engineer, so Wittgenstein's plans constitute the architecture of an engineer. They owe as much to theories of classical mechanics as the *Tractatus* owes to Heinrich Hertz's *Principles of Mechanics*. The front (south-east) elevation of the Kundmanngasse villa was conceived first in the architect's imagination as a square pasted over a rectangle. The square and the rectangle (we can extrapolate) would have had symmetrically arranged window cavities. Wittgenstein 'upsets' this original symmetry by lowering the left-hand side (as the viewer sees it) of the square. Suddenly the composition appears lop-sided. To reestablish equilibrium, Wittgenstein shifts the front portal off-centre, closer to the visually 'lighter' left side of the building. The mind's eye can then imaginatively lever one side of the building into equilibrium with the other side, and indeed does so intuitively, and without prompting.

A leveraged architectonics was one answer to the problem of the apparent aporia that arose in modern architecture once (Greek) post-and-beam or (Roman) arch devices were excluded from the imaginary of the architect. Leverage is apparent in a number of masterworks of modern architecture – notably in the cantilevered tectonics of Frank Lloyd Wright's Fallingwater and Richard Neutra's Lovell House (1927–9) in Los Angeles. Yet these buildings are atypical of modern architecture. Neutra (1892–1970), another Loos student, never designed anything again with the same power – the exquisitely balanced force of intersecting volumes – that marks the Lovell House. His later Los Angeles architecture retreats, like most moderns, into an acceptance of the dominance of the two-dimensional motif of the curtain wall.[14]

Such atectonic emasculation was by no means the intention of the prophets of modern architecture. Indeed the pioneering modern American architect Louis Sullivan (1856–1924) declared that architectural form should 'express' the structural nature of a building. He took this to mean that if a building had a steel frame, then this fact should be 'expressed' – that is, the building should appear as a skeletal frame instead of the building being made to imitate the poietics of solid masonry construction. The building should not be a false mimesis of nonexistent masonry load-bearing.

Sullivan intended that a building should be true to the nature of its structural frame. It should reveal, through its shape, the manner in which the building managed structurally the countervailing forces of nature. This had a certain merit. It did not shy away from the representation of the power of *phusis*. Sullivan's architecture was thus intended as an object lesson in how a building was composed or engineered. It consciously sought *not* to bury the forces of creation behind atectonic surfaces. At the same time, however, the interest of the architect in the tectonic was equated with the idea that a building should be *honest* – that it should *reveal* something of its 'inner nature'. In the architecture of classical antiquity, in contrast, a certain fiction was the order of the day. The façade of a Greek building mimicked the general structural *technē* (art) of the artisan builder (*tektainomenos*). It *re*-presented timber structure in stone. This was an act of deceit. Representing timber construction in stone alluded to the archaic origins of construction. But such fictions were never deployed for the sake of authenticity. For the Greek use of symmetry, proportionality, and rhythm always drew attention away from the carpenter's skill toward more abstract considerations of force, equilibrium and geometry.

The Greeks avoided the vicious paradox of deceit and honesty. Sullivan was not so lucky, or so careful. While calling for honesty in building, Sullivan's own works were extended essays in deceit. In the Wainwright Building (1890–1) in St Louis, Sullivan did the pioneering work of figuring out a distinctive form for the new skyscraper building type that had developed in America – in Chicago specifically.[15] The structure of the Wainwright Building was steel-framed with riveted columns and girders, with the steelwork encased in fire-proof tiles.[16] So far as structure is concerned, the steel frame was exactly the same in the lower stories as in the higher stories. Yet the masonry skin that Sullivan applied to the frame implied a base-superstructure model of construction. (It was as if, in America of the 1890s, a memory of the Marxism of the 1840s unconsciously asserted itself.) Sullivan thickened the brown sandstone ashlar walls of the lower stories of the building creating a fiction (an *aedifiction*) that they supported the higher red brick stories.

One of Sullivan's striking innovations in tall building design was his employment of visual devices that emphasized verticality. To create the impression that the Wainwright Building was a lofty creation, Sullivan simulated altitude by running continuous vertical piers from the fourth to the tenth floor. Yet this is another fiction. For the steel frame of the skyscraper is a cage-like structure in which neither verticals nor horizontals dominate. It is quite literally Max Weber's iron cage of modernity.[17] But the architect did not re-present this internal cage in the external form of the building. Rather he treated the building as an analogue of the classical column – with a sandstone base, redbrick shaft and a capital (a red terracotta cornice and a top storey of foliate design). The analogy with the classical column is underlined when Sullivan has the brick piers that dominate the shaft-like middle section of the façade mimic classical pilasters that in turn mimic the fluting of the classical column. There is no doubting either the ingenuity of such references or the appeal of this motif to later architects. Loos used the idea of the building-as-column for his 1923 design for the *Chicago Tribune* competition, and Philip Johnson used it for his AT&T Building in New York City (1984). But does the building-as-column have any architectonic significance? The column is a supporting member but this is a post-and-lintel architecture with the lintel struck out. So then does a post-without-lintel architecture have architectonic significance? Clearly the column is a highly adaptable form for the skyscraper. But a *free-standing* fluted column carries no weight. It has no tensile forces acting on it. It is a self-contained plastic volume. Its surface is corrugated with relief, the undulations of projection and recession. But it no longer has to equilibrate the forces of solid raised upon solid.

What if a flat plane surface is substituted for this? Can geometrical solids without relief, where these are counterposed, satisfy the need for architectonic representation? Can the intersection of volumes be understood as an alternative way of representing the clash of tectonic forces? Does cube against cube serve the same architectonic function as post and lintel?

Yes and no. When solid is leveraged against solid, it is as though the trace of the artisan carpenter transfigured in the stone architecture of the Greek temple is finally erased in favour of a pure Platonic geometry. Likewise the architect no longer wants to 'reveal' (expose) the structure beneath the surface. Instead, the architect wants *to show*, as a teacher might to a student, how forces balance each other. In such demonstrations, the teacher uses a *model*. The building-as-model is completely indifferent to the imperatives of truthfulness.

A model discloses nothing. A model *demonstrates*. The exhibitionary force of the model has no relation to an ethics of authenticity. Its ethic is geometrical, not expressive. The architect who creates models reveals no inner contents or hidden meanings, mysteries or truths. The architect instead shows, by way of the model, the stereometrical forms in which human beings can dwell, and that give shape (definition, order and meaning) to human lives.

Honesty has been the holy grail of modern ethics. When, in the modern era, honesty (truthfulness) replaced limit (boundary) as the sine qua non of the ethical, the whole question of structure, shape and form became much more perplexing. Where the classical ethos had been non-expressive (a matter of line and figure, contour and pattern), modern 'ethics' (even when it claimed some kind of 'objectivity') defined itself as an outward sign of some inner content – an expression, declaration or statement of an (inward) truth. Thus the notion that all imagination is a model of what is not (what is 'false') – and that a kind of 'lying' is intrinsic to social creativity and social form – eluded both the modern ethicist and the modern architect (Sullivan).

A building façade *may* 'tell the story' of structure by exposing or unveiling its structural members (piers, etc.), or by mimicking their lines on the surface of the building but only if the mimesis of the structure *also* conveys an 'image' of the 'order' achieved by the equilibrium of forces in the building. While many moderns believed that the human abode should reveal its own structural skeleton, such structuralism was not defended as a tectonic art but in the name of honesty – the modern virtue par excellence. Such 'expressive structuralism' was contrary to 'classical structuralism'. The latter did not set itself the task simply of making structural members visible, but rather of representing structural order – the 'moral arithmetick' of Shaftesbury. Such (classical) display is not an unconcealment (*alētheia*) of Being but rather an artificer's way of creating a representation of the ordered power of nature – sometimes an order that does not yet exist.

Sullivan's philosophy of 'honestly expressed structure' was realized most famously in Mies's Lake Shore apartment building in Chicago and his Seagram Building in New York City. Mies is a lot more truthful to structure than Sullivan. Mies understood that the structural form of the skyscraper is an iron cage, and proceeds on this premise. In certain ways, the Seagram building is the greatest building of the twentieth century simply because it replicates (with an unerring sense of proportion) the mesh-like structure of the iron cage of modernity. As Weber knew only too well, neither beam and post, nor arch, nor buttress but cage – with its net-like intersection of horizontals and verticals – was the structural image of modernity.

From a slightly different angle, Wittgenstein grasped this when he used the image of scaffolding in the *Tractatus*. To his mind, the geometry of the architect and the logic of linguistic philosophy were like a builders' scaffolding. Such scaffolding, like the skyscraper's structural cage, determines a space. 'In geometry and logic alike a place is a possibility: something can exist in it' (Tractatus 3.4111). In language, we fill in the scaffolding-cage. We do this when we create propositions – images of how things in the world are linked (images of 'states of affairs'). Such images have some of the characteristics of solid geometrical objects. 'A proposition, a picture or a model is, in the negative sense, like a solid body that restricts the freedom of movement of others, and, in the positive sense, like a space bounded by solid substance in which there is room for a body' (4.463). In language and architecture we create worlds (objectivations) that we can bump into and move around in. The difference in the 'propositions' that we create follows from the difference in the nets (the cage-like mesh) that we begin with. These cage-nets are 'different systems for describing the world' (6.341). The mesh we employ may be square, triangular, hexagonal and so on. The cage of logic therefore may help us to create scientific propositions (edifices) but there is also another kind of scaffolding, viz. that of geometry. As we build an edifice of science, we rest our ladder against the scaffolding of logic. Once that work is done, we can remove the scaffolding and throw away the ladder. To build the edifice of ethics, in contradistinction, we use the framework-scaffolding of geometry – the scaffolding not of words but of lines, planes and solids. For example, the horizontal and vertical lines that mesh into symmetrical planes – planes whose intersection with similar planes gives us Weber's iron cage.

Wittgenstein's Kundmanngasse building was an attempt by him to create an 'ethical abode' – *an edifice that is ethics* – using *the scaffolding of architectural geometry*. What were the qualities of this abode? Many moderns believed that the human abode should be 'honest' – that it should reveal its internal 'cage', its tectonic-structural 'skeleton' – as a token of modern openness. Yet there is nothing in Wittgenstein's architecture that suggests tectonic exposure. This is so even though Wittgenstein's own growing-up was dominated by strenuous demands for 'genuineness' in conduct. The strictures of 'genuineness' meant merciless honesty towards oneself and others. *Nothing hidden*. In the modern mind, the imperative of honesty is often allied with forms of puritanical asceticism. Genuineness in conduct is signified by the lack of pretence, false appearance or lying surface. Modern asceticism contributes to the aura of authenticity by renouncing embellishments of colour, pattern and contour. Plainness signifies honesty. Wittgenstein in his personal life never escaped the shadow of the demand for honesty. The bare white surface of the modern architect, a motif that Wittgenstein employed in the Kundmanngasse villa, is an ascetical sign. Wittgenstein's ethical impulse was in certain respects unambiguously ascetical. His 'Tolstoyan' decision to renounce his family inheritance, not to mention his attraction to sparsely furnished rooms, was typical of this deeply woven thread in his life. But, ultimately, what he created in the Kundmanngasse villa was not an architecture of ascetical renunciation but one of reason in the classical Shaftesburyian sense.

The idiomatic tensions of the philosopher – torn between renunciation and reason – recapitulate the whole history of ethics and of building. The history of building began with the subordination of the human being to the nomos of the earth. In archaic times, human beings dealt with the terrifying existential questions of human vulnerability and powerlessness via abasement to the forces (deities) of the earth. The arts and sciences of ancient Greece proffered another solution to the question of human powerlessness. These arts and sciences incubated rational strategies for the relatively powerless to deal with the overwhelmingly powerful. The Archimedean theory of the lever is an epitome of such strategies. When we use a lever, we find that which is relatively light can raise up that which is relatively heavy.[18] The Greeks grasped that geometric reason had social implications. Archimedes himself was a brilliant military engineer, and lost his life in the defence of Syracuse against the invading Romans in 212 BCE. Warfare demonstrates how, through the calculation of the ratio of forces, the weak can overcome their powerlessness. Such calculations made possible an ethos that no longer required abasement to the earth. Supposing that frail individuals or frail societies – and even the strongest of the Greek city-states was a frail entity by most standards – could think geometrically, then they could avoid being crushed by greater powers (social or natural).

The whole gamut of Greek engineering, mathematics, philosophy and architecture shared this ethos. At the time when Wittgenstein (himself steeped in engineering, mathematics and philosophy) turned his hand to architecture, the power of the archaic had begun to reassert itself over the European mind. Wittgenstein, however, showed no fascination with it. He was drawn rather to a much more modern form of self-abasement – that of puritanical renunciation. Moderns learnt to forgo money, pleasure, free time, friendship and so on in order to 'achieve goals'. This was a condition of the spectacular success of purposive-rational economic and technological systems. Modern economics made a virtue of renunciation just as modern architecture did. The house that Wittgenstein built has some marks of this. His carefully engineered door handles are an industrial counterpart of Shaker furniture. Wittgenstein's 'Spartan' light fittings are as ascetic as the modern imagination can conceive. Yet, on the whole, the simplicities of the Kundmanngasse villa are those of rational architecture, not those of modern asceticism. They are the simplicities of the geometric imagination – an imagination that finds pleasure and wealth, immediate gratification and lasting absorption in shape and form, and in subtle calculations of the equilibrium of forces. The Kundmanngasse villa was an attempt by Wittgenstein to create an ethical abode of a rational kind.

14 Greek Lessons: Mies van der Rohe in America

In many outward respects Mies was a paradigmatic modern. He believed that a building should reveal its internal structure. Therefore he designed his late masterworks as sublimely elegant steel cages. Yet, for all of his conspicuous modernism, Mies's steel cages were infused with a classical spirit. Mies provides us with an interesting case of a failed classicism. Interesting both because his modernism embodies a kind of classical reason and because the failure of his classicism is by no means absolute. Mies makes the very best fist of revealing the structural truth of the iron cage of modernity. At the same time, the elegant symmetries and beautiful proportionalities of his cages have Platonic qualities that ensure that his buildings have successfully outlived the circumstances and time of their creation. (Few of Mies's contemporaries have been so fortunate.) There is an ethical geometry in his work that goes far beyond the modern appetite for self-revelation and compulsive visibility.

As early as 1928, Mies declared his affection for certain classical qualities.[1] He offered these qualities as an antidote to the 'chaos' of modern life. Moderns, Mies knew full well, were brilliant at purposive organization but their grasp of 'value rationality' often failed them. Accomplished at realizing goals, moderns' sense of pattern, and their capacity for pattern-making, were in contrast weak. Mies generally avoided equating this pattern-making ability with the idea of form (*eidos*), and frequently used historicist terms like 'value' as synonym for this 'ordering'. But, whatever terms he employed, Mies's attraction to a certain kind of classical ethos – a modern classical ethos – is manifest.

'Order' was the precious gift of the ancients. However, that gift, Mies maintained, was not directly accessible to moderns. Each epoch of (Western) history was discrete. There was no unbroken linkage between Greeks, Romans, medievals and moderns. Yet, Mies conceded, a Platonic notion of order recurred in each of these periods.

[The] order of antiquity degenerated into late antiquity. But out of this chaos a new order arose, the order of the Middle Ages. On the basis of the Platonic theory of ideas, Augustine formulated the basic idea of medieval belief. In the medieval idea of order lived, even if in a totally new dimension, that spirit of proportion exemplified and proven by Plato. The noblest legacy of antiquity.

Faced with the totalitarian chaos of the mid-twentieth century, Mies insisted on the need for a coherent order.

For this to be realized, architecture had to be not only practical (purposive rational) in the way that functional social democratic and progressive architecture managed to be, but *beautiful* as well. 'It is a natural, human characteristic to consider not only the purposeful but also to search out and love beauty.'[2] Mies instinctively realized that the functional and the practical were no answer to the ominous and violent political movements of his time. In an address given while he was still in Germany, Mies expressed the wish that 'the chaos in which we live would give way to order and the world would again become meaningful and beautiful'.[3] The ultimate goal of architecture – Mies reflected on the occasion of his American exile – was 'to create order out of the godforsaken confusion of our time'.[4] Order was neither violent discipline nor rationalizing organization, but something akin to classical beauty. But what *exactly* was this beauty? Mies at first (in 1928) thought it 'something imponderable, something that lies in between things'.[5] He soon (1931) gave the name 'proportionality' to this imponderable. *'The artistic expresses itself in the proportions of things, often even in the proportions between things.'*[6] Mies made the point that *beauty was not expensive*. Beauty was not hostile to the imperative of economic rationality that preoccupied so many of his architect colleagues. Nor was it outside the reach of the poor or those who had to provide social housing. Beauty did not mean ruinous expenditure. Proportionality, Mies argued, 'is something immaterial, something spiritual, and thus independent of the material conditions of a period. It is a wealth that even a materially poor period need not renounce.'[7]

Mies's attraction to the classical was not unique. It parallels other exiles who, like Mies, came to Chicago in the 1940s and 1950s – most importantly Leo Strauss and Hannah Arendt, both of whom had been students of Heidegger. Their experience of *xeneteia* – of journeying among strangers – stimulated in these exiles a re-evaluation of both modernity and its radical other (conservative revolution). Not all exiles from European totalitarianism followed this course. In Los Angeles of the 1940s, Theodor Adorno and Arnold Schoenberg remained the kind of modernists for whom innovation in the aesthetic means of production allied with a romantic longing for a reconciliation with nature were the sine qua non of modernism. This kind of modernism found a mirror in the city of Los Angeles, even if the exiles rarely acknowledged the reciprocity between themselves and that city. Los Angeles was an aggressive innovator in the technical means of production, both in its culture and war industries. At the same time, it was home to a popular idiom of 'nature worship'. The deification of sun, sea and land was very popular. High European intellectuals looked askance at the enormous variety of Angelean pop romantic mysticisms and pantheisms. But in practice they were not so far removed from the archaicizing nature sympathies of the romantic.[8] The 'genius' of the Angelean was to embrace both enlightenment technical innovation and romantic nature philosophy. Even where European intellectuals gravitated to both (Adorno is a case in point), they did so without ever trying to blend them. Angeleans on the other hand in their 'naivety' thought both enlightenment and romanticism to be compatible. We see this mentality in post-1945 Angelean styles of vernacular building – modelled on the architectural modernism of Richard Neutra. This building style promoted itself as both the epitome of 'the future' and as suited to 'the climate'.

In Chicago a different atmosphere prevailed. Los Angeles was the 'promised land' for internal emigrants from the American South and the Midwest. These emigrants from the heartland, black and white alike, were immersed in traditions of Hebraic Protestantism. Chicago received its own waves of North-bound internal immigration, driven by visions of the industrial promised land, but in the period from the 1870s to the 1950s it was also an immigrant city for a Catholic Europe threatened by war, oppression and economic marginalization. Thus was exported to Chicago a certain Latin *universitas*, and one (in its higher moments) that was self-consciously aware of the manifold invisible threads of continuity with the Greco-Roman-Latin world that nineteenth-century historicism denied.[9]

Chicago became the Latinate heart of America for an extended period despite the fact that Los Angeles – and the strip of coastal California from San Francisco to San Diego – had been settled by the Spanish, and remained a Spanish possession till 1822. Though it persisted in the Californian atmosphere long after American annexation in 1848, the Iberian-Latin model was thoroughly romanticized in the nineteenth century. Under the influence of works like Helen Hunt Jackson's novel *Ramona* (1884), the humanist Latinity of California's Franciscan founders became a foil for the invention of a picaresque mythical past that owed more to William Morris-style romantic medievalism than it did to the adobe architectonics of the Franciscans.[10]

Like all American emigrant cities, Chicago organized itself around ethnic ward politics – yet, at the same time, the city harboured universalizing forces that cut across the divide of ethnic particularity. Common faith played its part in this, although the 'universal' church in Chicago was in everyday practice subdivided into ethnic parishes. In a more important and perhaps lasting way, it was in the institutions of higher learning that the Greco-Roman-Latin *universitas* was most influentially represented. One of the most interesting episodes in this story occurred when, under the leadership of Robert Hutchins, a group of Thomist Neo-Aristotelians was assembled at the University of Chicago (among them the Aristotle translator Richard McKeon and the Aristotle popularizer Mortimer Adler). Mies's arrival at the Illinois Institute of Technology complemented the Neo-Aristotelians at the University of Chicago. Mies had long harboured Thomist interests, and in the 1920s and 1930s had shared the company of German Catholic philosophers interested in rehabilitating a post-Kantian Plato.[11] Mies found a sympathetic intellectual environment in Chicago, and one that (there is every reason to think) provoked him to find some resolution of what had been a long-term process of thinking about the relationship of his architecture to the classical – an intellectual journey begun in the 1920s.

As well as the Neo-Aristotelians, Chicago became the intellectual home of Leo Strauss, whose 1949 Walgreen Lectures at the University of Chicago, *Natural Right and History*, dramatized a fundamental issue: the weakness of the modern tradition of natural right as against the classical idea of nature.[12] Chicago also welcomed fellow German-Jewish exile, Hannah Arendt. While Arendt had a more intermittent connection with Chicago, her major philosophical work, *The Human Condition*, was, as with Strauss, first presented publicly as Walgreen Lectures in 1956. (She later went back to Chicago to teach in the 1960s.) These two xenetics, Strauss and Arendt, sojourners in what (to European eyes) was the strangest of strange lands – America – were to produce a classicizing legacy in political thought that was both *universalizing* (it broke decisively with the 'cultural' Hellenism that had been a staple of romantic German nation-building and the leitmotif of their teacher, Heidegger) and at the same time addressed, for the first time in serious thought, the relationship of the New World to the classical world (via Arendt's 1962 meditations on the American Foundation and Strauss's recasting of American liberalism as a classical idea).[13]

Their fellow German sojourner among strangers, Mies, was also provoked in Chicago to depart from an existing template – not in his case, though, romantic 'cultural' Hellenism, but instead Weimar architectural modernism. Milieu played a decisive role in this. In Chicago, Mies formed one of those rare partnerships that was also a remarkable creative friendship – with the developer Herbert Greenwald. Before becoming a real estate developer, Greenwald had been a rabbinical scholar, and had supplemented his rabbinical studies with courses in (Hutchins' and Adlers') Great Books programme at the University of Chicago.[14] When they met in 1946, Mies was 60 and Greenwald was 29. For the next 13 years – till Greenwald's premature death in an aeroplane crash – their association coincided with the years in which Mies created his definitive American designs. In Mies's friendship with Greenwald one sees a mirror of Wittgenstein's friendship in the 1920s with Paul Engelmann and Arendt's friendship in the 1950s with the Catholic American novelist Mary McCarthy.

There is something decisive about such friendships. They are the crucible out of which the most brilliant creations come.[15] It is in this sense, then, that friendship is the middle term between the silence of architecture and the

Socratic volubility of philosophy. It stands between thought and expression, *eidos* and *logos*. It belongs fully neither to one nor to the other. It shares in characteristics of both. Friends are joined by conversation. They converse about the 'things that matter'. Yet friends are always aware that what is unspoken between them is as important as what is spoken. Between friends is *the silence of things*. In the silence of things lies the possibility of conversation. Without the silent intuitions – the always present unstated, to which the statements of friends allude – there is only 'chatter'. When Wittgenstein concluded in his *Tractatus, the most important things in life are unsayable*, his ongoing conversations with Paul Engelmann were the voluble silent partner of his paradoxical discourse on silence, and of his effort to find a logic that was not linguistic (a scaffolding of thought).

On the battlefields of Europe in 1914–18, where the *Tractatus* was written, Wittgenstein registered the pointlessness of all of the words that the wiseheads of the nineteenth century had spoken. From the perspective of a self-immolating Europe, the 'sign-language' of the age of historicism was a fraud. In its place, Wittgenstein postulated an image ('picture') language. This language worked something like an architect's blueprint that models, or representatively depicts, the essential aspects (the logical relations, the structure) of the world. With the aid of this *Bild*-language, Wittgenstein hoped to escape the paradox that afflicts all philosophy – viz. that it wants to speak of the unsayable. Philosophy cannot do without *logos* (speech-reason), but, as Plato and Aristotle already knew, its ultimate object (the Forms, the Unmoved Mover, God, Reason) is an object of thought (*nous*), not of speech (*logos*). Philosophy 'silently' apprehends the shape (*eidos*) of ultimate things. Thinking perceives and composes (rather than 'understands') the structure of the world. Correspondingly, philosophy succeeds in 'communicating' this only when it 'draws a picture' – when it 'outlines' the figure (image) of the limit of things. The *Bild*-language that it has to do this in is fraught with aporias. Indeed, so much so that Wittgenstein concluded his wartime reflections in the *Tractatus* by proposing that the highest things (ethics, values, the meaning of life) cannot be expressed in language. It is simply beyond the capacity of words (*logos*) to convey the structures (forms) perceived and composed by thought (*nous*).

This conclusion undoubtedly helped propel Wittgenstein to the second in his triptych of great works – his experiment in architecture, a work that stands up both as a minor masterpiece of twentieth-century architecture and as an illustrative theoretical-experimental attempt to step beyond language in order to adequately represent the scaffolding (the geometrical form-work) of the world, the structural frame of the building of the world. Architecture eminently suited Wittgenstein's intellectual purposes, because it is a speechless representation of form. The architect moves in the realm of the unspoken. But it is worth noting that Wittgenstein's plunge into built form also grew out of intensive conversations with his friend Engelmann (who had received the original commission for the Kundmanngasse house). Somehow in the conversation of friends, it is possible to speak of the unsayable – to use *logos* to engage in the experiments of the *nous*, to think aloud. In this, the conversation of friends is unique. It makes possible a translation of figures of thought into language. In the conversation of friends, the intuitions of the *nous* can be talked through.[16]

The Kundmanngasse house was Wittgenstein's most satisfactory attempt to deal with the fundamental paradox of philosophy. While philosophy utilizes the medium of words, the prime medium of the philosopher is thought. Thought is the thinking of the ethos (= rational abode or building) of humankind.[17] This ethos is not 'ethics' as conventionally understood – viz. a statement of norms, rules or principles. This ethos rather is the civitas in which the human being dwells. Thought is that which aims to give us an image (picture, outline or figure) of this abode. Thought is the 'imag(in)ing' of the abode of humankind.

Mies, an architect who had an intimate knowledge of philosophy, loved to quote Thomas Aquinas's definition of truth as the equation of thought and thing. This equating of thought and thing is the possible/impossible mission of thinking. In thought, one does not imagine words, but the thing-world. Thinking takes it upon itself to picture the forms – the foundational and structural members, the *res publica* – of the social and fabricated world. The tools – words – at its disposal, however, are ill suited to the task. We marvel at the ambition of philosophy, and the efforts devoted to it, but we know also that it is fatally exhausting. In its greatest moments, philosophy achieves an intimation of the figure of creation. But the cost of such moments is always the exhaustion of thought. For a superhuman energy is required in order for words to equate things – for words to be a picture-language. After that energy is expended, all that remains is deflation and expiration.

We might then ask: why persist in such a fraught enterprise? Why not go directly to the creation of figures (the shapes of the architect, the pictures of the painter, the musical figures of the composer)? Why permit the intercession of opaque words? After all, does not the outline of Hagia Sophia tell us much more about Byzantium than all its historians? Just as Ictinos and Callicrates's Parthenon tells us more about the nature of Periclean Athens than Plato. Why plunge into the endless labyrinth of words, only to conclude with a shrug: if you want to really understand America, visit its civic memorials. What is being admitted here are the limits of language. These limits were well assayed by Cornelius Castoriadis when he observed: 'That which cannot be said is that which makes us say; the unsayable is sayability itself, that to which the sayable owes its existence.'[18] Without *figures* of thought, we have nothing to say (certainly nothing worth saying). Conversely, we have something to say (something worth saying) because we want to communicate the figure (shape or pattern) of a world. This figure is the limit (*peras*) of that world, the container into which all of the contents of the world will be poured. A figure is not spoken – rather we speak (usually clumsily) about figures. So why persist with the discursive medium; why not forsake it entirely for a non-discursive medium, for images, for plans, for blueprints, for sound-figures? Why? Because even the painter, the architect, the composer have to translate the figures of thought into other kinds of figures. All media, discursive and non-discursive alike, are confounded by the allusiveness of the figures of thought. Only rarely, after all, is there produced a Hagia Sophia or a Pantheon.

As Wittgenstein was to experience for himself, the architectural, the figural, *does* stand closer to the unsayable, *but* there remains a *gap* between its figures and the figures of thought that one dreams in the imagination. How can one be made to map the other? How can we capture (on paper) the figures of thought? For such a purpose, even the architect finds it useful to *talk* about the unsayable, to use logos to engage in experiments of nous. In the conversations of friends, as between Wittgenstein and Engelmann, thought can find a stable point, some momentary fixity, enough for us to redraw the figure of our thoughts in some medium of objectivation (words, melodies and chords, plans, pictures and so on). In this aspect at least, philosophy and architecture move on a parallel track. That the philosophically well-read architect (Mies) should find friendship with the philosophically trained developer (Greenwald) is no less necessary to creation than that the philosopher (Arendt) should find unguarded friendship with the novelist (McCarthy).

Without the crucible of the conversations of friends, we could not imagine how such works – like those twin, symmetrical masterpieces of 1958: Arendt's *Human Condition* and Mies's Seagram Building – are possible.[19]

One thing is for certain – after the death of Herbert Greenwald, Mies's work loses something of its force. Nothing will again have the solicitous power of his masterpiece, the Seagram Building. Indeed Mies's last major commission is redolent with the echoes of the world of Leo von Klenze. Mies undertook the design of Berlin's National Gallery (1962–9). This was a project inextricably caught in the highly charged atmosphere of postwar German nation-building. It was constructed only a few blocks (but a world away) from the Altes Museum – the Schinkel building on the other side of the Berlin Wall, in the communist sector, a monument to the divided status of Cold War Germany. Like Germany in the age of Leo von Klenze, the bifurcated postwar German nation could not be defined territorially, but only culturally. Mies's last major work is at first glance an essay in aesthetic state building. Mies seemingly relearns the same 'Greek lesson' as his distinguished German forebear: it was the lesson of the cultural nation. Greece = culture; a great nation is defined by its cultural institutions.

Thus the late-period Mies appears to return to the historicism of the collector state that modernism in the 1920s had rebelled against. In his career, he had done few civic commissions. His practice had consisted overwhelmingly of university, corporate and domestic buildings. The irony was that when the opportunity of a state commission presented itself it was the kind of 'container' architecture – the museum – that was paradigmatic of the 'public' commissions of the nineteenth-century aesthetic state. These commissions emphasized culture in place of civilization. The symbolic forms of the civitas – public plaza and triumphal arch, fountains, stairs and riverside promenade – were rendered progressively less important in the course of the nineteenth century in preference to the museum, gallery and library. The latter emerged as the pre-eminent yet ambiguous 'public' architecture of the nineteenth century – 'storehouses' of 'culture' with uncanny echoes of the monumental storehouses of archaic societies. These were the public icons of aestheticized modernity. Despite this, Mies did offer a gesture of modernist defiance against the curatorial state. This is perhaps unsurprising. After all, the ethos of his glass house architecture of the 1930s and 1940s demanded the minimum of possessions. In the glass house the architect as a matter of principle provided little storage room, and the maximum visibility of the interiors from the outside was inhospitable to the collecting of things.[20] In this same spirit, Mies designed an exhibition hall for the National Gallery so massive that it dwarfed all contents, making itself the real work on show. Such daunting modernist space was indifferent to human scale, and the product of architectural hubris. Yet the cavernous emptiness also managed to recall a trace of the Greco-Roman legacy in its insistence that the edifice was more important than its contents.

Confronted with criticism of the massiveness of his Berlin exhibition space, Mies did not justify it as a study in openness, elevation or structural truth – although it was all of these. The transparent glass sheath of the museum ensured a permeable boundary between the cavernous-scaled interior and the outside. The immateriality of the glass boundary was such that the roof (composed of girders and steel plate) appeared, in typical Miesean fashion, to hover above the ground, while the eight steel columns on which the roof girders were poised were a consummate study in 'revealed structure'. Yet, when pressed about the collection-swallowing immensity of the exhibition space, Mies responded laconically: 'It is such a large hall that of course it means difficulties for the exhibiting of art. I am fully aware of that. But it has such potential that I simply cannot take those difficulties into account.' It did not matter in the least about the collection (of signs) housed within. Ictinos and Callicrates did not design the Parthenon with the needs of the Athenian treasury in mind. The 'storehouse' belongs to the spirit of archaic societies, not to the classical imagination. True, Mies's space violated classical precepts, even if its floor plan was laid out in an austere symmetry. This was a space 'out of proportion' not only with the exhibited paintings but with the viewers of those artworks as well. *And yet* – sitting on the Acropolis in 1959, looking at the Parthenon, Mies could not have but been reminded that the public building, not the storehouse of treasures, was the essence of the Greek world. His Berlin hall space was reserved for temporary exhibitions. Doubtless this pleased Mies in its sly renunciation of the patrimony of the aesthetic state. In the end the old modernist had the last (word): an affirmation of a constructive power that the modern 'museum city' and the aesthetic state was hard pressed to recreate.

Part Three
Modernity's Utopias

Introduction: Modernity's Utopias

The road to hell is paved with utopian dreams. It is not uncommon to find utopias filled with supremacism, narcissism, sadism or masochism. But, equally, a quietistic imagination that no longer thinks, and that adjusts itself completely to the horizon of its own time and place, is banal and defeated and uninteresting. If human beings can no longer speculate on what it is – in history or nature or production – that constitutes utopia, then they condemn themselves to a thoughtless routine of conformism and social dullness. Let us not forget that large slabs of human history can be described in terms of thoughtlessness. What makes the 'modern era' – the period between 1750 and 1950 – in Europe and America so important is that it was neither conformist nor banal. It was, though, filled with terrible dangers. Many of those dangers were due to the dystopian character of various of the utopias of the period.

Utopias allow social beings to look at their society from the outside. The logic, or in some cases illogic, of utopias is not governed by the norms of a particular time or a particular place. Thinking in a utopian manner is an activity that has great benefits for the expansion of the mind. But it also has great risks, for what the human imagination dreams up is not always affable or pleasant. Nor is it necessarily coherent or rational. Dystopias are common. But the risks of utopian thinking are outweighed on balance by the fact that where there is no utopian thinking there is also no possibility of great thought. Utopia is another word for imagination, and the strains of imagination is thought doing what is the most difficult thing of all. This is thought thinking through questions of beauty and happiness, freedom and necessity, spirit and soul. These questions cannot be answered just by the appeal to this or that social norm. Answering such questions requires some larger animating vision.

147

Modernity – meaning here the modernity of the nineteenth and twentieth centuries – oscillated around three key utopias. One was architectonic, one progressive and one romantic. These were the utopias of civilization, enlightenment and romanticism. In this, the third part of *Dialectic of Romanticism*, we examine each of modernity's utopias.

The first vision type is architectonic. It supposes that the most abiding issues of the human condition are in the end subsets of a more fundamental query about how the world is ordered. Art, science, religion and philosophy might help us to understand this, but they are all subject to an overarching rationalism of cognitive beauty – a rationalism of order, pattern and form. We discuss this vision in the following chapter, Modernity's Architectonic Utopia.

The second vision type is the archaic vision of an undifferentiated whole in which art and religion bind human beings into a sacrificial unity. Romanticism updates this archaic vision. Romanticism's art religion rests on the longing for totality. The third vision type is the vision of progress through ever-greater refinement of technology. Such progress supposes a division of labour in society between art and science, but an agreement nonetheless that what constitutes the human good comes about through the development of the means of production – be it artistic means of production or scientifically-enhanced material means of production. We discuss romantic and progressive visions of utopia in Chapter 16, Modernity's Aesthetic Utopias.

Modernity's first utopia, the utopia of civilization, placed its best hopes in the beautiful abstractions of form, proportion and rhythm. This utopia was a kind of recurrence. It was a return of the same utopia that underlay ancient Greek rationalism, Roman Stoic and Epicurean nature, Renaissance humanism and the Stoic-Epicurean elements of the Anglo-Scottish-Dutch enlightenment. This utopia underpinned the modernism of Loos, Mies, Wittgenstein, Stravinsky and their ilk. It was an architectonic, objective, unexpressive, unromantic modernism. Its concept of art was not aesthetic, but artisan-like. When Mies van der Rohe described the art of architecture as the art of building, or Stravinsky insisted that excitement in music was not created by emotive interpretation or by creative inspiration but by the exact length of a musical phrase, they were articulating a view that descended from Renaissance and classical art. This view long preceded, both conceptually and sociologically, Baumgarten and Kant's idea of aesthetics.[1] Its greatest advocate was Shaftesbury.[2]

In the artisan-like view of art, which was Plato's view also, art is not romantic, nor is it a version of Promethean science. It is about the exacting building of structure. It is cerebral, precise and unemotive. Its utopia is the cognitive utopia of form. Form should not be confused with the fetishism of technology, although currents in aesthetic modernism did just that. Those who make things do so with means. They employ technological media. However, the overriding concern of the anti-aesthetic artist is with the formative pattern of things, not with the progress of the means of aesthetic production. The 'civilizer as artist' is not indifferent to means, materials and mediums, but is not preoccupied with these in the way the progressivists and futurists who cluster around modernity's second utopia, the utopia of rationalization, are.

The second of modernity's utopias is a distillation of all of those widely held expectations that humanity's suffering can be overcome by the progressive rationalization of the aesthetic and material forces of production. Just as capitalism rationalized the physical means of production, creating machines to do the work of hands, so the abstractions of pointillism, cubism, futurism, the twelve-tone system, functionalism and the like, were imagined to be liberating aesthetic technologies that would usher in an age of human freedom – much as it was expected that capitalism would be rationalized, through utopian engineering, into a libertarian socialism. Technology, in this view, was an economizing and, at the same time, an emancipating power. In the hands of modernism, science and technology, artistic technique and technical innovation became the utopia of the future – the heroic-Promethean utopia of industrialism, or the orphic myth of post-industrialism. Progressives and futurists looked not to the quasi-mythical beginning of history but to the end of history when the laws of human and physical nature would be fully transparent and manipulable, and the division between subject and object could be dissolved into a man-machine interface.

Modernity's third utopia expressed longings for totalitarian community. These were longings for an undifferentiated social totality in which the divisions of society and of the arts were overcome, and cultural unity and social unanimity were achieved. This utopia was less concerned with technical development than with historical return. Its mentality was enchanted. It was romantic. Its dreams were of a past that was authentic, noble, or innocent – because it was undifferentiated. In undifferentiated times, suffering and hardship can be justified or overcome by a transcendent social whole in which human beings unselfishly and sacrificially participate through art and religion. In romanticism's art-religion, painting and music and poetry are fused with rite and ritual and self-effacement in the divine.

Romantic history is the account of the ascent to or descent from a founding time. This no time is the 'beginning' or mythical origin – the point outside time in which time (the processes of history) began. This 'point' outside historical time is the equivalent of a natural 'eruption'. It is the miraculous singularity at which history is reduced to nature, and the natural history of humankind begins. This history is not an enlightenment history of progress and rationalization. It is not a history of the stages of the human mind embodied in modes of production. Rather, it is the history of humanity's attempts to recapture the epiphany of a sublime sacrificial origin. History finally ends when a great conflagration plunges humankind into an abyss of self-immolation and nothingness – the epocalyptic repetition of the inimitable origin.

Romantic modernists placed their faith in nihilistic sacrifice to the mythical gods of origin. These gods were personified as creative genius, or as the aesthetic state, or the higher race or the redemptive people. Progressive modernists on the other hand believed in the inner logic of rationalization. In contrast to both futurism and romanticism, the utopia of civilization requires neither self-destructive unanimity nor the reductive equation of technique and spirit. Civilization's utopia is encapsulated in worlds of architectonic beauty and resplendent form. Civilization encompasses both the utopian glance to such worlds in the past and the anticipation of such worlds in the future. Its protagonists are sceptical about both mysterious origins and the indefinite progress of techniques.

The utopia of civilization assumes the power to create worlds. 'World making' is not measured by technical advances in the methods of aesthetic or material production, or by the retrospective glance back to an aesthetic dream time in which myth and ritual and heroism suffuse life. World making is rational. Civilizing is a collective activity without being sacrificial or totalitarian. It is trans-historical, meaning that it relates to past and future without deifying or demonizing either. The protagonist of civilization is not interested in the debate between the ancients and the moderns. Civilization is both classical and modern in spirit. Its advocates care for neither enchanted myth nor technological fetishism. They are interested, however, in how human beings create worlds for themselves through their rational gift for order-creating pattern and form. The greatest product of world making is the world city.[3]

From Miletus and Athens to Alexandria and Rome – and from Venice and Amsterdam to New York and Chicago – such cities have been great civilizing forces. Sometimes they have remained so for a long time; sometimes their moment was relatively short-lived. But, irrespective of longevity, what defines the practical utopianism of these cities is not the backward glance to an origin or the merciless forward progress of techniques, but a kind of circulatory movement – a backwards and forwards movement between the ancient and the modern. This is a rhythmical movement of 'revolution' between the classical and the modern urbs.

The world of the world city is an order or a pattern, not a technology or a siren song. Thus, the modernists who were adepts at ordering things were pattern creators. They were interested less in the pyrotechnics of aesthetic progress than in lucid structure, beautiful arrangement and memorable form. This stands in sharp contrast to the modernists who glorified art technologies of abstraction, serialism and functionalism in the name of the infinite self-development of art. It also stands in contrast to those who rallied Orpheus against Prometheus, or those others who played with the space between myth and technology – *vide* Thomas Mann's portrayal of Schoenberg as Doctor Faustus obsessed and enchanted with the musical technology of the twelve-tone system, or Isadora Duncan's demonstration of modern dance (the modern technology of the body) in an amphitheatre in Athens or, most spectacularly of all, Wagner's total work of art in which technological mastery of the most modern means of artistic production is conjoined with the re-enchantment of life through myth. In Wagner's case, mythology is redoubled by the modern 'myth of the artist' as the master of *all* artistic techniques (music, theatre, painting and the rest).

Modernism counterposed and interweaved myth and technology, enchanted history and mechanics – so much so that it is difficult in the end to decide whether modernism was progressive or reactionary. In truth, it was *both and neither*. For in the interstices of the modern age, we also find a utopia that is neither progressive nor reactionary. This utopia, modernity's first utopia, discounts the modern fable of the great artist who masters all mediums. Likewise it discounts the other beguiling modern legend – that of the great inventor whose technologies achieve utopian status and a reputation for social redemption. Modernity's first utopia was the work neither of demonic polymaths nor of master technologists. Standing outside the poles of progress and reaction, as we shall see, the significance of this utopia was that it was constructive rather than technological, and fictive rather than mythological.

15 Modernity's Architectonic Utopia

The year that his friend Herbert Greenwald died, Mies van der Rohe, by then the twentieth century's most influential architect, visited the Acropolis for the first time.[1] As he gazed out from the rocky hilltop, what did he think? In the past thirty years, he had travelled all the way from a youthful fascination with Schinkel's Altes Museum, through the firestorms of expressionist Berlin and the modernism of the 1920s, propelled by the anguish of totalitarian Europe and exile in America towards a serene, aloof, classicizing modernity of the 1950s. So many ghosts of the European past. How to make sense of them?

There is, extant, a blurry snapshot of Mies sitting on a rock on the Acropolis looking at the Erechtheum. In this pose, he appears like any one of the other millions of visitors to the Acropolis: sitting, observing, and musing. Why did Mies come to this place? Why would anyone travel to this hilltop filled with the rubble of the ages? To see a historic monument? Yes. To enjoy an architectural masterpiece? Doubtless. To experience a certain romantic nostalgia? Possibly. To experience something of the edifying power of the akrotic height? To listen for echoes of the distant Mycenean ancestry of the Attic acropolis, the prehistory of the Balkan dreams of a traumatized modernity? Perhaps.

One of the characteristics of ruined buildings is that they are stripped of their functionality, and (for the most part) of their decorative or utilitarian signifiers. What is left is something approximating a pure stereometrical object. While such structures are always approached (guidebook in hand) with an awareness of their historical associations and significances, some part of them always remains outside of time.

Sitting on the rock staring at the Erechtheum, the visitor probably knows

something about the Periclean age, and possibly bits and pieces of the Parthenon's later, fateful history. The more inquisitive visitor might also know a
little about classical Greek geometry. But all of this explicit knowledge is
trivial compared with the visitors' thoughts as they dwell on the elementary
shapes of creation – the shapes of solid geometry that the wear of centuries
has foregrounded. Even the processes of ruination are an aid to this thought-
projection. The mind, almost as a reflex, makes good the missing corners,
angles and tangents, the lines and planes that warfare and neglect have
erased. In the mind's eye, the original unadorned shapes of the geometer-
architect are restored.

In this act, the mind of the traveller engages with the universal – with a
pure reason that escapes the wear and tear of the empirical, the social
demands of the functional, and the contingencies of historical events. In con-
templation, the Parthenon becomes no longer a sense object (*aisthētos*) but a
thought object. The mind projects itself into a pure made-world of reason:
created from points, lines and planes – a made-world outside of society,
history and geography. This made-world is free from the rule of *aisthēsis* –
the rule of aesthetics. This made-world is the world of utopia.

Human beings get to begin to think about this utopian world by taking a
journey. Journeys are acts of estrangement. They impel the traveller into
unfamiliar surroundings. Sometimes they stimulate fascination or revulsion
with the law and customs, the *nomoi*, of unfamiliar places. In other cases they
present a radical provocation to grasp the universal. Finding oneself without
accustomed markers and signposts forces the question: is there something
'outside of place', a congenial nowhere (a utopia), where all strangers are welcomed – an 'outside place', a *temenos* (sacred temple precinct) where friendli-
ness towards strangers (*philoxenia*) is the prevailing ethos?

Travellers in strange lands love hospitality. As the humblest of guidebooks
will tell you, learn a little of the language and show respect for the local
customs, and you will be smiled upon. But the most adventurous sojourners
instinctively refuse the romantic demand to blend with the landscape. Instead,
they bring with them a gift, the gift of universality; the intuition that there are
silent forms of nature (*phusis*) that spiral up above all of the familiar signs
and marks of a place. Such forms define a 'nowhere' – a no-place where
everyone present is a stranger.

Such no-places are edifying – in the sense of *aedificium*. *Aedificium* is the
Latin term for structure or building – derived from *aedis* (dwelling) + *ficium*,
from *fingo* (to shape, fashion, form, mould).[2] No-places are constructs or artifices. They are the work of a builder (*aedificator*), not the weathered, striated
contours of topography, or the exclusionary zones of an ethnography
mapped over a topography. As the word-part 'ficium' suggests, there is a fictional element in the no-place. It has a made-up quality. What better or more
logical no-place for a stranger to dwell in than a 'fictional' one?

Utopia is a work of the imagination, the imag(in)ing of a place outside of
conventional social time and space. It may be a modest construct; it may be a
major work. In either case, the feeling of the visitor-stranger in its presence is

one of beautiful displacement. Utopia allows us to move away from everyday society into the sphere of ethical geometries – the world of beautiful-good forms. Cosmopolitan travellers intuitively search out no-places. Whatever other motives they have for their travels, they treasure most of all the moments that they can manage to set aside to see and enter these *aedifictions* and enjoy a 'time outside of time' spent lingering, rubbing shoulders and sharing a table with other strangers, in the presence of a poietic thing.

The aedifiction lifts us out of the ordinary. By this we most emphatically do not mean that it is magical or romantic. Nonetheless it has a quality of strangeness – not in the sense of odd or bizarre but in the sense of un-accustomed, un-familiar. This quality runs counter to the *nomoi* (conventions) of a specific place. It is a construction that is capable of turning even the most habituated local into a stranger, and thereby into a companion of the *xenos* – the guest-friend-stranger. Because aedifictions possess this power of defamiliarization, locals often avoid visiting the constructed no-places in their neighbourhood, while strangers will travel great distances to spend even a few minutes in their presence.[3] The no-place 'equalizes' stranger and local by allowing each to appear to the other as if behind a mask of estrangement.

This is not always pleasing to locals – especially those whose lives are defined by either idiomatic place or by romantic origin. In contrast to the idiomacies of landscape, ethnicity and birth, or the romantic desire to return to the source or origin, the mask of estrangement is the visage of universal justice. Among those who wear this mask, the power of local, organic and originary laws, myths and cultures are suspended. For this reason, the exile has a special attraction to aedifictions. The aedifiction represents a justice that exists apart from the local place. It is the justice of the no-place. The no-place is the visual image of a promise. It is the promise that those who experience the normative power of society as oppressive, discriminatory, superficial or stupid will find another, better, richer, deeper kind of order 'elsewhere'.

Exile is the human condition. Homo sapiens were always – and will always be – migratory, wandering, resettling creatures. The maxim of this peripatetic species is: *don't look back* – don't seek origins. Look instead to the no-where and timeless realm of ethical geometries and material forms. What does the no-place look like? Intuitively, we already know the answer to this question. We recognize immediately, even from photographs, the aedifictions that hold us in their thrall. We recognize them instinctively, even if it always proves difficult to *describe* these artifices.

The earliest accounts of something counterposed to the place and time, law and culture 'sprung from the earth' were furnished by the Ionian *phusikoi*, 'the first philosophers' of classical antiquity. It is not far-fetched to say that 'the first architect' – in the sense of the first creator of the universal place (the no-place) of the stranger – was one of these philosopher-*phusikoi*, because architecture, as opposed to vernacular building or even the work of the master builder, is an act of the mind. In this very strict sense, the philosopher Anaxagoras (500–428 BCE) can be thought of as the first architect. This is so not because this Ionian xenetic – who lived in Athens as a guest-stranger-friend of the city – built anything. He did not. But he, and others like him, certainly managed to infuse Pericles's public building programme of the 440s – a programme that produced the most wonderful aedifictions – with a sense of *theōria*. *Theōria* is the speculative reason of those who dwell in the strange interstices of the cosmopolitan city filled with strangers. These interstices are strange simply because they are rich in intimations of a no-where and a no-time outside of ordinary social place and social time.

Anaxagoras came from Clazomenae in Ionia. He was a close associate of Pericles – and of Phidias (who oversaw the building of the Parthenon), Hippodamus of Miletus and Euripides. Anaxagoras taught for almost thirty years (*c.* 460–430) in Athens. In the *Phaedrus*, Socrates credits Anaxagoras with Pericles's 'loftiness of mind'.[4] Pericles's ambitious scheme to rebuild Athens after the Persian invasion corresponded to the increasingly imperial self-confidence of a resurgent Athens, yet his guiding hand produced something decidedly more than mere imperial building – something that was indeed lofty. The greatest of the great works of the Periclean age displayed a sense of harmonious order that, quite evidently, emerged out of something more than simply the drive for power or domination. Such works were created out of a marvellous *power to arrange*. They came spilling forth out of the civilizing power of beauty.[5] We can give Anaxagoras some credit for this. Not that he was even the greatest of the diasporic Ionian intellectuals who came to Athens. But he managed to convey to his friend Pericles enough of the Ionian ethos of rational creation to make *out of something Attic, something also universal* – something that strangers from all over the world could admire and wonder at, and still do.

The Parthenon became a no-place – a universal place for the entirety of Western civilization. It was as if, in the Periclean character, Attic drive and Ionian internationalism were conjoined. The power politician's closeness to his Ionian intimates – Pericles's influential paramour Aspasia, Anaxagoras, and Hippodamus – found expression in the fusing of Attic ambitions with the Ionian 'philosophical' conception of things. This rational conception of things or *theōria* – the enduring legacy of the Ionians – was a *looking at the relation of things*. This 'looking at the relation of things' was dedicated to understanding the nature (*phusis*) of order or *kosmos*. Anaxagoras's strange theory – strange because of its seemingly contradictory propositions – set out a 'theory of ordering' that every 'arranger of things', every 'architect', must intuitively grasp. So many of the brilliant creations of Pericles's Athens were not Athenian in an ethnic or national sense. Rather, they were the joint work of Athenians and exiles. Figures like Anaxagoras brought to Athens a way of looking at the relation of things – sufficient to release Athens from its parochial past without causing it to become a derivative society.

Anaxagoras proposed that *in the beginning and now* everything is in everything. Things cannot exist separately (*chōris*) but everything shares a portion of everything. Things cannot be separated nor can they come to be by themselves (*eph' heautou*). Yet, at the same time, every ordering (*kosmos*) of things involves a differentiating of elements, a separating off (*apokrisis*). Thus the relating of things is both implied where things are undifferentiated and where they are differentiated. In an undifferentiated mass, things are related indifferently. The 'architect' begins by separating things, putting a space (*choros*) between things. But architecture is not the work of *choroi* – the spaces that separate things. For what is separated must be related (again). What is differentiated has to 'come together' in the act of *sunchōreō* (meeting).

In the representative Ionian conception of Anaxagoras, the universe had a structure that was the product of the *nous* (mind). The *nous* imparted – to the chaos of matter – shape and limit. It created austere, beautiful forms. These forms, in turn, allowed the human mind to look beneath the sensuous and aesthetic appearance of things. As human beings stared at this creation, as they grasped its order, they looked at it in wonderment. Yet, just as importantly, the human mind could also create its own forms on the model of the forms of nature. The human mind, at its greatest, was architectonic. It could, as if by virtue of its own nature (*phusis*), create forms that would be looked at in silent, astonished wonderment.

The architectonic is not easily achieved. Human society, from the simplest to the most sophisticated, organizes itself using patterns. The shape of the earth, of waves, leaves, the line of the sky and so on suggest forms for human beings to inhabit. But Ionian philosophy had a different conception of nature. Its order (kosmos) was mathematical (geometrical). By using the 'tools' of the mind (i.e. numbers) the human artificer could imitate the order of nature. The kosmos was not the local ground of the earth; it was not the familiar nature of the sky, leaf and cave of childhood experience. It was an intellectual object. With points were created lines, with lines were created planes, and with planes were created objects. Such a nature was only fully apprehensible to those who had 'left home', who had been ferried beyond their familiar place to live among strangers – in places where the heavens, the landscape, the birds and the trees, the shoreline and skyline looked different. In unfamiliar terrain, nature could be conceived as a mathematical construct. This was the task that philosophy set for itself – to think about nature as a universal rather than a local phenomenon.

Thales of Miletus participated in the Lydian campaign against Persia, and travelled to Egypt where he performed various mathematical experiments. Anaximander helped organize a Milesian colony at Apollonia on the Black Sea, and drew a map of the world. Pythagoras migrated from Samos to Croton in Southern Italy (to escape Polycrates's tyranny) and travelled to Egypt, Crete and Sparta (legend even had him in Babylonia). Xenophanes of Colophon left his city to escape the Persians. He journeyed to Malta, Pharos, Messana, Catania and Syracuse, and eventually settled in Elea in Southern Italy. Of Heraclitus, there is no record of him having travelled (perhaps it was enough that his thought was 'obscure').[6] Empedocles of Agrigentum ended his life as an exile in the Peloponnese, a 'wanderer gone astray'. Anaxagoras, as we have already observed, lived for thirty years in Athens. Protagoras of Abdera participated, along with Hippodamus, in the foundation of the Panhellenic colony of Thurii. Hippias of Elis was an ambassador to

Sparta, and travelled throughout Greece. Gorgias of Leontini was an ambassador of his city to Athens, and a Panhellenic visitor at Boeotia, Thessaly, Olympia and Delphi.

Socrates's only real absence from Attica, unless we count his war campaigning, was his absent-mindedness: the philosopher lost in the continent of thought. However his student, Antisthenes, the founder of the Cynic school, renounced altogether the idea of the 'homeland' (and the familiar life) for citizenship of the world. Antisthenes, memorable as a teacher who hated students, opened his school to foreigners and members of the lower classes – to the Cynics' beloved 'stray dogs'. These homeless dogs were the creators of the dog-like school of philosophy. The most famous of them, Diogenes, came to Athens from Sinope, a city on the Black Sea. Diogenes proclaimed that, so far as the stray dogs were concerned, 'the only real commonwealth is the whole world'. The Cynic was a citizen of the world (*kosmopolitēs*). The stray dog had no interest in a *patria* or native country. The dog was the archetypal expatriate.

Plato, that other student of Socrates, was only marginally more chained to his home city than the Cynics. After the execution of Socrates – the vengeance of Athenians who didn't like their local pieties being ridiculed – Plato lived abroad in Euclides (in Megara). Returning to Athens, he worked in a more or less conventional Socratic mode for ten years, and then travelled to Egypt, Kyrene, Tarentum and Syracuse – a journey that was a prelude to his mature thought. (His journeying nature also drew him to others with similar natures. Among his closest intellectual associates in Athens were figures like the great mathematician, Eudoxus, from Knidus, an island off the coast of Asia Minor.) Aristotle, who came from Stageira, spent twenty years in Athens – as a student of Plato's. Then, after Plato's death, he began his own journey of thought. He left Athens for Assus, and then on to Mitylene, and (finally) to Pella where he supervised the education of Alexander the Great.

Philosophers – the ones who are thinkers – are stuck with having to live on the fragile hospitality, the *philoxenia*, of others. It does not take too much to wear out one's welcome, especially if we suppose that philosophy is premised on the idea that the laws and conventions (*nomoi*) of the city can be replaced with something else – viz. a life according to *phusis*, ethical geometry, or laughter. Among ancient philosophers, the Presocratics presented nature as an alternative to the *nomoi*. Plato drew heavily on the Pythagorean ethical geometry of proportion and balance. The cynic's chortle was the laughter of the cosmopolitan. 'I have come to debase the coinage', explained Diogenes.

All of these currents converged in the person of Zeno of Citium (in Cyprus) – the founder of Stoicism. According to Diogenes Laertius, Zeno came to Piraeus from Phoenicia. (Like so many of the later Stoics who came from outside of Greek territories, he was not wholly Greek by birth – his mother was 'Phoenician', perhaps Semitic.) Zeno began his philosophical life under the tutelage of the Cynic Crates. The fragments of Zeno's early work – his *Republic* – that have survived have a strongly Cynical character. He proposes the abolition of marriage, temples and coinage (the apparatus of *nomoi*) in favour of the *phusis* of the anthropos (humankind). This human nature was the nature of the citizens of no-where. *Phusis* was counterposed to social place (status), to ethnos, to conventional social and moral judgements, to the property of the *oikos* (house), to geo-cultural boundaries and so on.

In this view, philosophy is a kind of homelessness – *not* as Novalis claimed a homesickness. This is so even despite the fact that philosophers often embark on a journey because they have no choice, because their views, or their associations, make them unpopular, and they are forced to leave for another city where (they hope) they will be more welcome – just as Anaxagoras was forced to leave Athens after the death of Pericles. Of course the paradigmatic philosopher (in modern eyes) – Socrates – was the one who refused to leave, and who preferred death at home to exile abroad. However, Nietzsche's intuition that Socrates is not the norm of philosophy was correct. For most philosophers, faced with a city tired of their reasoning or their laughter, will move on to some stranger city, some xenopolis – as Marx did in London, or as Nietzsche himself did, in his self-exile from German culture, living a peripatetic existence in hotels, among strangers, in Sorrento, Genoa, Venice, Nice and Turin.[7]

In the twentieth century, the importance of the experience of journeying among strangers to philosophy did not change. It is true that the 'greatest philosopher of the twentieth century' (Heidegger) stayed home, close to his native earth in defiance of the exilic condition of philosophy. But the traumatic self-destruction of Europe – during the 1910s to 1940s – nonetheless produced a brilliant generation of stray dogs who went into exile in America and England. The agonized peripatetics of Ludwig Wittgenstein are paradigmatic of the experience of this transplanted group. From 1908 to his death in 1951, he went from Vienna to Manchester and Cambridge, back to Vienna, back to Cambridge, with periods in London, Dublin, Norway and even the United States. The Wittgenstein case is replicated again and again: in the escape of Karl Popper from Nazified Vienna to New Zealand and eventually England; the flight of Cornelius Castoriadis from the death threats of Nazis and Communists in 1940s Athens to life as a Greek national in Paris; the equally troubled journeying of Simone Weil to Italy, civil-war Spain, her wartime flight to Vichy Marseilles, New York and London; Theodor Adorno's forced exile in 1940s Los Angeles; Hannah Arendt's displacement to Chicago and New York – all of these are typical of the philosophers' peripatetic fate of searching, or being forced to search, for an 'away home' (*apoikia*) for the homeless spirit.[8]

What does the 'away home for the homeless peripatetic' look like? How is it constructed? Can philosophy give an account of it?

We do not ordinarily think of philosophers as architects. Nevertheless the question of 'the away home of the homeless spirit' haunts philosophy. So philosophers are forced, even if only as a matter of personal fate, to sketch – in what are always allusive words – what others might build. Simone Weil turned to the Pythagoreans in order to conceive of a sacred (Christian-Greek) no-place, built with the invisible music-like metrics of classical geometry, in which all strangers might be able to find an ethical dwelling.[9] As we have already observed, Wittgenstein actually built his no-place, the Kundmann-gasse villa, in his home-town, in defiance of conventional Viennese taste – an away home that he would never inhabit in the very heart of his birthplace, created for his sister yet more the gift of a friend than of a sibling, a friend's house rather than the family/familiar house, a beautiful-strange composition, and the most radical gesture of the xenetic.

Above all, what characterizes Wittgenstein's philosopher's house is its geo-metric quality – its sparse, haunting, uncompromising measure of the earth. The house of the philosopher is an intellectual object. The compelling beauty and the affecting strangeness of such objects arise *inter alia* from their geome-tries. The ethical universality of such geometries places them outside all terrain, all territory and all conventional sense of place.[10] These geometries are the tools for creating an ethical abode that answers the question: what 'place' can there be for the person who is 'out of place'?

This question afflicts all travellers. But it is in the case of the philosophical wanderer that this affliction is most dramatically represented. Diogenes of Sinope put it bluntly: 'The porticoes and streets of Athens were built for me as a place to live.' The conventional household was uncongenial to the phil-osopher. He would rather lie down outdoors with stray dogs in public places. Philosophers have always got by with itinerant accommodation – living in hostels, hotels, with friends, or in institutional rooms and monasteries. Wittgenstein spent a life shuttling from friends' houses to Cambridge rooms to guesthouses. The *oikos* – both in the personal and symbolic sense – has always seemed at odds with the *phusis* and *logos* that the philosopher admires. Better then to accommodate oneself like a traveller.

Great architecture facilitates the creation of the universal no-place where those who are estranged can rest from their journey amidst the stereometrical depth of things. In such cases, the brilliance of objectivation matches the adventurousness of the xenoi. Through the concert of reification and estrangement, 'a world' comes into being. For the person who is a stranger, the capacity for world-making has a special significance. Invariably the stranger at some time will wonder whether there is anything more than the local habits and customs, laws and culture of idiomatic peoples? Anaxagor-as's world-making dialectic of separation (*chōrismos*) and joining (*koinōnia*) defines the logical tools that strangers use to compose the image of a world, ultimately of a world city or cosmopolis that escapes the destructive impera-tives of earth, terrain, archaic nature, locality, origin and genealogy.

A world (cosmos) is an arrangement. It is an arrangement in which things are delimited from and combined with each other. It is an arrangement that both separates and conjoins things. It is a *diairesis* (division, differentiation) and a *sunopsis* (seeing things as one, together). The simplest separation is two points a distance apart. The simplest join is the line that joins two points. The most elementary plane is the triangle (the triangulation of lines between three points that generates a plane figure with three angles and three sides). From the joining of triangles, other planes (such as squares and rectangles) and regular solid objects (cubes, prisms) can be created.[11] The beauty of creation is achieved by the proportional and symmetrical arrangement of lines, planes and solids. Symmetry governs the separation of parts; proportionality governs their joining. With the most elementary of means, then, the stranger can compose an image or model of a made-world – an image of the no-place.

World cities or cosmopolises are cities that are made-worlds. The cosmopolis is not defined by either the sheltering topographies of an idiomatic place or by the unbounded openness of modern space. Rather, it is distinguished by its poietic qualities. The comfort of the stranger in the cosmopolis is not the feeling of homeliness caused by contact with familiar places, nor is it the feeling of exuberance or expansiveness that open space (the 'open plan') engenders. The comfort of the stranger in the cosmopolis derives from pleasurable looking at the beautiful composition of buildings, squares, gardens and promenades. Being able to wander through the arcades and malls of the city eases the tensions of the stranger. The cosmopolis provides an intelligible order – intelligible to anyone, irrespective of language or culture. This order is lucid in contrast to the frequently impenetrable law of genos and ethnos. Since the time of the Ionic-Attic encounter (in the wake of the Persian Wars), there have been many kinds of cosmopolises. Some have flourished under auspicious circumstances; others under difficult conditions. All of these historical creations remain a kind of memorial to the possibility that something, some no-place, does exist beyond genos and ethnos.

Some of the most significant twentieth-century attempts to create a home for the homeless mind occurred in Central Europe. But these attempts, though, were almost an after-thought, an accidental by-product, of the prolonged self-demolition of Central Europe. They were akin to a reflex action by civilization as the Wilhelmine and Austro-Hungarian empires – and further afield the Russian and the Ottoman empires – began to collapse, unleashing enormous, vertiginous forces of barbarism. A number of brilliant characters managed to continue to think about reason and logic and form as the abyss of radical pan-nationalism, anti-Semitism and cultural ethno-nationalism opened up. But, strikingly, these resilient souls took many of their intellectual cues not from Central Europe but from the United States and England.

The other important thing to note is that the laboratory for their world making was not the public building or the agora but rather the *xenoikos*. This was yet another sign of the spiritual crisis of Central Europe. Those who understood something of the nature of civilizing forms had little opportunity to do publicly commissioned work. The house rather than the civic building became the crucible for their architectural and philosophical experimentation. In many cases, the domestic and familiar character of the house defeated these ambitions. But, in a handful of cases at least, this architecture managed to rise above the rule of conventional domestic norms to address the possibility of a 'home of the homeless spirit' and its promise that peripatetics would no longer have to sleep like dogs in the porticoes of the public street.

Adolf Loos is one who managed to do something out of the ordinary. Moravian born and Brno raised, educated in Bohemia and Dresden, Loos's own struggle with the troubling questions of his age took him to the United States for three years – in 1893–6. During that time away, he conceived the idea of a *sachlich* architecture. This 'objective' architecture was remarkable for one thing in particular: the idea of the 'spatial plan'. The phrase was a clumsy coinage (by one of Loos's followers). Its use of the word 'plan' was misleading. Yet it gave a name of sorts to something important. Loos's insight was that conventional architects worked with two-dimensional 'plans' – that is, primarily with planar surfaces in mind rather than with three-dimensional models.[12] He argued that, as an architect, he did not design plans, façades and sections but rather volumes.

Loos's specific innovation was to conceive of an architecture of interconnecting yet contrasting volumes: within one architectural container or shell, he could put together a high auditorium linked to a low annexe; a dining-room ceiling interlocked with a pantry of a different height; interconnecting areas on two different levels; a hall connected by steps to a slightly raised lobby; and so forth. Loos's key idea was to have two or three volumetric characters inhabiting the same architectural container. This was also a very American sense of volume. It is of crucial significance that Loos spent a year eking out an existence among penniless immigrants in Manhattan.[13] When he returned from America to Europe, it is evident that he came back with some nascent sense of how a *xenoikos* might be possible.

What was it in America that inspired his aedifiction? Was it the strong volumetric interplay columns – a recurring motif of American architecture based on the example of Jefferson's triptych of Monticello, the Rotunda at the University of Virginia and the Virginia Legislature? Was it this American echo of the Roman sense of space that attracted Loos?[14] As we've previously noted, the Romans closed in the public outdoors ambulatory space of the Greeks.[15] Where twin stoae faced each other, the Romans enclosed the ends, roofed over the structure, and cut clerestory windows under the line of the roof to light the enclosed space they had made. Thus was created the Roman court of law – the *basilica* – perfected in buildings such as the great Basilica Julia, 30–13 BCE. Romans enclosed space – whether it was the interior court-yard of the basilica or the peristyle villa or the atrium. They created enclosed indoor aedifictions for wandering around in – like Trajan's Market in Rome, with its elevated, vaulted basilica-like space lined with lower-level shops. The large enclosed volume contained smaller volumes, and human figures paced and strolled through this micro-cosmos. Something of this sense of space was duplicated in America. It ran like a thread from colonial houses, with their central octagons ringed by stairs and balustraded balconies, through to the great structures of the railroad age like New York's Roman Revival Pennsylvania Station (1902–10).

The American sense of the volumetric was not restricted to the overtly neoclassical structures either. Frank Lloyd Wright's iconic Larkin Building (1904) reminds us of the Basilica Julia without, in the slightest sense, being overtly related to it. In the mid-twentieth century, volumetric space became the American public norm – routinized in the shopping mall, a structure that for many purposes became the primary, sometimes the only, public space in mainstream American life. The 'New Rome' of America was the Rome of Trajan's Market.

Loos created a modern version of Roman 'container' architecture. Loos's modernism was a form of European and Western secondarity to Rome.[16] In his architecture, volumes within the volumetric container were connected in a flowing manner. This is not quite the 'open plan' of Mies van der Rohe. Nonetheless, it possessed a strong spatial quality, one that encouraged bodies to move through space. Movement is stimulated not across flat (two-dimensional) planar surfaces but rather up and down raised (mezzanine-style) volumes that evoke a profound sense of depth as well as length and breadth. Loos's raised/lowered volumes were not organized according to any strong classical definition. They displayed no particular proportionality or symmetry. Nonetheless, the volumetric sense of Loos strongly suggests a post-planar Platonic geometry of solids – the work of an '*object*-ive' architecture. Loos's general innovation was to draw attention to the third aspect of the Platonic architect's guiding maxim: with points are created lines, with lines are created planar surfaces, and with planes are created (volumetric) objects.[17] Hence the strongly 'cubic' feel of the more adventurous of Loos's designs.[18]

While Loos became famous for his polemics – notably his denunciation of ornamentation – his own self-understanding of the 'spatial plan' idea was rather limited. It was left to Loos's acquaintance, Wittgenstein, to bring to light the far-reaching implications of Loos's intuition. Like Loos, it was outside of the Central European maelstrom – in Manchester and Cambridge – that the preparatory thinking for this occurred.[19] As Wittgenstein grasped, to think in terms of *models* (volumetric figures) rather than *plans* (cross-sections, floor plans) represented an epistemological event of exceptional importance. The model – the *Bild* or image[20] – is like a wire-frame of three-dimensionality. Correspondingly, to think in images – to reason by invoking models – is to be able to conceive of a world.

Wittgenstein explained the notion of the model in the following way: The *Bild* – or model/image – of things represents how components of the world are related to each other.[21] The model or image does not represent the multiplicity of elements of a situation but rather the way in which elements are connected or structured. By constructing models, we can construct a world. In the model/image, we arrange the essential relations – or three-dimensional frame – of a world.[22] We devise a model so as to show or display the essential relations (forms, frames, patterns, structures) that order the multitudinous components of a made-world. The structure (the framework) of a world can only be shown. A model is a likeness (an *eikōn*) of the structure of a world. A world can only be represented *iconically* – in the sense that 'the world of Rome' is represented iconically by the Pantheon.

The peculiar privilege of the traveller (exile, wanderer, pilgrim, tourist, or peripatetic philosopher) is to view a model of the world such as the Pantheon with fresh eyes. On 'first view', an 'image of a world' has a much greater clarity and depth than when viewed with more familiar eyes. How many local inhabitants of Rome ever pay much attention to the model of the Pantheon? Habituation dulls the imagination. That is perhaps the ultimate justification of the traveller: to see a model of the world with fresh eyes.

Human beings can construct worlds. Human beings can act cosmopoieti-cally. Plato proposed a model for this constructive activity. Plato proposed that a *dēmiourgos*, an artisan (literally: a 'public worker') of the kosmos, as the model of all creation. How did this public worker create? Not by the act of *alētheia* (truth-revelation), but rather by the deployment of points, lines, shapes and volumes that are mathematically (proportionally, rhythmically) organized. Models are elegantly simple arrangements. They may be embellished and ornamented, but the creation of a basic model requires the ability to think, not in sensuous or aesthetic terms, but in terms of forms, frames and patterns.

To think in such sparse wire-frame terms requires a cognitive distance from the objects of the world in their everyday settings. This distance comes naturally to the stranger. The stranger stands at a tangent to everyday society. At 'home', the stranger looks at the local landscape with the eyes of the visitor. Abroad, the stranger is the 'perpetual visitor'. The stranger is the one who abstracts from the social. The stranger looks past the surfaces (the flat, two-dimensional aesthetic surfaces) of function, law, historical exigency and taste. The peripatetic stranger thinks in images, constructing three-dimensional models of inhabitable worlds – utopias of form and connection.

A model is a laboratory of creation. Such models may not, need not, be 'full scale'. Indeed often the most influential architectonics are no more than drawings or unexecuted scale models, i.e. thought experiments. Some of Loos's greatest creations – the 'Greek houses' he designed in the early 1920s – were never built.[23] Yet they are still an exquisite miniature of the utopia of civilization. They are beautiful abstractions of form. Their beauty intimates an ethical order. This order is utopian. It is not a function of *nomoi*, but an act of *phusis*. At their greatest, Loos's designs strip away the surface, ornamentation and style of society. What remains is the intimation of an order of beauty and justice, an order created through form. The plans for the Villa Stross (1922) and the Villa Simon (1924) brilliantly combine classical form with modernist simplicity and Loos's volumetric sense. They are modern and ancient, Greek and European, Roman and American. They are universal.

16 Modernity's Aesthetic Utopias

According to Schlegel, what distinguished modern art from the completed art of antiquity was its capacity for infinite reflexivity. Modern art opened the utopian horizon of a 'progressive universal poetry', born of the marriage of art and philosophy. This idea of the absolute work of art is the utopia of art as its own (infinite) end.[1] The idea resonates throughout the aestheticism of the nineteenth century from Flaubert to Mallarmé, and finds its continuation in the twentieth century in formalist theories of art. Formalist theories of art understand the process of aesthetic modernism in terms of a progressive abstraction from 'natural' conventions leading to an ever-purer self-reflexion of the medium.

What distinguished art from philosophy, according to Schelling, is its capacity to unite what thought divides. Art thereby becomes the organon of philosophy, and as such the anticipation of philosophy's return to the ocean of poetry – from which will arise a new mythology, the inspiration of a new *Gesamtkunstwerk*. Schelling thus stands at the beginning of the redemptive, rather than the progressive utopian, line of aesthetic modernism. In the progressive line the idea of the avant-garde can be seen as the vanishing point – both *telos* and limit – of a forward-looking 'aesthetic revolution' in the means of production; in the other redemptive-utopian line the idea of the total work of art functions as the vanishing point of 'aesthetic re-volution'.

The determining force of the second, romantic philosophical-historical horizon appears particularly clearly in Lukács's *Theory of the Novel*. Written under the impact of the First World War, it is an exemplary text of modernism. It turns to Hegel, Schlegel and Schelling to articulate the apocalyptic consciousness of the new epochal threshold of the War, which is seen as the overcoming of the unhappy consciousness of the moderns. The Hegelian opposition between ancients and moderns, Homeric epos and post-Cervantean novel, provides the backdrop to the characterization of Schlegel's romantic irony as the negative mysticism of a 'godforsaken age of sinfulness' (Fichte), whose coming end and redemption is adumbrated in the work of Dostoevsky, whose novels point beyond the novel to a coming return of the epos. *Theory of the Novel* not only provides a direct link between the epochal thresholds around 1800 and around 1910, it also demonstrates the continuity of a historicist matrix, which is inhabited from the beginning by a fundamental ambivalence towards the differentiation of art.

The emergence of autonomous art and the corresponding unifying concept of Art sets in train a process of purification of the individual arts in search of their intrinsic essence and logic. We could call this purification an ongoing process of the enlightenment of art, whose goal would be the absolute work of art, liberated from extrinsic considerations and constraints, the expression not so much of the subjectivity of the artist as of the sovereignty of the work. In the words of Clement Greenberg, 'a modernist work of art must try, in principle, to avoid dependence upon any order of experience not given in the most essentially construed nature of its own medium'.[2] This principle provides the basic schema of the progressive theories of modernism in painting, poetry, music and architecture. It is a teleological process governed by inner necessity and driven by the technical challenges posed by the material and the medium.

Thus Kurt Hübner describes painting from Impressionism through to Cubism as governed by a systematic study of perception under the spell of scientific ontology and technical civilization, which stripped the object of its mythical and religious, ethical and metaphysical dimensions.[3] Although the affirmative versions of the schema are usually identified with modernism, they share the same premise as the negative or tragic versions of this process: viz. the inner logic of the development of art is to be understood as the progressive self-critique of art. Suzi Gablik for instance equates progress in art with abstraction, in particular with the cognitive advance in perception realized in Cubism.[4] Cubism is likewise central to Greenberg's 'halcyon modernism of the first quarter of the century', since its elimination of the third dimension and the illusion of perspectival depth marks a decisive moment in the dissolution of content into the forward progress of art techniques, which gives free rein to a 'pure preoccupation with the invention and arrangement of spaces, surfaces, shapes, colours, etc.'[5] This self-purification announces a 'law of modernism',[6] e.g. the relentless discarding of conventions which has yet to run its course in painting (as opposed to literature or music), thus allowing Greenberg to hail the latest advance achieved by Abstract Expressionism. That this dynamic of self-critique, elevated to the creative principle of 'all art that remains truly alive in our time',[7] raises the question of the limits of progress does not seem to have concerned Greenberg, as it does Hans Sedlmayr, who observes that Duchamp's first readymades (1911) and Malevich's black paintings (1914) had already demonstrated the ultimate possibilities of the modernist paradigm of art.[8]

Writing like Adorno and Greenberg in the 1950s at the height of the ideology of modernism, Sedlmayr combines Greenberg's process of self-purification with Adorno's dialectic of aesthetic progress. He comprehends the revolution of modern art, this 'most monstrous of revolutions', which reached its extreme between 1905 and 1925, as the child of the enlightenment. The other, expressive side of modernism together with the fascination with the unconscious sources of creation is relegated, as with Adorno, to the role of irrational reaction to the utopian rationalism at work in modern art. The cultivation of chaos and madness, of the primitive and the absurd in Expressionism and Surrealism offers no more than a regressive counterfoil to the highest interests of modernism: the alliance of aestheticism, science and technology.[9]

Aestheticism appears in Sedlmayr's analysis as both cause and effect of the purification of the arts. The striving of the individual arts to become absolute is repeated on a higher level in the striving of art to become pure art. This logic of differentiation and universalization contains its own dialectic: the reversal of autonomy into heteronomy. Once the arts have been reduced to their 'essential' technical elements – lines, colours, words, twelve tones, etc. – in other words: emancipated from the grammar and syntax of their 'natural' languages, they are compelled to seek their new organizing principle in artificial systems of technical construction and composition. Surrender to the fetishism of self-posited brilliant techniques demonstrates the reversal of absolute subjectivity into blind objectivity – Sedlmayr's reference to Adorno's essay 'The Ageing of the New' underscores the parallels between the conservative anti-modernist and the tragic modernist. They both propose a self-cancelling dialectic of enlightenment as the key to modern(ist) art. But where Adorno unfolds in the wake of Simmel, Weber and Lukács the 'tragedy of culture', Sedlmayr expounds an exemplary fable of Faustian hubris.

Both Greenberg and Adorno identify modernism with an inner logic of rationalization, which defines the history of painting or of music as an unfolding series of technical problems. In this history of rigorous selection the moving arrow of the most advanced technical solutions serves to separate the sheep from the goats. Thus van Gogh, Munch, Böcklin, Klimt, Hodler, Schiele, Kokoschka, Chirico, the German Expressionists simply do not register on the flat surface of Greenberg's screen. Even Picasso is deemed to have failed to grasp the 'inherent laws of development' of Cubism.[10] Adorno's strait gate of election is even narrower and the path of progress even lonelier. Stravinsky or Hindemith are dismissed as technically reactionary, Bartók and Janáček scarcely merit mention, Shostakovich is consistently ignored. Schoenberg alone (exiled like Adorno in Los Angeles), in fulfilling the inherent laws of development of advanced music, poses the ultimate question of modernism: the fate of autonomous art, of the aesthetic in the dying epoch of bourgeois society and subjectivity. If there is an inner formal-aesthetic history of bourgeois music, as Adorno is never tired of insisting, it is because this history can only be comprehended within modernism's historicist matrix, which in imbuing art with an inherent *telos* (whether positive or negative) necessarily raises the question of the end of art and endows it with ambiguity. The dialectic traced by Adorno in *Philosophy of Modern Music* is that of a reversal of the historical dynamic of development – the compulsion (supposedly) inherent in the musical material – into stasis: the end of progress, which freezes the time of bourgeois music and philosophy into space, is also, however, the end of art's 'incurable affliction'. Beyond submission to the dialectical compulsion of necessity lies the longing to escape from the utopian iron cage of aesthetic progress.[11]

We can observe a comparable ambiguity in Sedlmayr's version of the dialectic of autonomy in *The Revolution of Modern Art*, where the first and second revolutions of architecture reveal the underlying dynamic of the whole epoch of modernism since the French Revolution. Sedlmayr's crown witness is the architecture of Boullée and Ledoux heralding and accompanying the Revolution, which already anticipates across the historicist revivals of the nineteenth century the anti-tectonic spirit of twentieth-century architecture.[12] Their designs, intended as prototypes of a revolutionary utopian architecture, are defined by the return to the elementary forms of geometry, yet not as ethical forms but as intimations of the romantic sublime. In particular, the sphere – as in Boullée's project for a cenotaph for Newton, based on the globe of the earth – was designed to transport the spectator into the infinity of space. Oversized and overpowering, Boullée's sphere is a symbol of romantic awe and mystery, about as far removed from the spherical architecture of the Pantheon as can be imagined.

The sphere – Boullée's image of perfection – symbolizes for Sedlmayr the negations of the very foundations of architecture, the radical break that points forward to Le Corbusier's claim that human freedom leads to the pure geometry of a machine-like modular perfection, or to El Lissitsky's utopian identification of freedom with the overcoming of the earthboundedness of the foundation – an overcoming that puts nothing but the infinite open sky in the place of the foundation. Sedlmayr also registers the spell of progressive rationalizing geometry in technical construction based on the use of the model to effect the serial construction of machines and of buildings according to the same principles. This is an engineer's utopia. It is Le Corbusier who asserts that his is the first generation to see the machine: 'The machine gleams with surfaces, spheres and cylinders of steel, of a precision never shown in nature. The machine is our great creation. Machine-making man acts like a god in perfection.'[13]

Sedlmayr's examples of the reversal of autonomy into heteronomy, which results in art's subordination to the functional requirements of society – a machine aesthetic for a machine age – invite a different reading. Where Sedlmayr observes the surrender of autonomy, one can with equal or greater justice perceive an intended sublation of autonomous art. The project of the utopian reconstruction of society, which inspires Le Corbusier and Lissitsky, necessarily involves going beyond the limits of the pure aesthetic in order to recover a public, socially defined function for art. Sedlmayr is right however to stress the anti-tectonic and anti-mimetic hubris of this futurism, which reached its climax in the manifestos of the avant-garde between 1905 and 1925. In their desire to escape the confines of an aesthetic practice, which reflected the uneasy symbiosis between (bohemian) artist and bourgeois society, the avant-gardist revolt brought to the fore those tendencies within modernism which tied the revolutionary transformation of art to the revolutionary transformation of society. The will to transform modernism's progressive logic of differentiation into the utopian logic of aesthetic and/or political totalization is shared by the avant-garde and the totalitarian movements that emerged from the First World War.

Thus, the sphere of the aesthetic is threatened not only by the avant-garde's technique-obsessed assault on the bourgeois 'institution of art'.[14] Romantic modernism also contests the autonomy of art in the name not of futurism but of the lost *Gesamtkunstwerk* of the past. Here too it is important to stress that modernism's historicist matrix encompasses both the idea of cultural revolution and of cultural re-volution, directed to cancelling the emancipation of art and recovering an undifferentiated social totality. From the perspective of re-volution the differentiation of the arts is to be grasped as the dissolution of the premodern harmony of the social, the political, the religious and the aesthetic, which gave style and unity to organic cultural epochs. The modern logic of functional differentiation amounts to a double negation of this social totality: on the one hand purity demands the separation of the arts and the elimination in each case of elements deriving from the other arts, on the other hand, the idea of pure aesthetic value is directly opposed to the romantic longing for the lost organic totality of culture, whether it be the archaic Greek polis of romantic Hellenism, the Catholic Middle Ages of romantic medievalism, or the theatrical splendour of court and church ceremony in the Baroque Counter-Reformation, 'in which the European spirit for the last time in history shaped for itself a completely adequate form that took in the whole sum of life'.[15]

The modern understanding of culture as a total work of art is a product of romantic historicism, that is, of the aestheticization of history since Winckelmann and Herder. It should be added that its inescapable institutional corollary is the museum. The museum (in its historical-hermeneutic as opposed to its natural scientific – taxonomic and evolutionary – mode) comes to occupy a central place in the historicist imagination of the nineteenth century and beyond. As a primary site of the comprehension of history as culture, it becomes the mausoleum of the *Gesamtkunstwerk* of the past (just as the exhibition, designed to display the wonders of science and technology, presents the *Gesamtkunstwerk* of the future). In this sense it replaces church and palace, which in turn are progressively transformed into monuments to their former social functions.

The museum documents the loss of cultural unity. Its very organization exemplifies the separation, decontextualization and aestheticization of the arts. In place of the lost cultural unity it offers a new organizing idea of national history. It is not by chance that the first museum to be organized according to the national-historical principle was established in Paris at the time of the Revolution.[16] Nor is it by chance that nineteenth-century nation-builders turned the city into a museum of architecture, notably in Munich and Vienna (the Ringstrasse). Renaissance universities, neo-Gothic town halls and railway stations, museums and stock exchanges in the form of Greek temples all testify to the loss of a unifying style which would be capable of renewing the lost totality of art-religion.[17]

The sentimental historicism of the museum extended its reach to include contemporary art in the twentieth century. An important date here is the founding of the Museum of Modern Art in New York in 1929. Just as contemporary art is produced more and more for the museum, so the museum becomes itself more and more a (total) work of art, and a central focus of architectural design from the Guggenheim to the Getty museums, from the Beaubourg to Bilbao.[18] The complement of the total work of art is the aesthetics of total illusion. The aesthetics of total illusion extends from Nash's Royal Pavilion at Brighton to the castles of Ludwig II, Las Vegas and Disneyland, from the cult of spectacle and effect in nineteenth-century opera to Hollywood, from Bayreuth to the Third Reich.

The rise of a sublime aesthetics of total illusion in the wake of the lost total work of art represents, together with the museum, the inescapable other side of avant-garde modernism. The consciousness of the social function lost to autonomous art accompanies and contests the history of aesthetic progress. This other occluded genealogy and lineage of modernism cannot be reduced, *pace* Sedlmayr or Adorno, to the workings of the one dialectic of rationalization and irrationalism. Rather than the one history and dialectic of progress we need to recognize here the constitutional division of aesthetic modernism. Its contrasted aesthetics derive from antithetical responses to the differentiation and secularization of art. Art may be the 'unanimous utopia of modernity'. However, this unanimity conceals sharply opposed conceptions of the ends of art.

The counter-position to the modern differentiation of art, to the aesthetic as such, appears particularly clearly in Gadamer's critique in *Truth and Method* of modern aesthetic consciousness, as exemplified in the concept of subjective experience (*Erlebnis*) and in Kant's doctrine of genius and taste. The subjectivization of aesthetics presupposes the historical consciousness of the enlightenment, which effects the break with the authority of tradition by the appeal to the autonomy of reason. The consequence of this break is registered in Hegel's *Aesthetics*: the historical knowledge of the end of art, i.e. the end of the religion of art and the transformation of art into nothing but art,[19] which entails the loss of the question of the truth of art. The retrieval of the ontological truth of art and its hermeneutic significance must therefore work through a critique of aesthetic consciousness, which reduces the work of art to an aesthetic object for a subject, if it is to recover the living continuity of tradition across the rupture of modernity. This is the task of historical hermeneutics, which is called upon to bridge the temporal distance between the past and the present through 'the miracle of understanding'.[20] Since historical hermeneutics has inherited the legacy of the religion of art, the aesthetic experience (*Erfahrung*) of understanding and the understanding of aesthetic experience find their model in the concept of play, which embraces both art and religion.

Gadamer distinguishes his concept of art-religious play from the subjective meaning the idea of play has acquired in modern aesthetics since Kant and Schiller: 'When we speak of play in reference to the experience of art, this means neither the orientation nor even the state of mind of the creator or those enjoying the work of art, nor the freedom of a subjectivity engaged in play, but the mode of being of the work of art itself.'[21] We gain access to this mode of being by playing the game, by adhering to the rules, which prescribe the field of the game. And, as with a game, religious or artistic representation enacts a self-presentation – 'the presentation of a god in a religious rite, the presentation of a myth in a play'[22] – whose reality surpasses the actors and spectators by transforming participation into the ideality of a structure. This self-transcendence of the game means that a dramatic action is entirely comparable to a religious act in that it rests absolutely in itself as a vehicle of higher truth, which accomplishes redemption into true being. If we are to escape modern *aesthetic differentiation*, we must return to the original meaning of the concept of mimesis (imitation, representation), which concerns the essential being of the work of art. *Aesthetic non-differentiation* looks not to form but to content. The experience of the work of art as a meaningful whole participates in 'the event of being which occurs in presentation'.[23]

Mimesis thus encompasses presentation, re-presentation and re-cognition. It denotes in Heideggerian terms the paradoxical idea of original repetition through which we respond to and appropriate past possibilities of historical being in an act of re-presencing. Such re-presencing belongs to historicity of being, which is temporal in a more radical sense than belonging to history since it is the being of becoming and return. Indeed, if it belonged solely to history the miracle of understanding could not bypass and surpass the historical consciousness of modernity. It could not be the miracle of historicity that reveals tradition and, belonging to tradition, as the eternal moment of presence beneath and above history – that is to say, the moment of contemporaneity (Kierkegaard), in which that which presents itself 'achieves full presence, however remote its origin may be'.[24] Gadamer's formulation here is exactly the opposite of Walter Benjamin's concept of aura. Both contemporaneity and aura, however, refer to the presence of the sacred, to the auratic quality of the work of art. Again, Gadamer insists on the religion of art: the 'being present', which characterizes participation in the redemptive event of religious ritual and the preaching of the Word, also holds for our experience of art: 'the ontological mode of aesthetic being is marked by parousia, absolute presence'.[25] The reference to the preaching of the Word points to the marriage of philosophy and theology as the source of Gadamer's historical hermeneutics: 'When the Greek idea of logic is penetrated by Christian theology, something new is born: the medium of language, in which the mediation of the incarnation event achieves its full truth.'[26] The paradox of original repetition returns here as the paradox of Gadamer's recovery of tradition: historical hermeneutics, rooted in the historicity of the event and truth of incarnation, is not only anti-historical, it is *essentially* ahistorical.

In other words, there is no place for historical discontinuity, for the historical rupture of modern historical, i.e. anti-traditional, consciousness. Historicity is Heidegger's answer to and negation of modern historicism. Aesthetic non-differentiation is Gadamer's answer to and negation of modern aesthetics. Familiar distinctions such as that between formalism and realism lose their purchase in Gadamer's perspective. A realism which reduces the world to the visible, as in French Impressionism, is itself part of a history of progress in which mimesis is reduced to technical problems of representation. Realism becomes an aspect of the inherent formalism of modern art, which can only pose the question of the truth of art, of 'the truth in painting' (Derrida),[27] self-referentially in the form of an interminable self-interrogation, whose vanishing point becomes that of modernism itself: 'La littérature va vers elle-même, vers son essence qui est la disparition.'[28] Maurice Blanchot's formulation encapsulates the modernist paradox of the coincidence of all and nothing, of self-creation and self-annihilation in the absolute work of art (cf. Malevich's paintings of Nothing or the absolute, self-cancelling il/logic informing the novels of Thomas Bernhard). Such a mysticism of form is defined by the self-reflexive knowledge of the *limits* of form, that is to say, *limits of the aesthetic* as such. When Lukács speaks of irony as the mysticism of a godforsaken age, he means the irony that contains the negative truth of form and conveys the negative theology of the aesthetic. The art that is nothing but art remains true to its essence by turning back upon itself in endless self-reflexion. Kafka's parable 'Before the Law' is perhaps the paradigmatic text of the (self-)defining limits of literary form.

The *mise-en-abîme* of the work of art, integral to romantic irony's interplay of mysticism and sovereignty (a sovereignty which belongs to the work rather than the subjectivity of the artist as Hegel and Kierkegaard too hastily concluded[29]), must be distinguished from the *mise-en-abîme* of the romantic sublime. A terminological clarification is called for here: despite its name, romantic irony always relates to the self-reflexion of autonomous art, i.e. to the dialectic of art and enlightenment, whose terminus Arthur Danto for instance sees in the philosophical disenfranchisement of art effected by Conceptual Art.[30] The sublime in modernism by contrast is always romantic in that it relates to the other side of the limits of form. It poses the question not of the truth of the aesthetic but of the truth of being from which the romantic work of art draws its being. At stake is not the mysticism of form and the infinite play of its sovereign possibilities but the infinite mystery of being, which aesthetic form necessarily conceals rather than reveals.

Where religion, philosophy, enlightenment strive to cover over the abyssal ground, art is called upon to shatter the closure of individuation, to rend the veil of Maya and uncover the originary chaos of being. With Artaud for instance it means life, 'that fragile, fluctuating centre which forms never reach': 'And if there is still one hellish, truly accursed thing in our time, it is our artistic dallying with forms, instead of being like victims burnt at the stake, signalling through the flames.'[31] As fundamental as this distinction is for the opposed aesthetics of modernism, the dividing line is nevertheless often difficult to draw. To take the apparently simple case of abstract painting: if Mondrian, or more recently Sol LeWitt, breathe the spirit of rationalism, 'the pursuit of intelligibility by mathematical means',[32] then Wassily Kandinsky and Jackson Pollock are masters of the media of colour and texture, while Mark Rothko or Barnett Newman have been persuasively claimed for the northern tradition of the romantic sublime since Caspar David Friedrich.[33] At the limit abstract painting may point to pattern creation, to the purely self-referential – 'What you see is what you see' – or to pure self-transcendence.

The romantic line of aesthetic modernism – to generalize – is thus characterized by an overt or covert ambivalence towards the principle of individuation, in relation both to the subject and to aesthetic form. The dynamic of romantic art runs directly counter to the *telos* of purification and abstraction. It seeks to renew and recharge itself by tapping the wellsprings of creativity, by breaking down the limits of expression in order to break out of the prison house of individuation. Death as the logic of passion – the inescapable theme of nineteenth-century opera – functions as the chiffre of the sacrifice of individuation, which opens the way to the momentary cancellation of the subject-object split in the romantic sublime – the very antithesis of the Kantian moral sublime. Post-Kantian aesthetics accordingly conceives of the sublime as chaos (Nietzsche's *deus sive chaos*), and as the magmatic ground of creativity. Hence the opposed imaginaries of creation running through the discourse of aesthetic modernism set vitalist ideas of spontaneity and self-expression against the sovereign rationality of aesthetic technology.

Schopenhauer's identification of music with the Will behind the phenomenal realm of subjective representation in space and time elevated music to the romantic art par excellence. Adorno's assumption that the 'blind' development of the productive forces of music since Beethoven harboured within itself the idea of the totally rationalized work, finally realized in the twelve-tone system of composition, simply takes for granted the dialectic of romantic expressivism unfolded by this 'blind' development. The progressive chromatic dissolution of tonality in the course of the nineteenth century was driven by the quest for ever more intense and overpowering means of expression, which reached its climax and limit in the first two decades of the twentieth century in such major works as Strauss's *Elektra* and *Salome*, Mahler's symphonies, Schoenberg's *Gurrelieder*, Scriabin's *Poème de l'ecstase* or Stravinsky's *Rite of Spring* and Bartók's *Miraculous Mandarin*.

This striving for total effect, for ecstatic experience, is of a piece with the collective intoxication that greeted the outbreak of war in 1914. Did not the war appear to transcend or at least suspend the reality principle of bourgeois order? Did not the war promise the breakthrough to a true reality? This is the Dionysian dynamic which infects the romantic versions of aesthetic utopia: the dream of the return of the *Gesamtkunstwerk* becomes caught up in a dialectic that transforms the higher reality of the total work of art into the surrender to collective experience. Thus Gottfried Benn in his radio talk 'The New State and the Intellectuals' (1933) pours scorn on the inability of enlightenment intellectuals to perceive the greater anthropological profundity of the Nazi Revolution's turn to the mythical collective, inspired by the great feeling for the sacrifice and loss of the self in the immanent totality of state and race.[34] But whether the goal is the cultural revolution of the avant-garde or cultural re-volution through the *Gesamtkunstwerk*, both are directed to overcoming the *differentia specifica* of modern art, and thus point – beyond their projections of an inner *telos* – to modernism's external ends in totalitarianism and the culture industry.

To recapitulate: aesthetic modernism must be grasped in terms of its divided unity, its dual genealogy and lineage in the enlightenment and in romanticism. We can speak here of counter-historicisms and counter-imaginaries. These are defined by contrary conceptions of the emancipation of art. In the narratives of art's progression towards its own essence, the drive to rationalization of the material goes together with the scientific spirit of experimental inquiry, invention and innovation. Teleology unfolds in the space opened by the freedom of (utopian) possibility. But where progress is equated with necessity, the coercion of technical form contracts into an iron cage of its own making, and modernism falls victim to the dialectic of enlightenment – a verdict generalized in postmodernist critiques, even though postmodernists do not share romantic modernism's dreams of redemption from the abstract freedom of autonomy through reconnection with the creative forces of nature, history and the psyche.

Formalist theories of art find it particularly hard to accommodate socially or politically engaged art (but also what has been aptly called the communicative rationality of realism with its shared world of meaning and values[35]). This is hardly surprising, given that the autonomy of art – if it is to have any meaning – can only mean a freedom of self-determination, independent of the now alien claims of religion and politics and the interests of the marketplace. And if autonomous art often compromises itself, such factual heteronomy only serves to reinforce the regulative idea of autonomy. Freedom of religious belief, freedom of political speech and freedom of artistic expression express three distinct but mutually supporting doctrines of autonomy, which signify the complete redefinition and recasting of the relations between religion, politics and art in the modern world. The mainstream narratives of modernism ratify this division of labour between the separate spheres of functionally differentiated society. Art now appears as a singular universal which exercises its retrospective reach through histories of art (painting, sculpture, architecture, music, poetry, drama), which effect the same decontextualization as the museum, thereby serving to elide (in the name of Art) the fundamental differences between the function and status of the arts in premodern and modern societies. This homogenizing effect is itself an index of the fundamental redefinition of the relations between art, religion and politics since the eighteenth century.

Nevertheless, the retrospective extrapolation and progressive confirmation of aesthetic differentiation present only half the story, whose other half is characterized by a trans-aesthetic attitude to the emancipation of art and all that it implies in terms of the severance of ties between art, religion and society. We should add however that the outcome is inherently contradictory. The revolt against autonomous art within the sphere of autonomous art betrays the double bind of romantic historicism: the idea of an organic solidarity of art and society, art and religion – like the idea of myth or community – is necessarily a post-enlightenment, in other words, a posthumous projection, which both illustrates and exemplifies the simultaneous return and retreat of the origin as the *fata morgana* of romanticism. Romantic protest only serves to endorse, it would seem, the irreversible process and progress of the differentiation of art, were it not for the fact that art came to represent and embody the unanimous utopia of the whole epoch of modernism. This unanimous utopia, born of the marriage of Art and History (the utopian or redemptive philosophies of history from the French Revolution to the Russian, Italian and German Revolutions) had at least one feature common to the diversity of its articulations: the image of aesthetic totality as the concrete promise of a coming society healed of its divisions. If the split between enlightenment and romantic conceptions of art bears witness to the *inner aesthetic* dimension of the self-contestation of autonomous art, the aesthetic utopias of modernism bear witness in turn to the *trans-aesthetic* dimension of this self-contestation: the dream of overcoming the modern separation of art, religion and politics delineates the utopian horizon and vanishing point of aesthetic modernism. And here the inner aesthetic split in modernism finds (in accordance with the historicist matrix of modernism) its twofold utopian projection in the idea of the avant-garde and in the idea of the *Gesamtkunstwerk*. It is precisely on the first threshold of aesthetic modernism that the first manifesto of the avant-garde – Schiller's *Letters on the Aesthetic Education of Man* – and the first manifesto of the *Gesamtkunstwerk* – the vision of the sublation of the 'mechanical state' through the highest idea of Beauty in *The Oldest System Program of German Idealism* – appear.

The theory and practice of the twentieth-century avant-garde movements from the first manifesto of Futurism (1909) to the last manifesto of Surrealism (1939) have been so exhaustively documented and analysed, by comparison with the idea of the *Gesamtkunstwerk*, that it is sufficient to confine discussion to some brief observations on the avant-garde and the end of modernism. The so-called historical avant-gardes, centred around the First World War, take on a new revolutionary quality in the face of the European crisis. The Great War marks the watershed between the old liberal bourgeois order and a new world to be constructed from its ruins. The pathos, utopianism and theoretical terrorism of the innumerable avant-garde manifestos of these years derive from the apocalyptic atmosphere of destruction and renewal, nihilism and voluntarism called forth by the spectacle of the suicide of European civilization. We need look no further to explain the radical will to make it new, to blow up the museum of dead tradition, and reconnect art and life. From Futurism to Dada, from Constructivism to Surrealism the avant-garde declares itself the exterminating angel of bourgeois art (and bourgeois society). At the same time however, these revolutionary gestures recall the revolutionary origins of utopian modernism: the enlightenment's radical critique of institutions and the terror of the French Revolution present the two sides of the rational reconstruction of society. The revolutionary ferment that accompanies the origins and end of the epoch of aesthetic modernism underscores the continuity of an enlightenment lineage across the aesthetic utopias of the nineteenth century.

Where the romantic utopias tend to assimilate the disenchanted world to a redemptive aesthetics, the avant-garde utopia typically seeks to assimilate the aesthetic (the differentiated sphere of art) to the utopian spirit of modernism. (We can think here of the avant-garde role allotted to artists in the reconstruction of society by Comte.) The avant-garde radicalism that negates the institution of art is not so very different however from the aesthetic radicalism that informs the drive for purification and abstraction. The inner aesthetic *telos* of the one is not at all incompatible with the social goals of the other, since both manifest a comparable utopian will to realize the essence of modernism. A commentator has described the idea of technologically progressive construction as a 'mythology of the modern, in which ideas of technological change and social liberation were interwoven with a belief in the power of geometric form, and in which a geometric, abstract art was part of a Utopian project'.[36] Fascination with machines and machine-like structures drove the transformation of ethico-geometry into techno-geometry. The avant-garde, in breaking with the concept of the work in autonomous art, posed in the most radical fashion the question of a new relation between technology and artistic production. Sedlmayr, however, stresses the continuity that transforms the techno-geometric spirit of abstraction in modernism into the triumph of the technological imagination in the avant-garde movements. Peter Bürger makes the avant-garde revolt against the institution of autonomous art central to his teleological theory of modernism and the avant-garde. Both perspectives are equally important for interpreting the ends of modernism.

The triumph of the technological imagination – along with its corollary: the negation of the modern hermeneutical imagination of tradition, enshrined in the museum – can hardly be separated from the unleashing of technology on the battlefields of the Great War. The new man, born of the mass slaughter, will be Ernst Jünger's Worker, anticipated in Futurism's dream of mechanical man, created from flesh and metal, as the symbol of the mobilization of technology, industry and the masses in warfare. The death of the bourgeois individual and bourgeois art announced mass society and the mass aesthetics of the age of mechanical reproduction. The competing totalitarian versions of mass culture revealed *pace* Benjamin the identity of politicized aesthetics and aestheticized politics.[37] They conceived and presented themselves as the negation and sublation of decadent bourgeois art thanks to the nihilistic dynamic that made them both the inheritors and liquidators of the avant-garde movements. For its part the capitalist version of mass culture presupposed and continued the avant-garde's demolition of the old cultural hierarchies.

Of comparable importance for the inner aesthetic *telos* and for the end of modernism was the radical self-critique of art undertaken by the avant-garde. If pure abstraction amounts to one ultimate possibility of modern art, Duchamp's readymades possess an equal significance, as Arthur Danto has insisted: the moment when the work of art becomes identical with its conceptual sublation, thereby ratifying Hegel's philosophical completion of the history of art. It is a moment comprehensible only within and against the matrix of teleological historicism. The vanishing point of Duchamp's readymades is to be sought, however, less in their (endlessly redundant) elucidation in Conceptual Art than in the overt cynicism of Pop Art: the mutation of the work of art into a commodity in the age of mechanical reproduction. The eternal return of the new in the culture industry daily proclaims the permanence of the avant-garde's dream of cultural revolution.

The paradoxes of modernism as it is usually conceived are paradoxes of progress. The modernism, which appeals to innovation, is tied to the self-consuming character of the new. It is connected to an avant-gardism that draws legitimation from its vision of creative destruction and reconstruction, and is tied to the ever-receding horizon of a future that failed. The history of modernism, written as a history of aesthetic progress and its (trans-)aesthetic *telos*, registers but does not recognize the other aesthetic lineage of modernism: the romantic critique of progress, which embeds the romantic idea of the work of art – reconnection with the mystery of being – in a counter-narrative of Art and History. This, the other founding narrative of aesthetic modernism, calls up the power of origin to redeem the contradictions of emancipated society. It is, however, the historical consciousness of the loss of the origin which governs and defines the eschatological structure of this historicism, whether we speak of the death of God and the coming god, of the loss of the organic community of the past and its recovery, or the loss of the total work of art and its redemptive revival. The romantic response to the revolutionary break of the Enlightenment and the French Revolution is not only nostalgic, it is also necessarily a product of reflexion: the idea of the naive is a sentimental invention. Hence the paradoxes of romantic historicism and the contradiction of its aesthetic utopia: the ontological truth of the work of art beyond the confines of the aesthetic (Wagner/Nietzsche I) is shadowed by the historical knowledge that art (the would-be total work of art) can offer no more than aesthetic illusion (Wagner/Nietzsche II). *The Birth of Tragedy* is angrily revoked in *The Case of Wagner*.

The modernist attempts to revive and revitalize the *Gesamtkunstwerk*, whose harmonious totality is to be the pledge of communal unity, appear in retrospect tainted by the ambivalence of aesthetic illusion revealed in the theatricalization of art and politics. Perhaps it is the loss of this sense of ambivalence and tension that distinguishes postmodernist attitudes from modernist positions. The end of modernism in Guy Debord's 'society of the spectacle'[38] – a last echo of Surrealism – or in Baudrillard's omnipresence of simulation – a last echo of Adorno – mark the transition to a desublimation and generalization of the aesthetic, which has apparently deconstructed the difference between depth and surface, (ontological) truth and appearance. On the other hand we might choose to see in the ironic, second order citation of (modernist) illusion an aesthetic and cognitive surplus, which defines at the same time our distance from the aesthetic utopias of modernism. Hans Jürgen Syberberg invites us in his film of the opera to re-view Wagner's *Parsifal* through the dual dis/enchanting optic of *The Birth of Tragedy* and *The Case of Wagner*. The film opens and closes with the very image of the *Gesamtkunstwerk* as the world and its representation: a crystal ball (over which broods a sybilline figure) enclosing the Bayreuth Festival Theatre. Wagner's world theatre, itself the inheritor and ambitious simulacrum of Schelling's construction of the universe as a work of art in his *Philosophy of Art*, thus forms the central point of reference and departure not only for the prophets of the *Gesamtkunstwerk* (from aestheticism through to the film and film theory of Eisenstein), but also for the (self-)critique of the aesthetic as illusion.

Danto, as we have seen, proposes with Hegel a terminal history of the philosophical disenfranchisement of art. Marquard proposes with Schelling a counter-history of the disenfranchisement of philosophy, the turn, that is, to art as the authorization and empowering of (total) illusion projected into the idea of the total work of art.[39] Of particular interest is Marquard's typology of the *Gesamtkunstwerk*, since each of the four types he constructs involves the question of the (internal or external) ends of modernism. In other words, he ties the question of modernism to the empowering of illusion, i.e. to the tendency to extinguish the boundary between reality and illusion. His first two types set up an antithesis between the directly positive and the directly negative *Gesamtkunstwerk*. The positive type, modelled on the Wagnerian conception, envisages the union of the arts under the (one-sided) form of a theatrical alliance between the arts and religious cult. The negative type, modelled on the avant-garde, seeks to overcome the separation of the arts from reality through the (one-sided) alliance with political agitation. The assault by Futurism, Dada and Surrealism on tradition intended the destruction of the individual arts in the total anti-work of art. Marquard somewhat ingeniously assimilates the avant-garde's determination to destroy aesthetic illusion to the overall dynamic of the empowering of illusion. Nevertheless it can be argued that the failure of these two, antithetical sublations of art – the failure, that is, to transform art through the aesthetic transformation of society – makes totalitarianism and the culture industry the heirs to the idea of the avant-garde and of the *Gesamtkunstwerk*, and exposes autonomous art to the social (political or economic) transformation of the aesthetic in totalitarianism and in capitalism, e.g. Marquard's third and fourth types: the aestheticization of politics in the totalitarian state, and the justification of the everyday world as an aesthetic phenomenon in liberal capitalist societies.

Unlike the theory and practice of the avant-garde movements, the *Gesamtkunstwerk* has attracted only sporadic attention. We do not have a history of its modernist manifestations as the basis for its theory, nor do we have, apart from the stimulating but somewhat apodictic typology of Odo Marquard, the outline of a theory that could provide an organizing perspective for its unwritten history. A few comments and some examples must suffice here. We can think of the Nazarenes, the Pre-Raphaelites and the Arts and Crafts movement as the 'avant-garde' of cultural re-volution against the whole direction of modern (art) history and at the same time as the precursors of Art Nouveau, whose importance as the last European movement inspired by the vision of a unifying style embracing all the arts has now, a century later, gained full recognition. One of the programmatic highpoints of the movement was the 14th Exhibition of the Viennese Secession, April to June 1902, dedicated under the artistic direction of Josef Hoffmann to the idea of the *Gesamtkunstwerk*. Designed as homage to Beethoven, the focal point of the exhibition was the figure of the composer sculpted by Max Klinger. Gustav Klimt's celebrated frieze, based on Wagner's interpretation of Beethoven's Ninth Symphony, leaves a gap, which opens onto a view of Klinger's figure, the gap which symbolizes the gulf between the real and the ideal worlds, the longing for happiness and its enemies in this world and the ideal world of fulfilment, which only art can bridge.

This collective homage to the redemptive powers of art belongs to the *art* religion rather than the art *religion* of modernism, which drives Mallarmé's and Scriabin's apocalyptic dreams (likewise indebted to Wagner) of the ultimate work of art, which would be artistic performance and liturgic rite in one.[40] Ultimate in the sense that the public reading of Mallarmé's *Livre* in a ritual lasting five days was to culminate in the abolition of phenomenal reality and the attainment of Nothingness, in the sense that Scriabin's *Mysterium*, to be enacted over seven days in a temple of his own design in the Himalayas, was to find its cosmic conclusion in the 'final chord of our race', powerful enough to separate soul and matter. The two (uncompleted and uncompletable) projects are complementary. The one proposes the *Gesamtkunstwerk* of negative theology: the Book, described as 'play, symphony, ballet, song, poem, theatre, hymn, opera', is declared to be 'like God, necessary, present, inexistent'. The other proposes a total feast of the senses, an orgiastic transcendence of the principle of individuation, achieved through the union of all the arts, which will reveal the identity of the human and the divine. More recently, we have Karl Stockhausen's cycle entitled *Licht*, conceived on a comparable cosmic scale as the union of the spheres of music, light and space in a sacred rite which re-presents over seven days the genesis of the world from inorganic darkness to the highest intensity of sound and light.

Susan Sontag has pointed to the close parallels between Artaud's *Theatre and its Double* and Nietzsche's *Birth of Tragedy*.[41] Both reassert the Dionysian cruelty of a theatre of presence against the subversion and denial of tragic experience by Socratic intellectualism and the primacy of the spoken word. Both are fascinated by the idea of the total work of art (Artaud speaks of a total spectacle) as a means of healing a sick society. The healing reunion of body and spirit calls for a reunion of theatre and rite, that is to say, in Gadamer's terms: the act of participation which continues the great play of tradition and renews the non-differentiated aesthetic of pre-secular society. Nietzsche's model is the Dionysian cult of Athenian drama, Artaud's model is the religious theatre of South East Asian (Cambodian and Balinese) civilization. In his *Second Manifesto for a Theatre of Cruelty* (1933) Artaud advances the idea of a metaphysical theatre, based on the oldest mythical and religious texts, which will address the total human being through a language of images, gestures, signs and magic incantations in order to create an atmosphere of hypnotic suggestion (1933!), aimed at cancelling the separation of stage and spectator, theatre and life.

The desire to recover the magic power of ritual and the sacred dimensions of art makes the theatre the primary medium of the modernist *Gesamtkunstwerk* (reflected in the great epoch of the building of opera houses, with Semper's Dresden Opera as the model, between 1850 and 1900). No longer subordinated to the architectural synthesis of the arts in the Renaissance and the Baroque, the theatre became the site of an imaginary fusion of the Dionysian and the Apolline, the site, that is, of the confusion of metaphysical reality and illusion. Nietzsche's late polemic against the former idol Wagner rests on equating the cultural decadence of the age with the triumph of the theatre. The leitmotif governing the argument of *The Case of Wagner* – 'That the theatre not become master over the arts' – declares that in a theatrical age the *Gesamtkunstwerk* is impossible, or rather, possible only as theatrical illusion, presided over by the 'Cagliostro of modernity', who satisfies the longing of the masses for the overwhelming experience of greatness, the sublime and the gigantic. With Wagner the actor has arrived in music – and politics – and effect has become everything.[42] Historical hindsight allows us to extrapolate: Wagner anticipates both the Third Reich and Hollywood, and to add: the double dialectic of romanticism evident here derives from the original contradiction of romanticism.

Adorno in his Wagner essay traces the line leading from the new mythology to Hollywood:

> Completed profanity would like to produce out of itself a sacral sphere.... No longer does the artwork follow its Hegelian definition as the sensuous appearance of the idea, rather the sensuous is arranged in order to appear as if it were capable of the idea: the transition of the opera to the autonomous sovereignty of the artist is bound up with the origin of the culture industry. The young Nietzsche mistook the artwork of the future: it is the event of the birth of the film from the spirit of music.[43]

One must not overlook the irony here: Nietzsche's and Adorno's critique of Wagner repeats Wagner's own attack on the operatic practice of the time, notably the Paris Opera: the triumph of 'industrial production' in Berlioz's use of the orchestra; the exploitation of 'mechanical illusion' in Meyerbeer's operas which leaves nothing to the imagination; the definition of sensation as 'effect without cause'; the hatred of 'Jewish' capital and the 'Jewish' culture industry.[44] If Hollywood represents the end of the line, it is important to distinguish between the dual genealogy of its 'dream factory': the power of 'mechanical illusion' should not be reduced to an epiphenomenon of capitalist 'industrial production'. Rather, it is the continuity of the critique of theatrical illusion that deserves attention, since it manifests the bad conscience of the longing for the total work of art. We must ask ourselves in retrospect whether this longing for totality – at odds with the mainstream modernist narratives of the demythologization of art – was not the primary motivating force which made art the unanimous utopia of modernity throughout the whole modernist epoch and in the speculative theory of art from Schelling and Novalis to Heidegger. What is Adorno's own rescuing critique of Schein – the rescue of the illusion of rescue through aesthetic illusion[45] – other than a last tribute to the redemptive dream of aesthetic modernism?

17   Utopia in the New World

The Wagnerian total work of art was the synthesis of all of the currents – progressive and reactionary – of modernity. Wagnerianism plundered mythological sources at the same time as it pushed forward the technical means of musical production and also propagated a new myth of the artist as the master of diverse artistic genres (drama, music, dance, poetry) and technological media. It was in the New World – in Hollywood – that the Wagnerian total work of art found its twentieth-century apotheosis. Hollywood did exactly what Wagner did. It ceaselessly retold fairy stories and myths and fables, and did so by continually refining the most up-to-date means of technical production, and it did so under the direction of great maestros (directors, producers and studio bosses). Here was a meta-modernism – myth and technology, romanticism and enlightenment, in a seamless conjunction. It was a bridging of modernity's divided unity.

What is particularly telling is that twentieth-century Wagnerianism not only found its artistic fulfilment in the New World but that it did so more particularly in Los Angeles under the aegis of an émigré (Central European) community in exile in the 1930s and 1940s. In the city of angels, the power of the American blend of myth and technology – evident from the days of the Pilgrims – proved fertile ground for Europeans schooled in the tracks of the Wagnerian imagination. America already had its *sui generis* romantic myth (the antinomian frontier) and its own enlightened obsession with technology (the Benjamin Franklin syndrome). On this terrain, Europeans – with their own advanced techniques and their vast cultural patrimony – could bring to fruition a mytho-technological fusion that hitherto was only latent in the American environment. The Europeans had fled home, and were strangers in an unfamiliar environment. They were cast into a West Coast America that was sometimes a source of great perplexity for them. Yet, in very short order, they adapted to this strange world. They assimilated by participating in the collective labour of a New Wagnerianism – the art of Hollywood film-making.

The New Wagnerianism was a neat synthesis of advanced aesthetic technology and romantic mythology. The one thing that this synthesis aggressively repelled was any sense of the architectonic. The culture of Los Angeles instinctively excluded works of strong plastic or architectonic character. One important exception to this rule was the music of Stravinsky. Stravinsky thrived in Los Angeles in part because he was not dependent on the studio system, and in part because music of any kind could be adapted to the dominant romantic paradigm of Hollywood. Everything was plundered for soundtracks, and subordinated to a larger Wagnerian musico-dramatic, techno-mythic multimedia fantasia. The other important exception to the exclusion of plastic mentalities was Orson Welles. But then Welles only survived as a living caricature of the myth of the 'great director'. The long tracking shot-cum-opening sequence of Welles's *Touch of Evil* (1958) is a superlative model of filmic architectonics. Welles's portrayal of architectonic depth is perhaps matched only by the work of British director Carol Reed in *The Third Man* (1949), a master interpretation of the city as the plastic embodiment of emotional intelligence.[1]

But the exception is not the rule, and the architectonic *is* the exception in Los Angeles. There is at least a small irony in this fact. After all, Los Angeles had begun its history as a Franciscan Spanish settlement, with all that implied. Spanish colonization, whatever else it may have been, was emphatically 'civilizing', which meant that its primary medium was the plastic construction of the city. The Spanish colonized by building urban settlements. While modest in size, Hispanic Los Angeles, like other Spanish settlements on the coastal strip between San Francisco and San Diego, was marked by the indubitable plastic quality of the Latin civitas. After California passed into the hands of the United States, this plastic sense was immediately romanticized, in the nineteenth-century 'Mission' literature and aesthetic.

Thus it came about that Los Angeles, the incubator of Hollywood, was a city that, through the twentieth century, has been almost bereft of 'plastic beauty'. Exceptions to this traded on their romantic nature. We see this in Abbot Kinney's (1905) attempt to recreate Venice in Los Angeles or A.M. Parsons's (1903) development of Naples (both on the Angelean coast). But, even if they were conceived in a spirit of romantic revivalism, both of these projects nonetheless betray a desire – or perhaps the nostalgia – for architectonic world making. Wherever this desire manifested itself in Southern California, it seemed always however to be over-determined by the romantic glance backwards – the *religio* – towards the European past. The tendency was for the fantasy of the Mediterranean or Hispanic city to over-determine the formative impulse of the plastic creator. Even so, in the predominately two-dimensional Los Angeles, where the intersection of lines and planes came to dominate the iconography of the city, such neo-romantic projects stand out as moments of interesting civic development. They appear as memories of 'cities of depth', intimations of cities of circulating reason – portal cities that never quite were. 'Venice' and 'Naples' were the failed utopias of coastal Los Angeles that eventually gave way to the Wagnerian stage fantasies of the Hollywood studio, the façade cities of romantic illusion of the film lots, and the phantasmagoria of Disneyland.[2]

The first Hollywood film was made in 1910. But the fantasies that drive Hollywood have their roots in a mentality that had already transformed the visual appearance and physical habitus of Los Angeles – well before the turn of the twentieth century. This fantasy complex found a willing partner in architectural movements, and its visual expression in the Queen Anne style of the 1880s. It culminated in the Craftsman-Bungalow movement of the 1910s. The former's medley of towers, turrets and gables evoked a heroic romantic past – an ideal world of fulfilment, totality and organic community – of a kind depicted in the versifying of William Morris. The latter evoked an earthier rustic romanticism typical of Morris's craft socialism.

The romantic spirit also over-determined the more substantial Hispanic-Mediterranean forms (Mission, Churrigueresque [Spanish Baroque], Moorish, Spanish Colonial) that formed much of the palette of nineteenth-century Californian architecture. Thus, turn of the century Los Angeles was a 'sound stage' in the making well before the Hollywood studio. Mid-westerners who settled the city were drawn to the mythical romance of Mission, Spanish Colonial, Gothic, Elizabethan and other potent mythemes. In these romances – all later Hollywood staples – history became naturalized, a still point of mock heroism or mysterious picturesqueness in the midst of the perpetual mobility of modern life. The moving picture, just like Angelean architecture, offered an 'escape' into nature. This was not the 'second nature' of quotidian society but the nature of artful romance. This was an aesthetic nature in which adventure, exoticism, love and heroism melded into an ersatz 'ethical totality' – an 'original, timeless (mythical) moment' in which history was frozen into a 'beautiful illusory nature'. This was a nature in which love or nobility or daring conquered all. Hollywood – like those other stage builders, the architectural stylists – was the master of numerous mythemes (Greek, Roman, medieval, Elizabethan, swashbuckling, Napoleonic, Revolutionary, Counter-Revolutionary, etc). Each of these mythemes, in their distinctive way, satisfied the romantic longing for a 'lost totality' of deed and feeling, intellect and sense.

This historicism confronted its nemesis in twentieth-century modernism. The explicit intention of the Modern Movement in literature and architecture was to put an end to the retrospective glancing of historicism. In architecture, this meant 'streamlining' design and emphasizing the formal qualities of geometry. In literature, the qualities of 'syntactical experimentation' or else 'unadorned prose' were stressed. Whether it pushed in the direction of functional simplicity or experimental difficulty, the Modern Movement sought a shift from romance to innovation. Experimentalism and innovation in the aesthetic means of production became enlightenment modernism's sine qua non. Innovation, though, tended to consume itself. Great modernism came not from experimentalism *per se*, but innovation modulated by form. The greatest works of modernism – say Cézanne, or Cubism or Constructivism in painting – had strongly Platonic qualities. Such qualities are a counterpoint necessary to produce any successful modern movement.

Many modern movements have been failures. Enlightenment persistently poses the question of how change and progress can be ordered? If it is not ordered, it becomes self-devouring. Thus, a strong Platonic sense of form is necessary for any successful modernity. Form provides an intimation of timelessness in time – 'a new order of the ages'. Kitsch modernisms like Art Nouveau offered neither the hard beauty nor the tough-minded natural order of timelessness in time. Rather, they were a sentimental, even romanticized, representation of the same. They turned timelessness in time into a memorial search for a lost totality.

While the International Movement of Mies van der Rohe, Le Corbusier, and the Bauhaus school had the will to resist such instant nostalgia, they were successful in doing so often only by mythologizing their own (European) origins. Progress requires an 'absolute' (natural) moment in order not to be buried under the weight of its own paradoxes. In high modernism, this nature was commonly thought of as the heroic origins of the modern – a self-referential myth. Aesthetic progress was anchored in the romantic mythology of the artist-genius who is ignored by society, but who struggles heroically against philistinism, is reluctantly recognized and eventually becomes a cultural giant. This mytheme played very well in an America that had offered sanctuary to European artists from Nazism.

But it would not be true to say that the International Movement found legitimacy only in the romantic myth of neglected cultural heroes and triumphant giants. It pivoted its legitimacy as much on its command of Platonic architectonic qualities as on hero worship. At its greatest, its mastery of depth and volume – composed out of both traditional and cubist planes, Euclidian and post-Euclidian geometries – was extraordinary. However, in replicating this in the New World – in the moment when twentieth-century modernism became an American movement – a strange bifurcation happened. The Platonism of Mies was amplified by the context of Chicago and New York. In contrast, in Los Angeles, the architectonic character of Loos-type modernism dissipated precipitously.

In the shift from Vienna to Los Angeles, the architectonic imaginary of Adolf Loos and Ludwig Wittgenstein was replaced by a graphical interface, i.e. thick-recession was replaced with thin-surface. In this was implicated the Los Angelean vision of the modern that was part-romantic, part-enlightenment, part-myth and part-technology. It is true that Mies van der Rohe already evangelized the shift from the thick masonry wall to the curtain-like glass wall in Berlin in the 1920s. What the Angeleans did was to exploit the glasshouse for the 'romantic view', the panoramic fantasy that had defined the late romantic vision of Karl Friedrich Schinkel. The glass wall broke down the barrier between the future and nature. The

Angelean was placed in the glasshouse looking out at the hills or the valley, or most potently of all – gazing at the Angelean plain that was overlain by the abstract plane-diagram of the city. What the Angeleans gazed at was a graphical nature ('the nature of the future'), an illusory nature with its lines flickering with daytime energy or night-time illumination. This was the nature of a flat-bed society of spectacle, its denizens mesmerized by endless pulsating loops of mobility, the frozen-motion of the end of history, the eternal city of angels.

Los Angeles of the twentieth century possessed none of the architectonic depth of a city like New York or Chicago. The influx of European émigrés made no difference at all to this, indeed it seems to have consolidated the illusory surface-character of the city. Architecturally, what Angeleans learnt from European modernism was not about the volumetric depth of Adolf Loos's 'spatial plan' but the two-dimensionality of the glass wall. Five decades after the generation of the exiles, Los Angeles's own 'Parthenon', the Getty Museum (1997) – designed by Richard Meier (b. 1934) – with its juxtaposition of plane against plane is perfectly emblematic of this depthless city. Los Angeles embodied the American myth (the myth of the lawless frontier) and technological obsession (the obsession with the automobile) to the point where the protagonist of plastic beauty and plastic power had no hope. The city was defined not by coastal portals (with their deep entry points of circulation) but by the plane geometries of its central flatland, and by the ecstatic high-points of its hills. The rule of 'the plane' is obvious even in the work of Loos's student, Richard Neutra, who, after early Angelean volumetric masterpieces like Heath House (1929), descended into work dominated by the juxtaposition of plane surfaces.

As an alternative to the classical collective work of creation of the city – typified by immigrant tenements in New York City or by the high art apartment building of Mies in Chicago – the modern Wagnerian myth propelled a different kind of collective work of creation, viz. the total work of art on which hundreds of artists might labour, controlled by the will of the Great Director. Where other European émigrés to the New World grappled with the issues of how a city of light and shadow might be created, the artists and technicians who flocked to Los Angeles made their Faustian bargain – the chance to participate in the Wagnerian total work of art in exchange for forgetting about such foolishness. Film noir was the collective conscience of those émigrés uneasy with the Wagnerian pact. Noir at least addressed the nature of the American city. But it also implied that the *phusis* of that city was terminally corrupted. It was nature as putrefaction.[3]

The New Wagnerianism of the Hollywood film industry was a prototype of what, in postwar America, was to become a powerful synthesis of romanticism and enlightenment. This synthesis was to solidify as a new ideational form – signalling the end of old Europe's 'dialectic of romanticism and enlightenment', and foreshadowing the appearance of a new kind of polarity in modernity.

Stimulated by the self-conscious intellectualism of the European exiles in

Los Angeles, and by the particular inclination of America (its instinct to blend technology and fantasy), the modern European ideologies of enlightenment and romanticism congealed into one common constellation in America – the Californian ideology. Its founding premise made the advancement of communicative-artistic technology the measure of enlightened progress. Communicative-artistic technologies were looked on as the obverse of industrial (or even craft) technologies. Their virtue was that they had a non-violent relation to external nature. Even if the film studio outwardly looked like a factory, aesthetic-communicative technology was not for the most part a controller of external nature, in contrast with paradigmatic industrial technologies like the steam engine or the assembly line. This also meant that aesthetic-communicative technologies did not undermine the second premise of the Californian ideology – the romantic idea of the reconciliation of humanity with external nature. Aesthetic-communicative technologies were 'soft' in contrast with the 'hard' technologies of the industrial era.

The leading intellectuals of the German exile community in Los Angeles – Adorno, Mann and Brecht – returned to Germany after the war (while Schoenberg died in California). But, even though they had departed, their ideas – especially those of Adorno – were kept very much to the forefront of American intellectual life due to the popularity of the work of their contemporary and fellow émigré, Herbert Marcuse, who chose to remain in America. Marcuse had been a student of Heidegger's and an associate of Adorno. He bridged the divided unity of modernism. From *Eros and Civilization* (1955) to *An Essay on Liberation* (1969), Marcuse stitched together a vision of a 'union of liberating art and liberating technology'[4] that owed the direction of its intellectual compass to a postwar America fascinated by West Coast utopias and the intellectual ballast of its ideas to the work of Adorno (and Heidegger). While Adorno is most often thought of as the definitive critic of the Californian 'culture industry', his measurement of progress, according to the most advanced art technologies and artistic forces of production (*Aesthetic Theory*), and his critique of the Enlightenment's mythologizing of the domination of external nature (*Dialectic of Enlightenment*) with the correlative repression of internal nature and construction of authoritarian personalities, are remarkably close in substance to the Californian ideology that took shape in the post-Second World War era. It is really only Adorno's relentless refusal of any concessions to nostalgic historicism that provides a dividing line between the full-fledged Californian ideology and Adorno's own aesthetic modernism.

After the 1940s, it took a full generation, and the rise of 'postmodernism', for a time-travelling historicism to gain intellectual respectability after being officially shunned during the High Modernist era (1920–60). By the end of the 1980s, the triptych of *a. art (communication) technology, b. reconciliation with nature, c. historicism (postmodernism)* had become not just California's but global society's most commanding ideology. One of the most successful local Californian interpretations of this was Charles Moore's Kresge College (1973) at the University of California at Santa Cruz. Moore's design merged the white flat planes of modernist enlightenment with the Californian wilderness and strong historicist reflections such as allusions to the medieval mixed-use street. Of the three components of the Californian ideology, historicism has been the quickest to fall in and out of focus according to cultural fashion. This is in part because any kind of 'revival' will only last for a limited time, while the 'cutting edge' of futurist technology (even of 'soft' information and art technologies) can be difficult to reconcile with the backward glance of historicism. Yet the power of the Californian ideology assuredly derives from its ability to fuse together romantic and enlightenment strains of European modernity.

In the less sunny regions of America, an alternative to the Californian ideology took shape in the 1940s and 1950s. This alternative constellation, the 'Chicago ideology', was concerned with long durational 'continuities', architectonic 'constructions', and the natural law of 'constitutionalism'. While it is true that New York City played a key role in the genesis of this counter-paradigm, the epochal Chicago constellation – of Mies van der Rohe at the Illinois Institute of Technology, and Hannah Arendt and Leo Strauss at the University of Chicago – nonetheless was decisive in the formation of what has proved to be the most formidable intellectual counter to the Californian ideology. All three – Mies, Arendt, Strauss – having adopted America as their home-in-exile sought to step out from the shadow of German romanticism and historicism – personified by Schinkel in Mies's case; and by Heidegger in Arendt's and Strauss's case. It cannot be said that any of the three entirely escaped the impress of the German ideology, but the toughness of mind displayed in each case held that influence at least at arm's length.

All three shared a fascination with 'the city', and a sense that the *civitas* provided a path beyond the banality of enlightened (*Bauhaus*) functionalism and beyond the nostalgic mythology of romanticism and historicism. At a quick glance, Mies looks like an unqualified enlightenment modernist but the classical nature of his American-period architectural forms belies this. At a similarly quick glance, Arendt and Strauss could be confused with romantic devotees of antiquity but what fundamentally interests them is not just the polis as an alternative to the ills of modernity but as a model for shaping modern life, not least American republican modernity. The Chicago constellation treats 'the city' as a trans-historical entity, an embodiment of *phusis* (the nature of the cosmos, the natural order of the *res publica*), and a place where human beings can give shape to the anonymous 'collective work' of city-making in contrast to the 'total work of art' of the Californian ideology.

It is too soon to judge which of these ideologies in the long run will have the greater influence over the American 'cosmos'. The trio of aesthetic-communicative technologies, romantic nature and historical mythology built into the Californian ideology without a doubt is enormously attractive. Together they inflame and seduce the imagination. On the other hand, the republican frame of American life carries indelible traces of the *civitas*. Try as it might, the American psyche cannot altogether escape this imaginary signification. For all of its failures,[5] the collective rational imaginary of the *civitas* has stimulated the creation of enduring architectonic forms like those of New York City and Chicago. This civic *poietics* is captured brilliantly in Aldo Rossi's 1986 project sketches for the Miami University campus.[6] Rossi's proposal draws analogies with the Roman Pantheon and with Jefferson's University of Virginia, but does so without relying on historical revival or motif. The architect's design uses geometrical forms (cylinders, domes), shadow and light, and stereo-metrical analogies (the plinth 'acropolis', the 'Venetian' library situated on the water and the cluster of university buildings compacted together like a city), in the creation of a civic form that comprehends its own pre-history while being contemporary in conception and timeless in spirit, an achievement of 'a new order of the ages'.

'A new order of the ages' is first and foremost an aspiration of the American New World. With too few exceptions, European modernism understood the 'newness' of the future and the 'ages' of history, but not the bridge between them, the syntax of architectonic 'order'. In part because of this, European modernism ends once it comes to America. European modernism recasts itself on American soil. In doing so, 'the dialectic of modernity' as it is commonly understood (the *agon* of romanticism and enlightenment) comes to an end, and a new modernism, one with global implications – the California constellation – quietly, unannounced, begins to take its place. Modernism's twin protagonists (enlightenment and romanticism) combine in a common constellation – the Californian ideology – in which progress, nature and historical mythology fuse. In the same epochal moment, a second, countervailing constellation – formed out of the elements of the trans-historical, the world city and *phusis* – appears as well. Both constellations aspire to modernity; both draw on modernist currents. Both have world-historical ambitions. In their laps, the future lies.

18 Conclusion: Modernity's Modernisms

The organic life of a culture ends, according to Spengler, in the sterility and entropy of civilization. Spengler dated the decadence of the West to the end of the Napoleonic Wars. We have argued that the emergence of the cultural interpretation of history in the second half of the eighteenth century signals the crisis of the trans-historical conception of civilization. More is involved here than an exchange of terms. Spengler represents a poisonous flowering of the romantic embrace of the inner, native powers of cultural creativity, which pitted autarchic natural development against universal natural law, originality against the lifeless doctrine of imitation, and vitalism against the soulless materialism of the French Enlightenment. The appeal to an intrinsic source in human nature, the privileging of authentic individuality against foreign models, underpinned the assertion of (German) culture against (French) civilization. Behind this ideological divide, which Norbert Elias analyses in *The Civilizing Process*, lies the larger question that Elias and other cultural historians do not address: the civilizational rupture and collapse implicit in the sense of an irreversible break with the past.[1] This notion of rupture and irreversible break was central to the emerging historicist self-understanding of modernity.

This profound sense of discontinuity is crystallized by the radical caesura of the French Revolution – or rather by the self-understanding of the revolutionaries that revolution was a caesura. This marks the crisis of the trans-historical conception of civilization that previously linked past and present, ancients and moderns, and that embodied the ever-present possibility of renewing history by making the old new, but that was also able to moderate the dynamism of the fresh and innovative with the rationalism and urbane spirit of the classical. In this non-historicist conception, the adjective 'modern' had functioned – since late antiquity – as a temporal index tied to the ever-moving present of a temporal continuum. This civilizational continuum linked together past, present and future. To be modern was not to be cut off from the past by an irreversible break – whether construed heroically or tragically. To be modern was to accept and to think together the creativity of imitation, in the form of renaissances, and the rich continuity of civilization. It meant, above all, the affirmation of the essence of European civilization – its creative 'secondarity'.

From the secondarity of the Greeks in relation to the Myceneans and the Phoenicians, of the Romans in relation to the Greeks, and of medieval Europe in relation to the dual Roman legacy of universal Empire and universal Church, European identity was carried forward and periodically renewed through the medium of this classical consciousness of rational continuity. The long nineteenth century looks very short against the *longue durée* of European civilization. It was long enough, however, to complete an intoxicating but self-destructive path – humanity to nationality to bestiality – which the Austrian writer Franz Grillparzer already foresaw and feared in 1848.

The civilizational rupture is implicit in the historical discontinuity that gave birth to the warring twins of enlightened and romantic European modernism. The fact of this discontinuity is pivotal to our critique of modernism. The romantic quest for origins turned against the legacy of classical continuity and secondarity to draw its energy from the search for revivifying original forces that would sweep away a tired civilization and the empty materialism of progress. That Horkheimer and Adorno's dialectic of enlightenment and Heidegger's metaphysical genealogy of nihilism stand as ultimate documents of the self-cancelling narratives of modernism is due not least to their projection of the closure of modern historicism into a blind denunciation of the history of the West. Fatally infected by Nietzschean genealogy (and its search for origins), they turn the totalitarian conclusions of the long nineteenth century into an indictment of European civilization as a whole, dismissing and discarding in the process the very idea of civilization (a lethally 'secondary' concept in Heidegger's eyes).

Their blindness to the romantic roots of their generalization of cultural critique into a total critique of civilization is matched by their concealment of the romantic inspiration of their critique of modernity. They register the entwinement of the twin dialectics of modernism only in the form of an elusive glimpse of the redemptive transcendence of the fallen world. Nevertheless, it is precisely this entwinement of enlightenment and romanticism that points beyond modernism's rival ideological narratives of scientific progress and aesthetic regeneration and the closure of their utopian/dystopian horizons. It is Heidegger who discerns in the ambiguity of the essence of technology a saving power that can come only from a reunion of the divided realms of *technē*.[2] Heidegger's *new alliance between technology and art*,[3] which calls us to keep watch over 'all essential unfolding on this earth',[4] like Critical

Theory's esoteric doctrine of the resurrection of nature, adumbrates an ecological vision of a reconciliation of technology and nature that continues to resonate. If the critique of western logocentrism made Heidegger and Adorno godfathers of postmodernism, their intimations of a new alliance of technology and art, technology and nature, mediated by Marcuse, are integral links between European modernism and its Californian transformations.

Although in postmodern fashion Californian modernism shed any explicit commitment to a philosophy of history, it continues to invoke the eternal return of the newest. Even when this is surrounded by the stage settings of an aesthetic historicism, all it does is to reduce the past to an ever-changing period film that is a surrogate for the present. Where a classic (from Sophocles to Shakespeare to Brecht) is forever fresh in its interpretations, aestheticism – so deeply appealing to the imagination – is trapped by its own time. European modernism, whether predicated on the 'modern' or the anti-'modern', was tied to what Habermas calls its 'core aesthetic meaning',[5] just as that aesthetic meaning was tied to the historicism which transformed history after 1750 into the singular universal History. To the modernist epoch of History corresponded the modernist epoch of Art, similarly singularized, universalized and endowed with a *telos* after 1750. This matrix – constituted by the interplay of Art and History, and consecrated by the discourse of philosophy of history and philosophy of art – provides the frame to the aesthetic utopias of European modernism. Jean-Joseph Goux's reflections on the postmodern eclipse of art bring out particularly clearly both the historicist matrix and the 'core aesthetic meaning' of modernism.

Perhaps it has not been taken sufficiently into account just how important was the exceptional consensus that united all the thinkers of modernity around art. From Kant to Heidegger, passing through Schiller, Comte, Schopenhauer, Nietzsche – and at the same time, for diverse reasons, Hegel, Freud, Sartre, and Bataille – art was constantly glorified as a uniquely special activity. Source of truth, paradigm of creative human activity, ideal reconciliation of opposites, openness to the world and so on – the arguments might differ or might be opposed, but one constant remains: the affirmation of an ontological pre-eminence of art over all the other human activities. We must finally recognize: art has been the unanimous utopia of modernity. In it were placed the most noble of hopes, the most demanding and the most serious of expectations. As instrumental reason became more and more important to social life, art became more and more desirable. As God retreated from a world rendered prosaic and profane, the last refuge of the lost dimensions of salvation, meaning and ideals came to be sought in art. Whether turned towards radiant futures filled with dialectic reconciliations of opposites, or towards distant epochs of past glories, the incomparable redemptive power of poetry, music and painting promised it all.[6]

The eclipse of art and its 'incomparable redemptive power' is identical with the dead ends and the exhaustion of modernism's futurist and archaizing visions. The collapse of the grand narratives of European modernism has not broken, however, the hold of historicism, even if this hold is only negatively evident in postmodernism's 'post-historicism'. The question of 'what comes after modernism?' seems incapable of generating a new sense of the modern, that is, an alternative conception of modernity, history and time. Postmodernism in this sense remains another historicist modernism of modernity, just as much in need of the corrective of the classically modern and the regulative idea of civilization as Europe's antagonistic modernisms were. Our architectonic conception of modernism, as opposed to the aesthetic conception, thus remains as relevant as ever. It stands for a perennial sense of the modern and of a modernism no longer trapped in an imaginary of beginnings and ends or of the pre-modern and the post-modern. Such an imaginary an anti-historicist modernism regards with scepticism. In saying yes to secondarity, it says no to enlightenment fantasies of a radical break with the past, and no to romantic fantasies of an aboriginal past. In saying no to fantasy, it says yes to reason.

Notes

Introduction: Three Modernisms

1. To take a representative text, Jürgen Habermas in *The Philosophical Discourse of Modernity* (Cambridge, MA: MIT Press, 1987) discusses only German thinkers for the whole period of modernism from Hegel to Heidegger and Adorno.

2. Georges Gusdorf, *Du Néant à Dieu dans le savoir romantique* (Paris: Payot, 1983), p. 183. For Isaiah Berlin the roots of the Romantic Movement, as the 'greatest single shift in the consciousness of the West' in the modern period, lie in Germany, *The Roots of Romanticism* (London: Pimlico, 2000), pp. 1, 6.

3. Bruno Latour, *We Have Never Been Modern* (Cambridge, MA: Harvard University Press, 1993), pp. 32–3.

Part One: Introduction

1. Robert Legros, *L'idée de l'humanité. Introduction à la phénoménologie* (Paris: Grasset, 1990).

2. Legros, *L'idée de l'humanité*, p. 189.

3. In the following we summarize the salient features of Legros's description of romanticism, ibid., pp. 45–137.

4. See Paul Hazard, *European Thought in the Eighteenth Century*, trans. J. Lewis May (Harmondsworth: Penguin, 1965); Peter Gay, *The Enlightenment. An Interpretation*: Vol. I *The Rise of Modern Paganism*, Vol. II *The Science of Freedom* (New York: Knopf, 1966, 1969).

5. The contrast between the universal and the particular underlies Charles Taylor's distinction between acultural (enlightenment) and cultural (romantic) theories of modernity. See Taylor, 'Inwardness and the culture of modernity', in Axel Honneth et al. (eds), *Zwischenbetrachtungen. Im Prozess der Aufklärung. Jürgen Habermas zum 60. Geburtstag* (Frankfurt: Suhrkamp, 1989), pp. 601–23.

6. See for a comprehensive overview James Engell, *The Creative Imagination. From Enlightenment to Romanticism* (Cambridge, MA: Harvard University Press, 1981).

7. Adam Müller (1779–1829), *Elemente der Staatskunst* (Berlin: Haude und Spener, 1968). See Hans Reiss, *Political Thought of the German Romantics 1793–1815* (Oxford: Blackwell, 1955).

8. Friedrich Daniel Ernst Schleiermacher (1768–1834), *On Religion. Speeches to its Cultured Despisers,* ed. Richard Crouter (New York: Cambridge University Press, 1996). See also David Jasper (ed.), *The Interpretation of Belief. Coleridge, Schleiermacher, and Romanticism* (Basingstoke: Macmillan, 1986). Friedrich Wilhelm Joseph Schelling (1775–1854), *System of Transcendental Idealism* (1800), trans. Peter Heath, introduction Michael Vater (Charlottesville: University of Virginia Press, 1978). See Werner Marx, *The Philosophy of F. W. J. Schelling. History, System, and Freedom*, trans. Thomas Nenon (Bloomington: Indiana University Press, 1984).

9. Legros, *L'idée de l'humanité*, pp. 190–5. This insight Legros attributes to Tocqueville, for whom democracy as the sphere of public political life is alone capable of mediating between the closure of tradition and the abstract individualism of denaturalization.

10. See G. P. Gooch, *Germany and the French Revolution* (New York: Russell & Russell, 1966). A good account of German history during the 'long nineteenth century' is David Blackbourn, *History of Germany 1780–1918. The Long Nineteenth Century*, 2nd edn (Oxford: Blackwell, 2003).

11. See note 2 above.

12. The indispensable account remains Friedrich Meinecke, *Historicism. The Rise of a New Historical Outlook,* trans. J. E. Anderson, Foreword Isaiah Berlin (London: Routledge & Kegan Paul, 1972). More critical is Georg Iggers, *The German Conception of History. The National Tradition of Historical Thought from Herder to the Present* (Middletown, CT: Wesleyan University Press, 1968).

13. Johann Gottfried von Herder (1744–1803), *Reflections on the Philosophy of the History of Mankind*, abridged, introduction Frank E. Manuel (Chicago: Chicago University Press, 1968); Isaiah Berlin, *Three Critics of the Enlightenment. Vico, Hamann, Herder* (Princeton: Princeton University Press, 2000); Wulf Koepke, *Johann Gottfried Herder* (Boston: Twayne, 1987).

14. See Philippe Lacoue-Labarthe, *L'imitation des modernes* (Paris: Galilei, 1986).

15. Johann Arnason, *Nation and Modernity* (Rejkjavik: Nordic Summer University, 1996), p. 34.

16. Michel Foucault, *The Order of Things. An Archaeology of the Human Sciences* (London: Tavistock Publications, 1970), p. 333.

17. ibid., p. 329.

18. Foucault, *The Order of Things*, p. 251.

19. For English romanticism see M. H. Abrams, *Natural Supernaturalism. Tradition and Revolt in Romantic Literature* (New York: Norton, 1973). Of fundamental importance for European romanticism is Jean-Jacques Rousseau's articulation of the myth of the Fall in terms of the contrast between natural innocence and the corruption of civilization. See Irving Babbitt's polemical *Rousseau and Romanticism* (New York: AMS Press, 1979).

20. Oswald Spengler (1880–1936), *The Decline of the West*, 2 vols, authorized translation with notes Charles Francis Atkinson (New York: Knopf, 1926–8); H. Stuart Hughes, *Oswald Spengler. A Critical Estimate* (New York: Scribner, 1962).

21. Charles H. Kahn, *The Art and Thought of Heraclitus. An Edition of the Fragments with Translation and Commentary* (Cambridge: Cambridge University Press, 1979).

22. Hans Joas, *The Creativity of Action* trans. Jeremy Gaines and Paul Keast (Chicago: Chicago University Press, 1996).

23. Jean-Luc Nancy, *The Inoperative Community* (Minneapolis: University of Minnesota Press, 1991), p. 45.

24. See Josef Chytry, *The Aesthetic State. A Quest in Modern German Thought* (Berkeley: University of California Press, 1989); Philip J. Kahn, *Schiller, Hegel and Marx. State, Society and the Aesthetic Ideal of Ancient Greece* (Kingston, ON: McGill-Queens University Press, 1982).

25. See E. M. Butler, *The Tyranny of Greece over Germany. A Study of the Influence Exercised by Greek Art and Poetry over the Great German Writers* (Cambridge: The University Press, 1935).

26. Philippe Lacoue-Labarthe, *La fiction du politique. Heidegger, l'art et la politique* (n. p.: Christian Bourgeois, 1987), p. 83.

27. Odo Marquard, *Transzendentaler Idealismus. Romantische Naturphilosophie. Psychoanalyse* (Cologne: Dinter, 1987).

1 The Idea of Natural History

1. Willem van Reijen, 'Die Dialektik der Aufklärung gelesen als Allegorie' in Willem van Reijen and Gunzelin Schmid Noerr (eds), *Vierzig Jahre Flaschenpost: Dialektik der Aufklärung 1947 bis 1987* (Frankfurt am Main: Fischer, 1987), pp. 192–209.

2. Martin Heidegger, *Sein und Zeit, Gesamtausgabe* [GA] 2, (Frankfurt: Klostermann, 1977), p. 508.

3. See Richard Wolin (ed.) *The Heidegger Controversy. A Critical Reader* (Cambridge, MA: MIT Press, 1993).

4. Heidegger, *Sein und Zeit*, GA 2, p. 509.

5. Heidegger, *Einführung in die Metaphysik*, GA 40, pp. 164–5.

6. 'The Oldest Systematic Programme of German Idealism', in Ernst Behler (ed.) *Philosophy of German Idealism* (New York: Continuum, 1987), pp. 161–3.

7. Theodor W. Adorno, 'Die Idee der Naturgeschichte', in Adorno, *Philosophische Frühschriften. Gesammelte Schriften* I (Frankfurt am Main: Suhrkamp, 1973), pp. 345–65.

8. Walter Benjamin, *The Origin of German Tragic Drama,* trans. John Osborne, introduction by George Steiner (London: NLB, 1977), p. 177.

9. Gunzelin Schmid Noerr, *Das Eingedenken der Natur im Subjekt. Zur Dialektik von Vernunft und Natur in der Kritischen Theorie Horkheimers, Adornos und Marcuses* (Darmstadt: Wissenschaftliche Buchgesellschaft, 1990), p. 25.

10. Adorno, 'Die Idee der Naturgeschichte', p. 363.

11. ibid., p. 365.

12. Jürgen Habermas calls Bloch a 'Marxist Schelling' in *Merkur* 11 (1960). See Schelling, *System of Transcendental Idealism* and Marx's definition of communism in 'Economic and Philosophical Manuscripts' (1844): 'Communism as completed naturalism is humanism and as completed humanism is naturalism. It is the genuine solution of the antagonism between man and nature and between man and man.' (Karl Marx, *Selected Writings*, ed. David McLellan (Oxford: Oxford University Press, 1985), p. 89). For Bloch see Gérard Raulet, *Humanisation de la nature, naturalization de l'homme. Ernst Bloch et le projet d'une autre rationalité* (Paris: Klinksieck, 1982); Wayne Hudson, *The Marxist Philosophy of Ernst Bloch* (London: Macmillan, 1982).

13. Ludger Heidbrink, *Melancholie und Moderne* (Munich: Fink, 1994), pp. 96–9.

14. Jürgen Habermas, 'The Entwinement of Myth and Enlightenment: Rereading Dialectic of Enlightenment', *New German Critique* 26 (1982), 13–30.

15. Max Horkheimer and Theodor Adorno, *Dialektik der Aufklärung*, in Adorno, *Gesammelte Schriften* 3 (Frankfurt am Main: Suhrkamp, 1984), p. 292.

16. Odo Marquard, *Transzendentaler Idealismus. Romantische Naturphilosophie. Psychoanalyse* (Cologne: Dinter, 1987), pp. 54–7.

17. For Hölderlin see Eric L. Santner (ed.), *Hyperion and Selected Poems* (New York: Continuum, 1990); Friedrich Hölderlin. *Essays and Letters on Theory*, trans. and

ed. Thomas Pfau (Albany, NY: State University of New York Press, 1988); Ray Fleming, *Keats, Leopardi, and Hölderlin: The Poet as Priest of the Absolute* (New York: Garland, 1987); Martin Heidegger, *Elucidations of Hölderlin's Poetry*, trans. and introduced Keith Hoeller (Amherst, NY: Humanity Books, 2000).

18. Heidegger, *Parmenides*, GA 54, pp. 113–14.

19. Heidegger, *Hölderlins Hymnen 'Germanien' und 'Der Rhein'*, GA 39, pp. 105–6.

20. ibid., pp. 290–2.

21. See Josef Chytry, *The Aesthetic State. A Quest in Modern German Thought* (Berkeley: University of California Press, 1989).

22. See E. M. Butler, *The Saint-Simonian Religion in Germany. A Study of the Young German Movement* (New York: Fertig, 1968).

23. Ernst Jünger, *Storm of Steel. From the Diary of a German Storm-troop Officer on the Western Front*, trans. Basil Creighton (London: Chatto & Windus, 1929). See also Thomas Nevin, *Ernst Jünger and Germany. Into the Abyss 1914–1945* (Durham, NC: Duke University Press, 1996).

24. See Richard Wolin, *The Heidegger Controversy* (Cambridge, MA: MIT Press, 1993).

25. Dana R. Villa, *Arendt and Heidegger. The Fate of the Political* (Princeton: Princeton University Press, 1996), p. 251.

26. Heidegger, *Hölderlins Hymnen 'Germanien' und 'Der Rhein'*, GA 39, p. 214.

27. Philippe Lacoue-Labarthe, *Le sujet de la philosophie. Typographies I* (Paris: Aubier-Flammarion, 1979), p. 97.

2 A New Mythology

1. Odo Marquard, *Transzendentaler Idealismus. Romantische Naturphilosophie. Psychoanalyse*, pp. 134 ff.

2. ibid., p. 137.

3. Friedrich Schiller (1759–1805), *On the Aesthetic Education of Man, in a Series of Letters*, ed. and trans. with introduction by Elizabeth M. Wilkinson and L. A. Willoughby (Oxford: Clarendon Press, 1992).

4. Cf. Bernhard Yack, *The Longing for Total Revolution. Philosophic Sources of Social Discontent from Rousseau to Marx and Nietzsche* (Princeton: Princeton University Press, 1986).

5. Friedrich Schiller, *Naive and Sentimental Poetry and On the Sublime* trans. with introduction by Julius A. Elias (New York: Ungar, 1966), p. 85.

6. Marquard, *Transzendentaler Idealismus*, pp. 151–2.

7. Phillippe Lacoue-Labarthe, *La fiction du politique. Heidegger, l'art et la politique* (n.p.: Christian Bourgeois, 1987), p. 83.

8. For the Jena romantics see A. Leslie Willson (ed.), *German Romantic Criticism* (New York: Continuum Books, 1982); Ernst Behler, *German Romantic Literary Theory* (Cambridge: Cambridge University Press, 1993); Philippe Lacoue-Labarthe and Jean-Luc Nancy, *The Literary Absolute: The Theory of Literature in German Romanticism*, trans. and introduced by Philip Barnard and Cheryl Lester (Albany: State University of New York Press, 1988).

9. Hans Freier, *Die Rückkehr der Götter. Von der ästhetischen Überschreitung der Wissensgrenze zur Mythologie der Moderne* (Stuttgart: Metzler, 1976), p. 134.

10. Georg Wilhelm Friedrich Hegel (1770–1831), *The Philosophy of Fine Art*, trans. F. Osmaston, 4 vols (New York: Hacker Fine Art, 1975). A good introduction to Hegel is Stanley Rosen, *G. W. F. Hegel. An Introduction to the Science of Wisdom* (New Haven: Yale University Press, 1974).

11. Heidegger, *Einführung in die Metaphysik*, GA 40, p. 135.

12. 'The Oldest Systematic Programme of German Idealism', in Ernst Behler (ed.), *The Philosphy of German Idealism* (New York: Continuum Books, 1987), pp. 161–3.

13. Friedrich Schlegel, 'Dialogue on Poetry', trans. Ernst Behler and Roman Struc in A. Leslie Willson (ed.), *German Romantic Criticism* (New York: Continuum, 1982), pp. 84–133.

14. For the importance of Spinoza for German romantic pantheism and mythology see Walburga Lösch, *Der werdende Gott. Mythopoetische Theogonien in der romantischen Mythologie* (Frankfurt: Lang, 1996).

15. See for Jacob Boehme (1575–1624), Andrew Weeks, *Boehme. An Intellectual Biography* (Albany: State University of New York Press, 1991).

16. Johann Gottlieb Fichte's (1762–1814) *Grundlagen der Wissenschaftslehre* (1794) was of crucial importance for the Jena romantics. See *Science of Knowledge with the First and Second Introductions*, trans. Peter Heath and John Lachs (New York: Appleton Century Crofts, 1970).

17. Chytry, *The Aesthetic State*, Part III.

18. For the instituting and instituted symbolic and the concept of the political sublime, see Marc Richir, *Du sublime en politique* (Paris: Payot, 1991).

19. Philippe Lacoue-Labarthe and Jean-Luc Nancy, *The Literary Absolute: The Theory of Literature in German Romanticism*, trans. and introduced by Philip Barnard and Cheryl Lester (Albany: State University of New York Press, 1988).

20. Friedrich Wilhelm Schelling, *System of Transcendental Idealism (1800)*, trans. Peter Heath, introduction Michael Vater (Charlottesville: University of Virginia Press, 1978), p. 12.

21. ibid., pp. 231, 232–3.

22. Schelling, *The Philosophy of Art*, ed., trans. and introduced by Douglas W. Stoll (Minneapolis: University of Minnesota Press, 1989).

23. Ernst Cassirer, *Freiheit und Form* (Darmstadt: Wissenschaftliche Buchgesellschaft, 1961), pp. 349–51.

24. Schelling, *Of Human Freedom* trans. James Gutman (Chicago: Open Court, 1936), pp. 31–4.

25. Heidegger, *Schelling: Vom Wesen der menschlichen Freiheit (1809)*, GA 42, pp. 194–9.

26. Karl Jaspers, *Notizen zu Heidegger*, ed. Hans Saner (Munich: Piper, 1978), p. 102.

27. For the German mystic tradition see Andrew Weeks, *German Mysticism from Hildegard of Bingen to Ludwig Wittgenstein: A Literary and Intellectual History* (Albany: State University of New York Press, 1993).

28. Georges Gusdorf, *Du Néant à Dieu dans le savoir romantique* (Paris: Payot, 1983), pp. 127–43.

29. ibid., p. 134.

3 The Disenchantment of Romantic Nature

1. Schelling, *System of Transcendental Idealism*, pp. 12, 230.

2. Marquard, *Transzendentaler Idealismus*, p. 126.

3. ibid., p. 157.

4. ibid., pp. 89, 95, 105.

5. ibid., p. 116.

6. ibid., p. 161.

7. ibid., pp. 43–6.

8. ibid., p. 148.

9. ibid., p. 143.

10. ibid., pp. 186–9, 192.

11. Gusdorf, *Du Néant à Dieu*, pp. 115–26.

12. ibid., p. 47.

13. Marquard, *Transzendentaler Idealismus*, pp. 201–2, 187.

14. See Manfred Frank, *Der kommende Gott. Vorlesungen über die Neue Mythologie* (Frankfurt: Suhrkamp, 1982).

15. See the article 'Nihilismus', in Joachim Ritter and Karlfried Gründer (eds), *Historisches Wörterbuch der Philosophie*, Vol. 6 (Darmstadt: Wissenschaftliche Buchgesellschaft, 1984).

16. See for Hegel the critique of romantic irony in the Introduction to *The Philosophy of Fine Art*, Vol. 1 (New York: Hacker Fine Art, 1975), taken up by Kierkegaard in *The Concept of Irony with Constant Reference to Socrates*, ed. and trans. by H. V. Hong and Edna Hong (Princeton, NJ: Princeton University Press, 1989), and for Carl Schmitt his *Political Romanticism* (Cambridge, MA: MIT Press, 1986).

17. Max Horkheimer and Theodor W. Adorno, *Dialectic of Enlightenment*, trans. John Cumming (London: Allen Lane, 1973), p. 33.

18. Cf. Honoré de Balzac, *The Unknown Masterpiece* (Berkeley: Creative Arts Book Co., 1984) and Gottfried Keller, *Green Henry* (London: Calder, 1960).

19. Goethe, *The Sorrows of Young Werther* (New York: Penguin, 1989), letter of 18 August.

20. Marquard, *Transzendentaler Idealismus*, pp. 203–9.

21. Nietzsche, Aph. 1067, *The Will to Power*, ed. Walter Kaufmann, trans. Walter Kaufmann and R. J. Hollingdale (New York: Vintage Books, 1968), p. 550.

22. The basic text is still Fritz Stern, *The Politics of Cultural Despair. A Study in the Rise of the German Ideology* (Berkeley: University of California Press, 1961).

4 Original Imitation

1. See Jacob Burckhardt on the primacy of 'romantic' as opposed to 'classical' Greece, *Griechische Kulturgeschichte* Vol. 1, *Gesammelte Werke* Vol. 5 (Basel: Schwabe, 1956), p. 36.

2. The main works of Friedrich Meinecke (1862–1954) are *Cosmopolitanism and the National State* (Princeton, NJ: Princeton University Press, 1970) and *Historicism. The Rise of a New Historical Outlook*, trans. J. E. Andersen, Foreword by Isaiah Berlin (London: Routledge & Kegan Paul, 1972).

3. Friedrich Meinecke, *Die Entstehung des Historismus*, ed. and introduced by Carl Hinrichs (Munich: Oldenburg, 1965), p. 580.

4. ibid., pp. 500, 301.

5. Johann Winckelmann (1717–68), *Reflections on the Painting and Sculpture of the Greeks* (London: Routledge, 1999); *History of Ancient Art*, trans. Alexander Gode, 4 vols (New York: Ungar, 1968). See also Alex Potts, *Flesh and the Ideal. Winckelmann and the Origins of Art History* (New Haven: Yale University Press, 1994).

6. Meinecke, *Die Entstehung des Historismus*, pp. 425, 417, 439.

7. ibid., p. 503.

8. ibid., pp. 417, 337.

9. ibid., pp. 389–90.

10. ibid., p. 571.

11. ibid., p. mxli.

12. Meinecke, *The German Catastrophe. Reflections and Recollections* (Boston: Beacon Press, 1950).

13. Heidegger, *Hölderlins Hymnen 'Germanien' und 'Der Rhein'*, GA 39, p. 3.

14. Meinecke, *Die Entstehung*, p. 373.

15. ibid., pp. 564–5.

16. Jürgen Scharfschwerdt, *Hölderlin. Der Dichter des deutschen 'Sonderwegs'* (Stuttgart: Kohlhammer, 1994).

17. Heidegger, *Contributions to Philosophy (From Enowning)*, trans. Parvis Emad and Kenneth Maly (Bloomington: Indiana University Press, 1999).

18. See for Ludwig Klages (1872–1956) Roland Müller, *Das verzwistete Ich. Ludwig Klages und sein philosophisches Hauptwerk 'Der Geist als Widersacher der Seele'* (Bern: Lang, 1971).

19. Heidegger, *Einführung in die Metaphysik*, GA 40, par. 15, pp. 48–51.

20. Philippe Lacoue-Labarthe, *L'imitation des modernes* (Paris: Galilei, 1986), pp. 103–4.

21. Goethe's 'Literarischer Sansculottismus' (1795) appeared in Schiller's journal *Die Horen* in the same year as Schiller's *Letters on the Aesthetic Education of Man*.

22. Cf. Rainer Marten, 'Heidegger and the Greeks' in Tom Rockmore and Joseph Margolis (eds), *The Heidegger Case* (Philadelphia: Temple University Press, 1992), pp. 167–87.

23. Karl Marx, 'Towards a Critique of Hegel's "Philosophy of Right": Introduction' (1844) in K. Marx, *The Early Texts*, ed. D. McLellan (Oxford: Oxford University Press, 1971), pp. 115ff.

24. Lacoue-Labarthe, *L'imitation des modernes*, p. 119.

25. Habermas, *The Philosophical Discourse of Modernity* (Cambridge, MA: MIT Press, 1987), ch. 4.

26. Louis Dumont, *The German Ideology* (Chicago: University of Chicago Press, 1994), p. 25.

27. Lacoue-Labarthe, *L'imitation des modernes*, p. 195.

28. Heidegger, GA 40, 164–5. *An Introduction to Metaphysics*, trans. Ralph Manheim (New Haven: Yale University Press, 1959), p. 155.

29. For Alfred Baeumler see Roger Wood, *The Conservative Revolution in the Weimar Republic* (London: Macmillan, 1996); Ilse Korotin (ed.), *Die besten Geister der Nation. Philosophie und Nationalsozialismus* (Vienna: Picus, 1994).

30. Alfred Baeumler, 'Bachofen der Mythologe der Romantik', in Bachofen, *Der Mythos von Orient und Occident*, ed. Manfred Schroeter (Munich: Beck, 1956).

31. Johann Jakob Bachofen (1815–87), *Myth, Religion and Mother Right. Selected Writings of J. J. Bachofen*, trans. Ralph Manheim (London: Routledge & Kegan Paul, 1967).

32. Bachofen, *Der Mythos*, p. ccli.

33. ibid., p. xxv–xxxi.

34. ibid., p. clxix.

35. ibid., p. cxciv.

36. ibid., p. lxvii.

37. ibid., p. ccli.

38. Joseph Görres (1776–1848), 'Exposition d'un système sexuel d'ontologie', in Görres, *Gesammelte Schriften 2.2* (Cologne: Bachen, 1934), pp. 201–36. See Reinhardt Habel, *Joseph Görres. Studien über den Zusammenhang von Natur, Geschichte und Mythos in seinen Schriften* (Wiesbaden: Steiner, 1960).

39. Bachofen, *Der Mythos*, pp. clxxi–clxxx.

40. ibid., p. clxxxviii.

41. ibid., pp. xciii, ccxiii.

42. Georg Friedrich Creuzer (1771–1858), *Symbolik und Mythologie der alten Völker*, 6 vols (New York: Arno Press, 1978).

43. Bachofen, *Der Mythos*, p. ccxlvii.

44. ibid., pp. cxxi, cxxii.

45. See Manfred Frank, *Gott im Exil. Vorlesungen über die Neue Mythologie* (Frankfurt: Suhrkamp, 1988), pp. 128ff.

46. Heidegger, *Hölderlins Hymnen 'Germanien' und 'Der Rhein'* GA 39, pp. 98–100.

5 Metaphors of Creation

1. J. L. Talmon, *Romanticism and Revolt. Europe 1815–1848* (London: Thames & Hudson, 1967), pp. 58-68.

2. See the chapters 'Nature as Source' and 'The Expressivist Turn' in Charles Taylor, *Sources of the Self. The Making of Modern Identity* (Cambridge, MA: Harvard University Press, 1989).

3. See for instance Goethe's celebration of the artist creator as God in 'Von deutscher Baukunst' (1770) and for the development of the idea of the genius Jochen Schmidt, *Die Geschichte des Genie-Gedankens in der deutschen Literatur, Philosophie und Politik 1750–1945* (Darmstadt: Wissenschaftliche Buchgesellschaft, 1985).

4. Ernst Cassirer, *The Philosophy of the Enlightenment* (Boston: Beacon Press, 1955), pp. 35, 29, 32.

5. Cassirer, *Freiheit und Form. Studien zur deutschen Geistesgeschichte* (Darmstadt: Wissenschaftliche Buchgesellschaft, 1961), p. 82.

6. Gilles Deleuze, *Spinoza et le problème de l'expression* (Paris: Editions de Minuit, 1968), pp. 299–311.

7. Immanuel Kant, 'Rezensionen von J.G. Herders "Ideen zur Philosophie der Geschichte der Menschheit" ', Part I, Appendix (Beilage) in Kant, *Schriften zur Geschichtsphilosophie*, ed. Manfred Riedel (Stuttgart: Reclam, 1974), pp. 49–51.

8. Dumont, *The German Ideology* (Chicago: Chicago University Press, 1994).

9. Thomas Nipperday, 'Auf der Suche nach der Identität: Romantischer Nationalismus', in Nipperday, *Nachdenken über die deutsche Geschichte* (Munich: Beck, 1986), pp. 110–25.

10. See chapter 2, 'Metaphors of creativity', in Hans Joas, *The Creativity of Action* (Chicago: Chicago University Press, 1996).

11. Richard Wagner, *Prose Works* Vol. I, trans. William Ashton Ellis (London: Kegan Paul, 1895), pp. 52–3.

12. ibid., p. 55.

13. ibid., p. 88.

14. Joas, *The Creativity of Action*, p. 116.

15. ibid., 125. Hans Schnädelbach sees the antagonism of life philosophy to the whole tradition of European rationalism as the signature and sum of the post-1848 epoch. See ch. 5 in Schnädelbach, *Philosophy in Germany 1831–1933* (Cambridge: Cambridge University Press, 1984).

16. Theodor Adorno, *Negative Dialektik* (Frankfurt: Suhrkamp, 1966), p. 111.

17. Axel Honneth, 'L'esprit et son objet – Parentés anthropologiques entre la dialectique de la raison et la critique de la civilisation dans la philosophie de la vie,' in Gérard Raulet (ed.), *Weimar ou la explosion de la modernité* (Paris: Anthropos, 1984), pp. 97–112. See also Georg Stauth, 'Critical Theory and Pre-Fascist Social Thought', *History of European Ideas*, xviii (1994), 711–27.

18. See Roger Wood, *The Conservative Revolution in the Weimar Republic* (London: Macmillan, 1996); Martin Travers, *Critics of Modernity. The Literature of the Conservative Revolution in Germany 1890–1933* (New York: Lang, 2001).

19. Thomas Mann, 'Deutsche Ansprache. Ein Appell an die Vernunft' in *Politische Schriften und Reden*, Vol. 2 (Frankfurt: Fischer, 1968). See Marianne Baeumler (ed.), *Thomas Mann und Alfred Baeumler. Eine Dokumentation* (Würzburg: Königshausen & Neumann, 1989).

6 Newly Invented Myths: Wagner

1. Philippe Lacoue-Labarthe, *Musica Ficta, Figures of Wagner* (Stanford: Stanford University Press, 1994), p. xix.
2. ibid., p. xx.
3. Quoted from L. J. Rather, *The Dream of Self-Destruction. Wagner's 'Ring' and the Modern World* (Baton Rouge: Louisiana State University Press, 1979), p. 48.
4. ibid., p. 7.
5. ibid., p. 15.
6. Adorno, *In Search of Wagner*, trans. Rodney Livingstone (London: NLB, 1981), p. 137.
7. Richard Wagner, *Prose Works*, Vol. I, trans. William Ashton Ellis (London: Kegan Paul, 1895), p. 24.
8. ibid., p. 35.
9. ibid., p. 166.
10. ibid., pp. 208, 210.
11. Wagner, *Oper und Drama* (Stuttgart: Reclam, 1984), p. 39.
12. ibid., p. 101.
13. See Lesley Sharpe, *Friedrich Schiller. Drama, Thought, and Politics* (Cambridge: Cambridge University Press, 1991); T. J. Reed, *Schiller* (Oxford: Oxford University Press, 1991).
14. Wagner, *Oper und Drama*, p. 199.
15. ibid., p. 113.
16. Theodor Adorno, *In Search of Wagner* (London: New Left Books, 1981), p. 122.
17. Wagner to Liszt, 11 February 1853, in *Selected Letters of Richard Wagner*, trans. and ed. Stewart Spencer and Barry Millington (London: Dent, 1987).
18. Carl Dahlhaus, *Richard Wagner's Music Dramas* (Cambridge: Cambridge University Press, 1979), pp. 140–2.
19. Warren Darcy, ' "The World belongs to Alberich!" Wagner's changing attitude to the "Ring" ' in Stewart Spencer (ed.), *Wagner's Ring of the Nibelungen. A Companion* (London: Thames & Hudson, 1993), pp. 48–52.

7 Myth and Enlightenment: Nietzsche

1. Friedrich Nietzsche, 'Der Fall Wagner', in *Werke in zwei Bänden*, Vol. II (Munich: Hanser, 1967), p. 298.
2. *The Birth of Tragedy and the Case of Wagner*, trans. with commentary by Walter Kaufmann (New York: Vintage Books, 1967), p. 25.
3. ibid., p. 45.
4. Arthur Schopenhauer, *The World as Will and Representation*, Vol. I, trans. E. F. J. Payne (New York: Dover, 1969), p. 266 (§52).
5. *The Birth of Tragedy*, p. 52.
6. Richard Wagner, 'Beethoven', *Gesammelte Schriften und Dichtungen*, ed. Wolfgang Golthe, Vol. 9 (Berlin: Bong, n.d.), p. 121.
7. *The Birth of Tragedy*, p. 64.
8. Wagner, 'Beethoven', p. 69.
9. ibid., p. 109.
10. ibid., pp. 69–70.
11. ibid., pp. 78, 105.
12. *Birth of Tragedy*, p. 103.
13. ibid., p. 137.

14. ibid., p. 136.
15. Heinz Röttges, *Nietzsche und die Dialektik der Aufklärung* (Berlin: de Gruyter, 1972), p. vi.
16. ibid., p. 125.
17. *Birth of Tragedy*, p. 141.

8 Mytho-Logics

1. M. H. Abrams, *Natural Supernaturalism. Tradition and Revolution in Romantic Literature* (New York: Norton, 1973), pp. 27–31. See also E. D. Hirsch, *Wordsworth and Schelling. A Typological Study of Romanticism* (New Haven: Yale University Press, 1960).
2. *Natural Supernaturalism*, p. 30.
3. Heidegger, *Nietzsche*, Vol. 3–4 (New York: HarperCollins, 1991), p. 204.
4. Heidegger, 'Six basic developments in the history of aesthetics', in *Nietzsche*, Vol. 1–2 (New York: HarperCollins, 1991), pp. 77–91.
5. ibid., p. 85.
6. See Joachim Köhler, *Wagners Hitler. Der Prophet und sein Vollstrecker* (Munich: Blessing, 1997).
7. Heidegger, *Einführung in die Metaphysik*, GA 40, pp. 168, 140.
8. 'The origin of the work of art', in David Farrell Krell (ed.), *Martin Heidegger. Basic Writings* (London: Routledge, 1993), p. 189.
9. ibid., pp. 196, 200–1.
10. ibid., p. 202.
11. ibid., p. 168.
12. ibid., p. 201.
13. Marc Richir, *Du sublime en politique* (Paris: Payot, 1991), pp. 51–81.
14. Jean-Luc Nancy, *The Inoperative Community* (Minneapolis: University of Minnesota Press, 1991), p. 45.
15. ibid., p. 11.

Part Two: Introduction: Artifice and History

1. Michael Crozier and Peter Murphy, 'Introduction: In search of the civic center', in *The Left in Search of a Center* (Urbana-Champaign: Illinois University Press, 1996), pp. 1–30.
2. Hannah Arendt, *On Revolution* (Harmondsworth: Penguin, 1963).
3. The 'classicizing-modernizing impulse' in Britain was wide-ranging, and it deeply affected the British state. Examples varied from the utilitarian reformism of the classical historian George Grote in Victorian England to the institutional pluralism and Aristotelian syndicalism of the twentieth-century English political theorist Ernest Barker. See, for example, Grote, *History of Greece* (New York: Harper, 1875), *Plato, and the other Companions of Sokrates* (London: J. Murray, 1888); Barker, *Principles of Social and Political Theory* (Oxford: Clarendon Press, 1951), *The Ideas and Ideals of the British Empire* (Cambridge: Cambridge University Press, 1941), *Essays On Government* (Oxford: Clarendon Press, 1951), *Greek Political Theory; Plato and his Predecessors* (London: Methuen, 1947).
4. On classical rationalism and modern deployments of it, see Peter Murphy, *Civic Justice: From Greek Antiquity to the Modern World* (Amherst, NY: Humanity Books, 2001).

5. Leo Strauss, *Natural Right and History* (Chicago, IL.: University of Chicago Press, 1953); *The City and Man* (Chicago: Rand McNally, 1964); *Liberalism, Ancient and Modern* (New York: Basic Books, 1968); *Thoughts on Machiavelli* (Glencoe, IL.: Free Press, 1959); *What is Political Philosophy? and Other Studies* (Glencoe, IL.: Free Press, 1959).

6. For Popper, Athens was characterized by a cosmopolitan empire, anti-slavery murmurings, and by the disavowal of myth and magic. As the first open society, Athens went a long way toward replacing custom with law, landed aristocracy with commerce, and establishing its politics on the basis of reason rather than tribalism. Popper's portrait of Athens was deliberately conceived as a counter to the constellations of ethnonationalism and historicist cultural nationalism. These idea sets had come to dominate Central Europe, and the Vienna that Popper was forced to flee from. Written in exile in wartime New Zealand, *The Open Society and its Enemies* (London: Routledge, 1947) was a cosmopolitan philosophical response to the dialectic of romanticism. His critique of the Doric character of Plato's thought was intended as a critique of the totalitarian Doric politics of the Nazis.

7. This is not unlike what Stravinsky in contradistinction to Wagner envisaged for music – the synchrony of the non-synchronous. See David Roberts, *Art and Enlightenment: Aesthetic Theory after Adorno* (Lincoln: University of Nebraska Press, 1991), p. 209.

8. Stravinsky is a paradigm example. See ibid.

9. Peter Murphy, 'Metropolitan rhythms: a preface to a musical philosophy for the New World', *Thesis Eleven* 56 (1999), pp. 81–105.

9   The Gate

1. Peter Gay's terminology. See his *The Enlightenment: An Interpretation. Vol. I: The Rise of Modern Paganism* (London: Weidenfeld & Nicolson, 1966).

2. On this, see Peter Murphy, 'Romantic Modernism and the Greek Polis', *Thesis Eleven* 34 (1993), pp. 42–66.

3. The nineteenth-century American pragmatist philosopher and scientist Charles Sanders Peirce made much of the spontaneous causes in nature, laying the groundwork for the pragmatic cast of American philosophical and technological thought, a cast of mind that manages to elide the distinction between romanticism and enlightenment.

4. Cornelius Castoriadis makes an analogous point when he suggests that:

'The genius of Aeschylus or Sophocles is inseparable from the genius of the Athenian demos, just as the genius of Shakespeare is inseparable from the genius of the Elizabethan public. ... These communities instituted themselves in this creative type of relation with creative workers in various fields. I am not speaking in a nostalgic mood nor am I implying that there was an idyllic relationship between the artist and the public. It is well known that the burghers of Leipzig wanted to have Telemann as Kapellmeister. But Telemann was not available, so they hired Johann Sebastian Bach as the second best. History has decided otherwise. But the fact is that they did hire Bach, and also that, after all, Telemann was a very good musician.

Philosophy, Politics, Autonomy (Oxford: Oxford University Press, 1991), pp. 229–30.

5. Nietzsche, *Beyond Good and Evil*, translated, with commentary, by Walter Kaufmann (New York: Vintage Books, 1966), Section 224.

6. ibid., Section 223.

7. ibid., Section 224.

8. Cornelius Tacitus, *Histories* IV, trans. K. Wellesley (Harmondsworth: Penguin, 1975), p. 74.

9. Allan Janik and Stephen Toulmin, *Wittgenstein's Vienna* (New York: Simon & Schuster, 1973), p. 97.

10. Franz Schulze, *Mies van der Rohe: A Critical Biography* (Chicago: University of Chicago Press, 1985), p. 7.

11. Erwin Panofsky, *Renaissance and Renascences in Western Art* (New York: Harper & Row, 1972 [1969]), chapter 2.

12. Aldo Rossi, *The Architecture of the City* (Massachusetts, MA: MIT Press, 1984), p. 51.

13. ibid., p. 87.

14. ibid., p. 174.

15. To cite another Rossi example: could not one say that the cathedrals and churches scattered throughout the world together with St Peter's in Rome constituted the universality of the Catholic Church?

16. Wilhelm Dilthey, *Pattern and Meaning in History*, ed. H. P. Rickman (New York: Harper & Row, 1962), p. 157.

17. ibid., p. 156.

18. ibid., p. 156.

19. ibid., p. 156.

20. ibid., pp. 142–3.

21. ibid., p. 143.

22. Jacob Burkhardt is a partial and important exception to this. Burkhardt understood the power of renaissance. Perhaps because of his reluctance to embrace the ambition of Hegel's philosophy of history, Burkhardt still treated Western history, and its civilizing turning points, episodically rather than as part of a grand narrative. However, without Burkhardt, and his inspiration to the discipline of art history, there would have been no Ernst Gombrich and no volumes like *The Story of Art*.

23. Dilthey, p. 120–1.

24. ibid., p. 167.

25. Niccolo Machiavelli, 'Letter to Francesco Vettori' in John Plamenatz (ed.), *Machiavelli, The Prince, Selections from The Discourses and other writings* (London: Collins, 1972), p. 360.

26. Should the reader doubt this, then take a walk through the vast galleries of the Louvre in Paris that are filled to brimming with second and third-rate French painting. The relief of getting to the Italian Renaissance paitings (stolen by Napoleon's armies) and the Impressionist and Post-Impressionist sections is palpable and overwhelming.

27. The latest of such projects (both from the 1990s) was to reorientate the Basque city of Bilboa around the Frank Gehry-designed Guggenheim Museum, and Richard Meier's kitsch modern, acropolitically sited Getty Museum in Los Angeles.

28. Nikolaus Pevsner, *A History of Building Types* (Thames & Hudson: London, 1976), pp. 117–20.

29. Due to the federalist form of the American Republic.

30. This is not to say that cities did not engage in wars – on the contrary they could at times be very warlike, but their wars concerned trade routes and territory, not national or ethnic self-assertion. Even when, as in the case of Athens, the city's territory sometimes took on a quasi-deified character, history does not bequeath to us stories of the 'internment' or slaughter of aliens; on the contrary, the long-term history of these cities is one of openness to foreigners, including those they had conquered. On the attitudes of city-states to foreigners and aliens, see Peter Murphy, *Civic Justice: From Greek Antiquity to the Modern World* (Amherst, NY: Humanity Books, 2001).

10   Civilization and Aestheticism: Schinkel

1. Quoted in Barry Bergdoll, *Karl Friedrich Schinkel* (New York: Rizzoli, 1994), p. 64.
2. ibid., p. 65.
3. Peter Collins, *Changing Ideals in Modern Architecture* (London: Faber, 1965), p. 203.
4. Marc-Antoine Laugier, in his 1753 *Essay on Architecture*.
5. Bergdoll, p. 216.
6. This is beautifully described by John Carroll in his *The Western Dreaming* (Sydney: HaperCollins, 2001), pp. 149, 175.
7. The film director Alfred Hitchcock was a master of portraying this vertigo plunge.
8. The archaic power of the mountain was invoked in the Arnold Frank–Leni Riefenstahl 'mountain films' of the mid-1920s. When Riefenstahl the actress debuted as a film director (in her 1926 film *The Blue Light*), it was again a mountain film, one in which the lead character is enchanted by alpine crystals.

11   Truth in Building: Mies van der Rohe

1. Mies van der Rohe, 'Building' published in the constructivist journal *G*, 2 (September 1923), p. 1 and reprinted in Fritz Neumeyer, *The Artless Word: Mies van der Rohe on the Building Art* (Cambridge, MA: MIT Press, 1991), p. 243.
2. Mies's axiom of 'truth in construction' was not an original programmatic idea, even if Mies's pursuit of the idea was to be executed in an unprecedented fashion. Already in 1672 the French architect N. F. Blondel had defined architecture as the art of building. In 1753, Marc-Antoine Laugier, in his *Essay on Architecture*, argued that the orders of architecture must be employed in such a way as not only to decorate a building but also to constitute it. The French 'classical rationalist' tradition equated truth and beauty in contrast to the Greek equation of the good and the beautiful. The truth-beauty of a building was its architectural integrity. J. G. Soufflot (1713–80) advised that aesthetic effects should follow from the nature of structural components. J. A. Borgnis, in his *Elementary Treatise on Construction* (1823), argued against the Roman practice of carving the appearance of a structural frame on the surface of a building. Borgnis reasoned that architecture should not be reduced to a species of painting. Where the painter sketched from nature, the method of the architect was reliant on physico-mathematical sciences. In this view, architecture was productive of mathematical structure rather than reproductive of (painterly) nature.

Borgnis's argument was not new. In 1789, in a memorandum distributed to the revolutionary French National Assembly, J. B. Rondelet, the supervising architect for Soufflot's Sainte-Geneviève (the Parisian Pantheon) wrote that, since the time of Renaissance, architects had been too preoccupied with decoration, and had made this accessory part of architecture their principal aim. Rondelet's explanation, as Peter Collins observes, was quasi-historical:

> The origin of abuse, he said, could be traced to the fact that when Goth architecture was abandoned in Italy, the first architects to follow the new fashion had been painters and draftsmen, who thus had nothing but decoration in mind. Hence this part of architecture was more congenial to them than planning and construction, because the latter demanded specialised knowledges. Hence, also, the products of the first architects consisted mainly of decorative elements, which did not form an essential part of the building, and resulted in a heavy and expensive veneer of architecture in which everything was subjected to the decorators' caprice. (Peter Collins, *Changing Ideals in Modern Architecture* [London: Faber, 1965], p. 203)

The effect of this privileging of decoration was to cause architects to abandon the study of planning and construction.

3. Collins, *Changing Ideals*, p. 203.

4. Mies van der Rohe, 'Building art and the will of the epoch', originally published in *Der Querschnitt* 4(1) (1924), pp. 31–2 and reprinted in Neumeyer, p. 245.

5. ibid.

6. ibid.

7. Mies van der Rohe, 'Where do we go from here?', originally published in *Bauen und Wohnen* 15(11) (1960), p. 391, and reprinted in Neumeyer, p. 332.

8. ibid.

9. Mies was not an especially political figure, although he did design the memorial (1926) for the slaughtered revolutionary council communists Rosa Luxembourg and Karl Liebknecht, as well as a house extension (1928) for communist party figure and historian Eduard Fuchs. Mies's exercises in 'historical understanding' in the 1920s at times have echoes of the marxisant historicism of Karl Korsch. See Korsch, *Marxism and Philosophy* (London: New Left Books, 1970 [1928]).

10. 'Two large building domains lie before us as we survey the development of building. One realm concerns building for life in a general sense, the other is intimately connected with specific spiritual atmospheres that we perceive as characteristic cultures.' From an unpublished manuscript, 17 March 1926, reprinted in Neumeyer, p. 253.

11. ibid.

12. ibid.

13. Mies, 'Building art and the will of the epoch' (1924), reprinted in Neumeyer, pp. 245–7.

14. Unpublished lecture, 17 March 1926, reprinted in Neumeyer, pp. 252–6.

15. Unpublished manuscript of a lecture given on 14 March 1927, reprinted in Neumeyer, p. 262.

16. Mies, 'The preconditions of architectural work', lecture presented February and March 1928 and reprinted in Neumeyer, pp. 299–301.

17. ibid.

18. Mies, 'Inaugural address as director of architecture at Armour Institute of Technology', 20 November 1938, reprinted in Neumeyer, pp. 316–17.

19. ibid.

20. Lecture, 17 March 1926, reprinted in Neumeyer, pp. 252–6.

21. Mies, 'The preconditions of architectural work' (1928) reprinted in Neumeyer, pp. 299–300.

22. ibid., p. 300.

23. ibid.

24. ibid.

25. Mies, 'Building art and the will of the epoch', reprinted in Neumeyer, p. 245.

26. Aldo Rossi, *The Architecture of the City* (Cambridge, MA: MIT Press, 1984).

27. Mies, 'Building art and the will of the epoch', reprinted in Neumeyer, p. 245.

28. ibid.

29. ibid.

30. Mies, 'Building art and the will of the epoch', reprinted in Neumeyer, pp. 245–7.

31. ibid.

32. Mies, 'Industrial building', first published in *G*, 3 (June 1924), pp. 8–13 and reprinted in Neumeyer, pp. 248–9.

33. ibid.

34. ibid. Such charges against modern materials remain in currency; indeed continue to be mounted with great plausibility.

35. Mies was not always dismissive of the complaints about modern materials, however. In 'Building' published in *G*, 2 (September 1923), and reprinted in Neumeyer,

pp. 242–3, he commented that 'the disadvantage of ferroconcrete, as I see it, lies in its low insulating property and its poor sound absorption'.

36. Mies, 'Introductory remarks to the special issue "Werkbundausstellung: Die Wohnung"', first published in *Die Form* 2:9 (1927), and reprinted in Neumeyer, p. 261.

37. Mies, 'The preconditions in architectural work', reprinted in Neumeyer, pp. 299–301.

12   The House of the Gods: Heidegger

1. This was echoed in a mass longing to 'return to the land'.

2. 'Balkan' was originally an Ottoman word for mountain. On the ideology of the mountain, see Peter Murphy, 'The seven pillars of nationalism', *Diaspora: A Journal of Transnational Studies* 7: 3 (2000).

3. On the idea of *kosmopoiēsis*, see Peter Murphy, *Civic Justice: From Greek Antiquty to the Modern World* (Amherst, NY: Humanity Books, 2001).

4. On the Greek breakthrough, see Johann Arnason and Peter Murphy (eds), *Agon, Logos, Polis: The Greek Achievement and its Aftermath* (Stuttgart: Franz Steiner, 2001).

5. Vincent Scully, *Architecture: The Natural and the Manmade* (London: Harper-Collins, 1991), pp. 33–7.

6. Alan Gowans, *Styles and Types of North American Architecture* (New York: HarperCollins, 1992), p. 204.

7. ibid., p. 173.

8. Contrary to what Gowans, *op. cit.*, argues.

9. Gowans, p. 174.

10. Quoted in Marcus Whiffen, *American Architecture since 1780* (Cambridge, MA: MIT Press, revised edn, 1992), p. 202.

11. The first treatise by an architect of this generation (Francisco Mujica) on the topic of the American skyscraper noted that the new style of the skyscraper 'strikingly recalls the Pre-Columbian architecture with its palaces and pyramids with small cornices and magnificent decorations carved in big dominating surfaces', Francisco Mujica, *History of the Skyscraper* (New York : Da Capo Press, 1977), p. 33.

12. This was despite Mies's protestations in the 1920s that industrial materials were as good as artisan materials.

13. See Heidegger, 'The question concerning technology', in *The Question Concerning Technology and Other Essays* (New York: Harper & Row, 1977), p. 25 especially; and 'The origins of the work of art' in *Poetry, Language, Thought* (New York: Harper & Row, 1971), p. 45 especially.

14. Heidegger, 'The origins of the work of art', p. 41.

15. On Mies's interest in Aquinas, see Franz Schulze, *Mies van der Rohe: A Critical Biography* (Chicago: University of Chicago Press, 1985), pp. 13, 93–4, 138, 172–3, 193, 214.

16. Heidegger's last attempt to do this was in *Being and Time* (1927), a book notably that he couldn't finish.

17. 'The question concerning technology', p. 10.

18. Heidegger, 'Origins', p. 54.

19. Heidegger, 'Origins', p. 41.

20. Heidegger, 'Origins', p. 54.

21. Heidegger, 'Origins', p. 42.

22. Heidegger, 'Origins', p. 42.

23. Heidegger, 'Origins', p. 42.

24. Heidegger, 'Origins', p. 43.

25. Heidegger, 'Origins', p. 53.

26. Heidegger, 'Origins', p. 40.

27. Heidegger, 'Origins', pp. 40–1.

28. Heidegger, 'Origins', p. 41.

29. Heidegger, 'Origins', p. 42.

30. Wilhelm Dilthey, *Pattern and Meaning in History*, ed. H. P. Rickman (New York: Harper & Row, 1962), p. 130.

31. Heidegger, 'Origins', p. 47.

32. Heidegger, 'Origins', p. 46.

33. Heidegger, 'Origins', p. 47.

34. Heidegger, 'Origins', p. 48.

35. Heidegger, 'Origins', p. 49.

36. Heidegger, 'Origins', p. 49.

37. It made little difference that those on the left often identified themselves with modernism in order to demarcate themselves from the völkisch geopolitics of rightist movements.

38. On the way in which Neohellenic modernism was guided by the principle of autochthony, see Artemis Leontis, *Topographies of Hellenism* (Ithaca, NY: Cornell University Press, 1995), p. 115.

39. Franz Schulze, *Philip Johnson: Life and Work* (Chicago: University of Chicago Press, 1994), pp. 109–19.

40. Heidegger, 'Origins', p. 49.

41. Mies's acolyte Philip Johnson repeated the temple reference when he designed his Glass House (1949) in New Canaan, Connecticut, although Johnson's design lacked the radicalism of Mies – its slab-floor rests on the ground, instead of being raised above it.

13   The Iron Cage: Wittgenstein

1. The idea was adapted by Philip Johnson for his 1980 Crystal Cathedral, designed for the televangelist Robert Schuller, in Garden Grove, California.

2. These motifs reached an international audience through Mie's design of the German government-sponsored Barcelona Pavilion (1929).

3. The geometric aspect of this modernism shared affinities with the paintings of the Cubists and of Giorgio de Chirico, though in the painters' case interest in four-dimensional space-time supplanted more traditional three-dimensional architectonics. Corbusier's own painting style gravitated to the two-dimensional, exploring the superposition of plane upon plane. Corbusier's architecture of the 1920s on the other hand utilized classical geometries for the purpose of a rather aggressive celebration of a machinic future. It might be said that Corbusier's modernism was a futurist Neoplatonism in which the ubiquitous white-painted concrete was the symbol of enlightenment.

4. For a discussion of Loos's notion of the Roman, see Massimo Cacciari, *Architecture and Nihilism* (New Haven: Yale University Press, 1993), pp. 133–8.

5. As Michael Grant observes of classical Greek life: 'Sky and scenery were never far away, because life was mostly lived out of doors' (Grant, *The Ancient Mediterranean* [New York: Penguin, 1969], p. 202).

6. The closest Loos came to this was the Scheu building of 1912/13.

7. For their role in classical architecture, see Alexander Tzonis and Liane Lefaivre, *Classical Architecture: The Poetics of Order* (Cambridge, MA: MIT Press, 1986), pp. 101–8.

8. The dimensions of the hallway (1:1), Saal (1:2), dining room (2:3), and breakfast

room (5:6), and those of the vestibule (1:1), library (2:3), and the salon (3:4) follow Pythagorean musical ratios. On this, see Paul Wijdeveld, *Ludwig Wittgenstein Architect* (London: Thames & Hudson, 1994), p. 167.

9. This was not Loos's term. It was invented by one of his followers after Loos's death.

10. Interestingly, the geometric centre of the building thus lies between two entranceways.

11. Alan Colquhoun, *Modernity and the Classical Tradition* (Cambridge, MA: MIT Press, 1991), p. 110.

12. Wittgenstein's sensitivity to architectonics was no doubt due to the fact that he trained as an engineer before he taught himself architecture. Indeed, he was one of the few significant cultural figures of the modern era, at least in a biographical sense, who bridged the chasm that had appeared in the nineteenth century between architecture and engineering. Whereas engineers remained sympathetic to a constructivist (rationalist) idea of the classical, nineteenth-century architects by and large came to see themselves as designers – masters of style – rather than choreographers of force. Peter Collins, in *Changing Ideals in Modern Architecture* (London: Faber, 1965), outlines the subjection of architecture to the 'arts of drawing', and the teaching of architecture as simply a matter of dramatic pictorial representation (pp. 202–3). For this reason some of the most resonant, visually compelling 'classic'-like structures of the historicist era – such as John A. Roebling's Brooklyn Bridge (1883) – were created by engineers, not by architects whose work had been aestheticized and who came to excel in scholarly recreations that in situ were stilted memories rather than architectonic masterpieces. These 'academic revivals', even if at times resplendent, lacked power.

13. Wittgenstein's engineering studies on jet propulsion at the University of Manchester, in a parallel manner, were based on the idea of Hero of Alexander, whose work Wittgenstein had read in his father's library.

14. Indeed, the Lovell House lacked the stereometrical bravery of the Kundmanngasse villa.

15. William LeBaron Jenny had first used the idea of a metal frame to support exterior walls in the Home Insurance Building in Chicago in 1884–5.

16. What follows draws from the technical detail of Hugh Morrison, *Louis Sullivan: Prophet of Modern Architecture* (NY: Norton, 1962 [1935]).

17. Max Weber coined the phrase 'the iron cage' after his breakthrough trip to America in 1902. The phrase appeared in what was first published as a two-part essay *The Protestant Ethic and the Spirit of Capitalism* in 1904–5 in the *Archiv fur Sozialwissenscaft und Sozialpolitik* [cf. chapter 5, 'Asceticism and the Spirit of Capitalism' (London: Allen & Unwin, 1976), p 181.] Unlike most of his German colleagues, Weber was not scornful of what he saw on his trip to America. Indeed, the skyscrapers that he saw in New York City and Chicago reminded him of 'the old pictures of the towers in Bologna and Florence'. Weber, with his acute sense of the comparative at work, also noted the difference between the image of 'the towering fortresses of capitalism' and the quite unpalatial dimensions of the American apartment house: 'the home of Professor Hervay, of the German department in Columbia University, is surely a doll's house with tiny little rooms, with toilet and bath facilities in the same room (as is almost always the case). Parties with more than four guests are impossible (worthy of being envied!) and with all this it takes one hour's ride to get to the center of the city' (quoted in Hans Gerth and C. Wright Mills, *From Max Weber: Essays in Sociology*, New York: Oxford University Press, 1973 [1946]), p 15).

18. 'Give me a place to stand,' remarked Archimedes, 'and I shall move the earth.'

14   Greek Lessons: Mies van der Rohe in America

1. Mies, 'The preconditions of architectural work', reprinted in Fritz Neumeyer, *The Artless Word: Mies van der Rohe on the Building Art* (Cambridge, MA: MIT Press, 1991), p. 299.

2. Mies, 'Build beautifully and practically! Stop this cold functionality' first published in the *Duisburger Generalanzeiger* 49 (26 January 1930) and reprinted in Neumeyer, p. 307.

3. Lecture (undated) reprinted in Neumeyer, p. 325.

4. Mies, 'Inaugural address as director of architecture at Armour Institute of Technology' (20 November 1938) in Neumeyer, pp. 316–17.

5. Mies, 'Build beautifully and practically! Stop this cold functionality' first published in the *Duisburger Generalanzeiger* 49 (26 January 1930) and preprinted in Neumeyer, p. 307.

6. Mies, 'Radio address', August 1931 reprinted in Neumeyer, p. 311.

7. ibid.

8. After all, Wagner was a vegetarian as well as a socialist, nationalist, proto-fascist, and anti-Semite.

9. This Catholic universalism had much more difficulty, though, finding a place in its schemas for the post-Protestant 'pagan enlightenment' of the seventeenth and eighteenth centuries.

10. On the romanticization of the Spanish legacy in California, see Harold Kirker, *California's Architectural Frontier: Style and Tradition in the Nineteenth Century* 3rd edn (Salt Lake City: Peregrine Smith, 1986), chapter 1; Harold Kirker, *Old Forms on a New Land: California Architecture In Perspective* (Niwot, CO: Roberts Rinehart, 1991), chapter 5; Charles Gibson, *Spain in America* (New York: Harper, 1966), pp. 202–4.

11. Most crucial of all was the Italian philosopher of religion at the University of Berlin, Romano Guardini.

12. Leo Strauss, *Natural Right and History* (Chicago, IL: University of Chicago Press, 1953).

13. Even when, say, Arendt retained some of the vocabulary of German romanticism, for example its ur-concept of 'beginnings', she translated it into the 'Roman' lexicon of mimetic re-creation.

14. Franz Schulze, *Mies van der Rohe: A Critical Biography*, p. 239.

15. On the nature of such friendships, see Peter Murphy, 'Friendship's eu-topia' in the Friendship special issue of *South Atlantic Quarterly* 97: 1 (Winter 1998), pp. 169–86.

16. In contrast, Hannah Arendt, who turned to the problem of thinking in her later life, was wrong to treat *nous* as an internal dialogue (of I and me). Such internal dialogues occur, of course, but like external dialogues they occur in the effort to tease out the allusive grasp we have of the figures of thought and to find words (metaphors, descriptions) for them.

17. Vassilis Lambropoulos, 'The rule of justice', *Thesis Eleven* 40 (1995), especially p. 2.

18. Cornelius Castoriadis, 'The sayable and the unsayable' in *Crossroads in the Labyrinth* (Cambridge, MA: MIT Press, 1984), p. 139.

19. When friendships are severed (as Engelmann's was with Wittgenstein: Engelmann was not the first nor the last to be unequal to the force of Wittgenstein's personality), or else when one of the friends dies, the crucible is broken. The question then is posed: is there left any way for the figures of thought to find representation? To find words (logoi) for the unsayable is achieved in such cases through an enconium for the friend, or else a new 'prime friendship' is struck. Otherwise the thinking being retreats inwards, into solitude, into thought, into reflection.

20. Notably, Philip Johnson, with his own glasshouse, New Canaan (1949), had to design a painting gallery (1965) separate from the house in order to exhibit his private collection. He designed it as a burial chamber – on the model of the Treasury of Atreus, a Mycenean underground tomb dating from the 14th century BCE. Cf. Franz Schulze, *Philip Johnson: Life and Work* (Chicago: University of Chicago Press, 1994), p. 288.

Part Three: Introduction: Modernity's Utopias

1. Alexander Baumgarten, *Aesthetica* (1750). Baumgarten derived the term aesthetics from the Greek word *aisthanomai*, meaning perception by means of the senses.

2. Shaftesbury [Anthony Ashley Cooper, 3rd Earl of Shaftesbury] *Second Characters, or The Language of Forms* (Cambridge: Cambridge University Press, 1914 [1711–13]).

3. The nature of the world city is discussed in Peter Murphy, 'Marine reason', *Thesis Eleven* 67 (2001), pp. 11–38.

15 Modernity's Architectonic Utopia

1. A belated opening to Greece occurred in the late 1950s/early 1960s, after decades of civil war and dictatorship. Lewis Mumford visited for the first time in the summer of 1960, traveling to Athens and Delphi. Hannah Arendt visited in 1963. Mies's visit in 1959 took him to Athens, Delphi, Epidaurus and Nafplion.

2. Related to the Latin *fingo/fingere* is *fictus* (false, feigned), *fictio* (a forming, fashioning), *fictor* (image-maker, moulder, maker, sculptor, contriver). The *aedificator* is the builder; the *aedificium*, the building; *aedificatio*, the act of building.

3. Even in antiquity this was so. Pliny the Younger observed that 'we travel long roads and cross the water to see what we disregard when it is under our eyes'. Pliny explained that this was 'either because nature has so arranged things that we go after what is far off and remain indifferent to what is nearby, or because any desire loses its intensity by being easily satisfied, or because we postpone whatever we can see whenever we want, feeling sure we will after get around to it'. (Pliny, Ep 8: 20: 1–2.)

4. *Phaedrus*, 270 A.

5. 'In everything there is present a portion of everything; and in some things mind also is present.'

6. It is said that he did not get along well with his countrymen. Perhaps he was what in the twentieth century was called an internal exile – an exile of the spirit.

7. A tourists' habit, already established in the ancient world, was to visit the itinerant houses of great thinkers – the house where Plato allegedly stayed at Heliopolis in Egypt when he went to learn from the priests there; Pythagoras's house at Metapontum in Southern Italy, etc.

8. On the Greek concept of the apoikia or away home, see Peter Murphy, *Civic Justice: From Greek Antiquity to the Modern World* (Amherst, NY: Humanity Books, 2001), pp. 23–4.

9. See, for example, the selections from her notebooks, published as Simone Weil, *The Intimations of Christianity among the Ancient Greeks* (London: Routledge, 1957).

10. This is like Hobbes's discovery of Euclid – and the science of politics – in Geneva. From John Aubrey's colourful account in *Brief Lives*, we learn that, during his stay in Geneva (April–June 1630), Hobbes read Euclid's *Elements* – an event that was to prove a turning-point in Hobbes's intellectual life:

> He was 40 yeares old before he looked on Geometry, which happened accidentally. Being in a Gentleman's Library, Euclid's Elements lay open, and 'twas the

47 el. libri 1 ['Pythagoras's theorem']. He read the proposition. By G—, sayd he (he would now and then swear an emphaticall Oath by way of emphasis) this is impossible! So he reads the Demonstration of it, which referred him back to such a Proposition, which proposition he read. That referred him back to another, which he also read. *Et sic deinceps* that at last he was demonstratively convinced of that trueth. This made him in love with Geometry.

11. When Plato, in the *Timaeus*, adapted this schema of world-creation from the Pythagoreans, he fused it with certain mythopoietic elements – for him, geometrical solids equated the elements of archaic nature. The cube equated the earth; the pyramid = fire; octahedron = air; icosahedron = water; dodecahedron = kosmos.

12. For a treatment of the social-theoretical significance of multi-dimensionality, see Johann Arnason, 'Culture and imaginary significations', *Thesis Eleven* 22 (1989), pp. 25–45 and 'Civilization, culture and power: reflections on Norbert Elias' Genealogy of the West', *Thesis Eleven* 24 (1989), pp. 44–70.

13. Loos remained a traveller all of his life. He even became interested in the design of hotels – and developed projects for a Grand Hotel Babylon in Nice (1923) and for a hotel on the Champs Elysées in Paris (1924).

14. Loos returned from America with the very American idea in mind that the true classical moment was Roman. 'Our civilization is based on a recognition of the insurpassable grandeur of classical antiquity. From the Romans we have derived the technique of our thought and of our way of feeling. It is to the Romans that we owe our social conscience and the discipline of our souls.' Loos, *Architektur*, 1910, quoted in Benedetto Gravagnuolo, *Adolph Loos: Theory and Works*, trans. C. H. Evans (New York: Rizzoli, 1982), p. 37.

15. Loos understood this in the following terms: 'The Greeks wasted their imaginative force in the order of columns, the Romans applied theirs in designing buildings' (Loos, *Architektur*, 1910, quoted in Gravagnuolo, *Adolph Loos: Theory and Works*, p. 37).

16. The term secondarity comes from Remi Brague, *Eccentric Culture* (South Bend, IN: St Augustine Press, 2001). His argument is that the classical makes the old new in the sense that Rome is secondary to Greece, Christianity is secondary to Judaism, and Europe is Greek and Jewish because it is Roman. Its centre is eccentric.

17. 'I have taught my pupils to think in three dimensions, to think in the cube' (Loos, *Meine Bauschule*, 1913, quoted in Gravagnuolo, *Adolph Loos: Theory and Works*, p. 41).

18. Like the Scheu House (1912/13), Strasser House (1918/19), his unbuilt project for the Villa Stross (1922), the Villa Moissi (1923), Möller House (1927/28), and Müller House (1928–30).

19. In 1908 Wittgenstein went to Manchester to do research in aeronautics at the University of Manchester. In 1911, he left Manchester to study mathematical logic with Russell in Cambridge. This was a period of preparation for the thinking that was to produce his *Tractatus*. To formulate those ideas, though, he had to escape the mindless chatter of Cambridge academic life. In 1913, he headed off to the solitary world of Skjolden in Norway. He returned from England to Austria when war broke out in 1914.

20. The picture, photo, film frame or drawing that re-presents that which is recessed or shaped or formed or moulded.

21. 'The fact that the elements of a picture are related to one another in a determinate way represents that things are related to one another in the same way' (Wittgenstein, *Tractatus Logico-Philosophicus*, trans. D. F. Pears and B. F. McGuinness [London: Routledge, 1961 (1921)], 2.15). On theories of *Bilder* propounded by Wittgenstein's contemporaries – from Klages to Benjamin – see John Ely, 'Intellectual friendship and the elective affinities of critical theory' in P. Murphy (ed.), Special Issue on Friendship, *South Atlantic Quarterly* 97:1 (Winter 1998), 187–224.

22. 2.0272 The configuration of objects produces states of affairs.

2.03 In a state of affairs objects fit into one another like links in a chain.

2.031 In a state of affairs objects stand in a determinate relation to one another.

2.033 Form is the possibility of structure.

2.034 The structure of a fact consists of the structure of states of affairs.

2.04 The totality of existing states of affairs is the world.

23. 'Greek' houses because they had columns in contradistinction (as Loos saw it) to the Roman building. As well as these houses, Loos's (temporary) re-evaluation of the Greek column also yielded his entry in the *Chicago Tribune* Building competition.

16 Modernity's Aesthetic Utopias

1. On the idea of absolute art or the 'literary absolute', see Philippe Lacoue-Labarthe and Jean-Luc Nancy, *The Literary Absolute. The Theory of Literature in German Romanticism*, trans. and introduced by Philip Barnard and Cheryl Lester (Albany: State University of New York Press, 1988).

2. Clement Greenberg, *Art and Culture. Critical Essays* (Boston: Beacon Press, 1965 [1961]), p. 139.

3. Kurt Hübner, *Die Wahrheit des Mythos* (Munich: Beck, 1985), pp. 293, 296.

4. Suzi Gablik, *Progress in Art* (London: Thames & Hudson, 1976), followed however in 1991 by *Reenchantment of Art* (New York: Thames & Hudson, 1991).

5. Greenberg, *Art and Culture. Critical Essays* (Boston: Beacon Press, 1965), p. 61.

6. ibid., p. 7.

7. ibid., p. 208.

8. Hans Sedlmayr, *Die Revolution der modernen Kunst* (Reinbek bei Hamburg: Rowohlt, 1953), p. 113.

9. ibid, p. 95.

10. Greenberg, *Art and Culture*, p. 64.

11. Theodor W. Adorno, *Philosophy of Modern Music* (London: Sheed & Ward, 1973).

12. Sedlmayr, *Die Revolution der modernen Kunst*, p. 66.

13. ibid., p. 69.

14. Peter Bürger, *Theory of the Avant-Garde*, Preface by Jochen Schulte-Sasse (Minneapolis: University of Minnesota Press, 1984).

15. Friedrich Blume, *Renaissance and Baroque Music* (London: Faber & Faber, 1973), p. 125.

16. Alexandre Lenoir's Musée des monuments français. See Stephan Bann, 'The premisses of modern art', in Christos M. Jochimedes and Norman Rosenthal (eds), *The Age of Modernism, Art in the Twentieth Century* (Berlin: Gerd Hatje, 1997), p. 517.

17. Hans Sedlmayr, *Der Verlust der Mitte. Die bildende Kunst des 19. und 20. Jahrhunderts als Symptom und Symbol der Zeit* (Frankfurt: Ullstein, 1959), pp. 35–45.

18. These cathedrals of cultural tourism manifest our postmodernist fascination with our own modernist culture as well as our romantic longings for the organic and the authentic, whose ubiquitous expression extends from the touristic transformation of the world and its 'cultures' into an imaginary museum to the ever growing aestheticization of daily life and the consumerist packaging of lifestyles and the resultant 'experience economy'. For the 'experience economy' see Jeremy Rifkin, *The Age of Access: The New Culture of Hypercapitalism* (New York: Tarcher/Putnam, 2000).

19. Hans-Georg Gadamer, *Truth and Method*, 2nd revised edn (London: Sheed & Ward, 1993), p. 574.

20. ibid., p. 311.

21. ibid., p. 101.
22. ibid., p. 109.
23. ibid., pp. 116–17.
24. ibid., p. 127.
25. ibid., p. 128.
26. ibid., p. 428.
27. See Jacques Derrida, *The Truth in Painting* (Chicago: University of Chicago Press, 1987).
28. Maurice Blanchot, *Le livre à venir* (Paris: Gallimard, 1959), p. 237.
29. See the section on irony in the Introduction in Georg Hegel, *The Philosophy of Fine Art*, Vol. 1 (New York: Hacker Fine Art, 1975) and Søren Kierkegaard, *The Concept of Irony with Constant Reference to Socrates*, ed. and trans. by H. V. Hong and Edna Hong (Princeton, NJ: Princeton University Press, 1989).
30. Arthur C. Danto, *The Philosophical Disenfranchisement of Art* (New York: Columbia University Press, 1986).
31. Antonin Artaud, *The Theatre and its Double* (New York: Grove, 1958), p. 13.
32. Donald Kuspit, 'Sol LeWitt: the look of thought', *Art in America* LXIII (September/October 1975), p. 48.
33. Robert Rosenblum, *Modern Painting and the Northern Romantic Tradition. Friedrich to Rothko* (London: Thames & Hudson, 1975).
34. Gottfried Benn, 'Der neue Staat und die Intellektuellen' in Benn, *Essays. Reden.Vorträge* (Wiesbaden: Limes Verlag, 1959), pp. 440–9.
35. Astradur Eysteinsson, *The Concept of Modernism* (Ithaca: Cornell University Press, 1990), p. 195.
36. Briony Fer, 'The language of construction', in Briony Fer, David Batchelor and Paul Wood, *Realism, Rationalism, Surrealism. Art between the Wars* (New Haven: Yale University Press, 1993), p. 95.
37. See the epilogue to 'The Work of Art in the Age of Mechanical Production': 'The logical result of Fascism is the introduction of aesthetics into politics. ... Communism responds by politizing art'. Walter Benjamin, *Illuminations. Essays and Reflections*, edited with an Introduction by Hannah Arendt (New York: Schocken Books, 1969), pp. 141–2.
38. Guy Debord, *Society of the Spectacle* (Detroit: Black and Red, 1983).
39. Odo Marquard, 'Gesamtkunstwerk und Identitätssystem', in *Der Hang zum Gesamtkunstwerk. Europäische Utopien seit 1800* (Aarau: Sauerländer, 1983), pp. 40–9.
40. See Klaus Englert, 'Two Versions of the Symbolist Apocalypse: Mallarmé's *Livre* and Scriabin's *Mysterium*', *Criticism* 28: 3 (1986), 287–306.
41. Susan Sontag, 'Approaching Artaud', in *Under the Sign of Saturn* (New York: Farrar, Straus & Giroux, 1980).
42. Nietzsche, *The Birth of Tragedy and The Case of Wagner*, trans. Walter Kaufmann (New York: Vintage Books, 1967).
43. Theodor W. Adorno, *In Search of Wagner*, trans. Rodney Livingstone (London: New Left Books, 1981), p. 122.
44. Richard Wagner, *Opera and Drama*, trans. William Ashton Ellis (Lincoln: University of Nebraska Press, 1995), Part I, and 'Judaism in Music' in *Judaism in Music and Other Essays*, trans. William Ashton Ellis (Lincoln: University of Nebraska Press, 1995).
45. Norbert Bolz, *Eine kurze Geschichte des Scheins* (Munich: Fink, 1991), p. 108.

17 Utopia in the New World

1. Directed by Carol Reed; produced by Alexander Korda, Reed and David O. Selznick; screenplay by Graham Greene.

2. On this, see Reyner Banham, *Los Angeles: The Architecture of Four Ecologies* (Harmondsworth: Penguin, 1971), pp. 125–7.

3. The outstanding 'literary child' of this mentality was Mike Davis, and his noir vision of Los Angeles in *City of Quartz excavating the future in Los Angeles* (London: Pimlico, 1998).

4. Herbert Marcuse, *An Essay on Liberation* (Harmondsworth: Penguin, 1972 [1969]), p. 54.

5. See Peter Murphy, *Civic Justice: From Greek Antiquity to the Modern World* (Amherst, NY: Humanity Books, 2001).

6. Gianni Braghieri, *Aldo Rossi*, 2nd edn (Barcelona: Editorial Gustavo Gili, 1993), pp. 214–18.

18 Conclusion: Modernity's Modernisms

1. Norbert Elias, *et al.*, *The Civilizing Process* (Oxford: Blackwell, 1994).

2. Martin Heidegger, *Basic Writings*, ed. David Farrell Krell (New York: Harper-Collins, 1993), p. 334.

3. ibid., p. 340.

4. ibid, p. 337.

5. Jürgen Habermas, *The Philosophical Discourse of Modernity* (Cambridge, MA: MIT Press, 1987), p. 8.

6. Jean-Joseph Goux, 'The Eclipse of Art?' *Thesis Eleven* 44 (1996), pp. 57–8.

Bibliography

Abrams, M. H., *Natural Supernaturalism. Tradition and Revolution in Romantic Literature* (New York: Norton, 1973).

Adorno, Theodor, 'Die Idee der Naturgeschichte', in Adorno, *Philosophische Frühschriften. Gesammelte Schriften I* (Frankfurt: Suhrkamp, 1973), pp. 345–65.

Adorno, Theodor, *In Search of Wagner*, trans. Rodney Livingstone (London: New Left Books, 1981).

Adorno, Theodor, *Negative Dialektik* (Frankfurt: Suhrkamp, 1966).

Adorno, Theodor, *Philosophy of Modern Music* (London: Sheed & Ward, 1973).

Arendt, Hannah, *On Revolution* (Harmondsworth: Penguin, 1963).

Arnason, Johann, 'Civilization, culture and power: reflections on Norbert Elias' Genealogy of the West', *Thesis Eleven* 24 (1989), pp. 44–70.

Arnason, Johann, 'Culture and imaginary significations', *Thesis Eleven* 22 (1989), pp. 25–45.

Arnason, Johann, *Nation and Modernity* (Rejkjavik: Nordic Summer University, 1996).

Arnason, Johann and Peter Murphy (eds), *Agon, Logos, Polis: The Greek Achievement and its Aftermath* (Stuttgart: Franz Steiner, 2001).

Artaud, Antonin, *The Theatre and its Double* (New York: Grove, 1958).

Babbitt, Irving, *Rousseau and Romanticism* (New York: AMS Press, 1979).

Bachofen, Johann Jakob, *Myth, Religion and Mother Right. Selected Writings of J. J. Bachofen*, trans. Ralph Manheim (London: Routledge & Kegan Paul, 1967).

Baeumler, Alfred, 'Bachofen der Mythologe der Romantik', in Bachofen, *Der Mythos von Orient und Occident*, ed. Manfred Schroeter (Munich: Beck, 1956).

Baeumler, Marianne (ed.), *Thomas Mann und Alfred Baeumler. Eine Dokumentation* (Würzburg: Königshausen & Neumann, 1989).

Balzac, Honoré de, *The Unknown Masterpiece* (Berkeley: Creative Arts Book Co., 1984).

Banham, Reyner, *Los Angeles: The Architecture of Four Ecologies* (Harmondsworth: Penguin, 1971).

Bann, Stephan, 'The premisses of modern art', in Christos M. Jochimedes and

Norman Rosenthal (eds), *The Age of Modernism, Art in the Twentieth Century* (Berlin: Gerd Hatje, 1997).

Barker, Ernest, *Essays on Government* (Oxford: Clarendon Press, 1951).

Barker, Ernest, *Greek Political Theory: Plato and his Predecessors* (London: Methuen, 1947).

Barker, Ernest, *Principles of Social and Political Theory* (Oxford: Clarendon Press, 1951).

Barker, Ernest, *The Ideas and Ideals of the British Empire* (Cambridge: Cambridge University Press, 1941).

Behler, Ernst, *German Romantic Literary Theory* (Cambridge: Cambridge University Press, 1993).

Benjamin, Walter, *Illuminations. Essays and Reflections*, edited with an Introduction by Hannah Arendt (New York: Schocken Books, 1969).

Benjamin, Walter, *The Origin of German Tragic Drama*, trans. John Osborne, introduction by George Steiner (London: NLB, 1977).

Benn, Gottfried, 'Der neue Staat und die Intellektuellen', in Benn, *Essays. Reden. Vorträge* (Wiesbaden: Limes Verlag, 1959).

Bergdoll, Barry, *Karl Friedrich Schinkel* (New York: Rizzoli, 1994).

Berlin, Isaiah, *The Roots of Romanticism* (London: Pimlico, 2000).

Berlin, Isaiah, *Three Critics of the Enlightenment. Vico, Hamann, Herder* (Princeton: Princeton University Press, 2000).

Blackbourn, David, *History of Germany 1780–1918. The Long Nineteenth Century*, 2nd edn (Oxford: Blackwell, 2003).

Blanchot, Maurice, *Le livre à venir* (Paris: Gallimard, 1959).

Blume, Friedrich, *Renaissance and Baroque Music* (London: Faber & Faber, 1973).

Bolz, Norbert, *Eine kurze Geschichte des Scheins* (Munich: Fink, 1991).

Braghieri, Gianni, *Aldo Rossi*, 2nd edn (Barcelona: Editorial Gustavo Gili, 1993).

Brague, Remi, *Eccentric Culture* (South Bend, IN: St Augustine Press, 2001).

Burckhardt, Jacob, *Griechische Kulturgeschichte* Vol. 1, *Gesammelte Werke* Vol. 5 (Basel: Schwabe, 1956).

Bürger, Peter, *Theory of the Avant-Garde*. Preface by Jochen Schulte-Sasse (Minneapolis: University of Minnesota Press, 1984).

Butler, E. M., *The Saint-Simonian Religion in Germany. A Study of the Young German Movement* (New York: Fertig, 1968).

Butler, E. M., *The Tyranny of Greece over Germany. A Study of the Influence Exercised by Greek Art and Poetry over the Great German Writers* (Cambridge: The University Press, 1935).

Cacciari, Massimo, *Architecture and Nihilism* (New Haven: Yale University Press, 1993).

Carroll, John, *The Western Dreaming* (Sydney: HarperCollins, 2001).

Cassirer, Ernst, *Freiheit und Form. Studien zur deutschen Geistesgeschichte* (Darmstadt: Wissenschaftliche Buchgesellschaft, 1961).

Cassirer, Ernst, *The Philosophy of the Enlightenment* (Boston: Beacon Press, 1955).

Castoriadis, Cornelius, *Crossroads in the Labyrinth* (Cambridge, MA: MIT Press, 1984).

Castoriadis, Cornelius, *Philosophy, Politics, Autonomy* (Oxford: Oxford University Press, 1991).

Chytry, Josef, *The Aesthetic State. A Quest in Modern German Thought* (Berkeley: University of California Press, 1989).

Collins, Peter, *Changing Ideals in Modern Architecture* (London: Faber & Faber, 1965).

Colquhoun, Alan, *Modernity and the Classical Tradition* (Cambridge, MA: MIT Press, 1991).

Creuzer, Georg Friedrich, *Symbolik und Mythologie der alten Völker*, 6 vols (New York: Arno Press, 1978).

Crozier, Michael and Peter Murphy (eds), *The Left in Search of a Center* (Urbana-Champaign: Illinois University Press, 1996).

Dahlhaus, Carl, *Richard Wagner's Music Dramas* (Cambridge: Cambridge University Press, 1979).

Danto, Arthur C., *The Philosophical Disenfranchisement of Art* (New York: Columbia University Press, 1986).

Darcy, Warren, ' "The World belongs to Alberich!" Wagner's changing attitude to the "Ring" ', in Stewart Spencer (ed.), *Wagner's Ring of the Nibelungen. A Companion* (London: Thames & Hudson, 1993), pp. 48–52.

Davis, Mike, *City of Quartz excavating the future in Los Angeles* (London: Pimlico, 1998).

Debord, Guy, *Society of the Spectacle* (Detroit: Black and Red, 1983).

Deleuze, Gilles, *Spinoza et le problème de l'expression* (Paris: Editions de Minuit, 1968).

Derrida, Jacques, *The Truth in Painting* (Chicago: University of Chicago Press, 1987).

Dilthey, Wilhelm, *Pattern and Meaning in History*, ed. H. P. Rickman (New York: Harper & Row, 1962).

Dumont, Louis, *The German Ideology* (Chicago: University of Chicago Press, 1994).

Elias, Norbert, *The Civilizing Process* (Oxford: Blackwell, 1994).

Ely, John, 'Intellectual friendship and the elective affinities of critical theory', in P. Murphy (ed.), Special Issue on Friendship, *South Atlantic Quarterly* 97:1 (Winter 1998), pp. 187–224.

Engell, James, *The Creative Imagination. From Enlightenment to Romanticism* (Cambridge, MA: Harvard University Press, 1981).

Englert, Klaus, 'Two Versions of the Symbolist Apocalypse: Mallarmé's *Livre* and Scriabin's *Mysterium*', *Criticism* 28: 3 (1986), pp. 287–306.

Eysteinsson, Astradur, *The Concept of Modernism* (Ithaca: Cornell University Press, 1990).

Fer, Briony, 'The language of construction', in Briony Fer, David Batchelor and Paul Wood (eds), *Realism, Rationalism, Surrealism. Art between the Wars* (New Haven: Yale University Press, 1993).

Fichte, Johann Gottlieb, *Science of Knowledge with the First and Second Introductions*, trans. Peter Heath and John Lachs (New York: Appleton Century Crofts, 1970).

Fleming, Ray, *Keats, Leopardi, and Hölderlin: The Poet as Priest of the Absolute* (New York: Garland, 1987).

Foucault, Michel, *The Order of Things. An Archaeology of the Human Sciences* (London: Tavistock Publications, 1970).

Frank, Manfred, *Der kommende Gott. Vorlesungen über die Neue Mythologie* (Frankfurt: Suhrkamp, 1982).

Frank, Manfred, *Gott im Exil. Vorlesungen über die Neue Mythologie* (Frankfurt: Suhrkamp, 1988).

Freier, Hans, *Die Rückkehr der Götter. Von der ästhetischen Überschreitung der Wissensgrenze zur Mythologie der Moderne* (Stuttgart: Metzler, 1976).

Gablik, Suzi, *Progress in Art* (London: Thames & Hudson, 1976).

Gablik, Suzi, *Reenchantment of Art* (New York: Thames & Hudson, 1991).

Gadamer, Hans-Georg, *Truth and Method*, 2nd revised edn (London: Sheed & Ward, 1993).

Gay, Peter, *The Enlightenment. An Interpretation*: Vol. I *The Rise of Modern Paganism*, Vol. II *The Science of Freedom* (New York: Knopf, 1966, 1969).

Gerth, Hans and C. Wright Mills, *From Max Weber: Essays in Sociology* (New York: Oxford University Press, 1973 [1946]).

Gibson, Charles, *Spain in America* (New York: HarperCollins, 1995).

Goethe, Johann Wolfgang, *The Sorrows of Young Werther* (New York: Penguin, 1989).

Gooch, G. P., *Germany and the French Revolution* (New York: Russell & Russell, 1966).

Görres, Joseph, 'Exposition d'un système sexuel d'ontologie', in Görres, *Gesammelte Schriften 2.2* (Cologne: Bachen, 1934), pp. 201–36.

Goux, Jean-Joseph, 'The Eclipse of Art?', *Thesis Eleven* 44 (1996), pp. 57–8.

Gowans, Alan, *Styles and Types of North American Architecture* (New York: HarperCollins, 1992).

Grant, Michael, *The Ancient Mediterranean* (New York: Penguin, 1969).

Gravagnuolo, Benedetto, *Adolph Loos: Theory and Works*, trans. C. H. Evans (New York: Rizzoli, 1982).

Greenberg, Clement, *Art and Culture. Critical Essays* (Boston: Beacon Press, 1965 [1961]).

Grote, George, *History of Greece* (New York: Harper, 1875).

Grote, George, *Plato, and the other Companions of Sokrates* (London: J. Murray, 1888).

Gusdorf, Georges, *Du Néant à Dieu dans le savoir romantique* (Paris: Payot, 1983).

Habel, Reinhardt, *Joseph Görres. Studien über den Zusammenhang von Natur, Geschichte und Mythos in seinen Schriften* (Wiesbaden: Steiner, 1960).

Habermas, Jürgen, 'The Entwinement of Myth and Enlightenment: Rereading Dialectic of Enlightenment', *New German Critique* 26 (1982), 13–30.

Habermas, Jürgen, *The Philosophical Discourse of Modernity* (Cambridge, MA: MIT Press, 1987).

Hazard, Paul, *European Thought in the Eighteenth Century*, trans. J. Lewis May (Harmondsworth: Penguin, 1965).

Hegel, Georg Wilhelm Friedrich (1770–1831), *The Philosophy of Fine Art*, trans. F. Osmaston, 4 vols (New York: Hacker Fine Art, 1975).

Heidbrink, Ludger, *Melancholie und Moderne* (Munich: Fink, 1994), pp. 96–9.

Heidegger, Martin, *An Introduction to Metaphysics*, trans. Ralph Manheim (New Haven: Yale University Press, 1959).

Heidegger, Martin, *Basic Writings*, ed. David Farrell Krell (London: Routledge, 1993).

Heidegger, Martin, *Contributions to Philosophy (From Enowning)*, trans. Parvis Emad and Kenneth Maly (Bloomington: Indiana University Press, 1999).

Heidegger, Martin, *Elucidations of Hölderlin's Poetry*, trans. and introduced Keith Hoeller (Amherst, NY: Humanity Books, 2000).

Heidegger, Martin, *Nietzsche*, Vol. 1–4 (New York: HarperCollins, 1991).

Heidegger, Martin, *Poetry, Language, Thought* (New York: Harper & Row, 1971).

Heidegger, Martin, *The Question Concerning Technology and Other Essays* (New York: Harper & Row, 1977).

Heidegger, Martin, *Gesamtausgabe* (Frankfurt: Klostermann, 1977–).

Heidegger, Martin, *Einführung in die Metaphysik*, GA 40.

Heidegger, Martin, *Hölderlins Hymnen 'Germanien' und 'Der Rhein'*, GA 39.

Heidegger, Martin, *Parmenides*, GA 54.

Heidegger, Martin, *Schelling: Vom Wesen der menschlichen Freiheit (1809)*, GA 42.

Heidegger, Martin, *Sein und Zeit, Gesamtausgabe*, GA 2.

Herder, Johann Gottfried von, *Reflections on the Philosophy of the History of Mankind*, abridged and introduction by Frank E. Manuel (Chicago: Chicago University Press, 1968).

Hirsch, E. D., *Wordsworth and Schelling. A Typological Study of Romanticism* (New Haven: Yale University Press, 1960).

Hölderlin, Friedrich, *Essays and Letters on Theory*, trans. and ed. Thomas Pfau (Albany, NY: State University of New York Press, 1988).

Honneth, Axel, 'L'esprit et son objet—Parentés anthropologiques entre la dialectique de la raison et la critique de la civilisation dans la philosophie de la vie', in Gérard Raulet (ed.), *Weimar ou la explosion de la modernité* (Paris: Anthropos, 1984), pp. 97–112.

Horkheimer, Max and Theodor W. Adorno, *Dialectic of Enlightenment*, trans. John Cumming (London: Allen Lane, 1973).

Horkheimer, Max and Theodor Adorno, *Dialektik der Aufklärung* in Adorno, *Gesammelte Schriften* 3 (Frankfurt: Suhrkamp, 1984).

Hübner, Kurt, *Die Wahrheit des Mythos* (Munich: Beck, 1985).

Hudson, Wayne, *The Marxist Philosophy of Ernst Bloch* (London: Macmillan, 1982).

Hughes, H. Stuart, *Oswald Spengler. A Critical Estimate* (New York: Scribner, 1962).

Iggers, Georg, *The German Conception of History. The National Tradition of Historical Thought from Herder to the Present* (Middletown, CT: Wesleyan University Press, 1968).

Janik, Allan and Stephen Toulmin, *Wittgenstein's Vienna* (New York: Simon & Schuster, 1973).

Jasper, David (ed.), *The Interpretation of Belief. Coleridge, Schleiermacher, and Romanticism* (Basingstoke: Macmillan, 1986).

Jaspers, Karl, *Notizen zu Heidegger*, ed. Hans Saner (Munich: Piper, 1978).

Joas, Hans, *The Creativity of Action*, trans. Jeremy Gaines and Paul Keast (Chicago: Chicago University Press, 1996).

Jünger, Ernst, *Storm of Steel. From the Diary of a German Storm-troop Officer on the Western Front*, trans. Basil Creighton (London: Chatto & Windus, 1929).

Kahn, Charles H., *The Art and Thought of Heraclitus. An Edition of the Fragments with Translation and Commentary* (Cambridge: Cambridge University Press, 1979).

Kahn, Philip J., *Schiller, Hegel and Marx. State, Society and the Aesthetic Ideal of Ancient Greece* (Kingston, ON: McGill-Queens University Press, 1982).

Kant, Immanuel, 'Rezensionen von J.G. Herders "Ideen zur Philosophie der Geschichte der Menschheit" ', Part I, Appendix (Beilage), in Kant, *Schriften zur Geschichtsphilosophie*, ed. Manfred Riedel (Stuttgart: Reclam, 1974), pp. 49–51.

Keller, Gottfried, *Green Henry* (London: Calder, 1960).

Kierkegaard, Søren, *The Concept of Irony with Constant Reference to Socrates*, ed. and trans. by H. V. Hong and Edna Hong (Princeton, NJ: Princeton University Press, 1989).

Kirker, Harold, *California's Architectural Frontier: Style and Tradition in the Nineteenth Century* 3rd edn (Salt Lake City: Peregrine Smith, 1986).

Kirker, Harold, *Old Forms on a New Land: California Architecture in Perspective* (Niwot, CO: Roberts Rinehart, 1991).

Koepke, Wulf, *Johann Gottfried Herder* (Boston: Twayne, 1987).

Köhler, Joachim, *Wagners Hitler. Der Prophet und sein Vollstrecker* (Munich: Blessing, 1997).

Korotin, Ilse (ed.), *Die besten Geister der Nation. Philosophie und Nationalsozialismus* (Vienna: Picus, 1994).

Korsch, Karl, *Marxism and Philosophy* (London: New Left Books, 1970 [1928]).

Kuspit, Donald, 'Sol LeWitt: the look of thought', *Art in America* LXIII (September/October 1975).

Lacoue-Labarthe, Philippe, *La fiction du politique. Heidegger, l'art et la politique* (n. p.: Christian Bourgeois, 1987).

Lacoue-Labarthe, Philippe, *L'imitation des modernes* (Paris: Galilei, 1986).

Lacoue-Labarthe, Philippe, *Le sujet de la philosophie. Typographies I* (Paris: Aubier-Flammarion, 1979).

Lacoue-Labarthe, Philippe, *Musica Ficta, Figures of Wagner* (Stanford: Stanford University Press, 1994).

Lacoue-Labarthe, Philippe and Jean-Luc Nancy, *The Literary Absolute: The Theory of Literature in German Romanticism*, trans. and introduced by Philip Barnard and Cheryl Lester (Albany: State University of New York, 1988).

Lambropoulos, Vassilis, 'The rule of justice', *Thesis Eleven* 40 (1995).

Latour, Bruno, *We Have Never Been Modern* (Cambridge, MA: Harvard University Press, 1993).

Legros, Robert, *L'idée de l'humanité. Introduction à la phénoménologie* (Paris: Grasset, 1990).

Leontis, Artemis, *Topographies of Hellenism* (Ithaca, NY: Cornell University Press, 1995).

Lösch, Walburga, *Der werdende Gott. Mythopoetische Theogonien in der romantischen Mythologie* (Frankfurt: Lang, 1996).

Machiavelli, Niccolò, *The Prince, Selections from The Discourses and other writing*, edited by John Plamenatz (London: Collins, 1972).

Mann, Thomas, 'Deutsche Ansprache. Ein Appell an die Vernunft' in *Politische Schriften und Reden*, Vol. 2 (Frankfurt: Fischer, 1968).

Marcuse, Herbert, *An Essay on Liberation* (Harmondsworth: Penguin, 1972 [1969]).

Marquard, Odo, 'Gesamtkunstwerk und Identitätssystem', in *Der Hang zum Gesamtkunstwerk. Europäische Utopien seit 1800* (Aarau: Sauerländer, 1983), pp. 40–9.

Marquard, Odo, *Transzendentaler Idealismus. Romantische Naturphilosophie. Psychoanalyse* (Cologne: Dinter, 1987).

Marten, Rainer, 'Heidegger and the Greeks', in Tom Rockmore and Joseph Margolis (eds), *The Heidegger Case* (Philadelphia: Temple University Press, 1992), pp. 167–87.

Marx, Karl, *Selected Writings*, ed. David McLellan (Oxford: Oxford University Press, 1985).

Marx, Karl, 'Towards a Critique of Hegel's "Philosophy of Right": Introduction' (1844), in K. Marx, *The Early Texts*, ed. D. McLellan (Oxford: Oxford University Press, 1971).

Marx, Werner, *The Philosophy of F. W. J. Schelling. History, System, and Freedom*, trans. Thomas Nenon (Bloomington: Indiana University Press, 1984).

Meinecke, Friedrich, *Cosmopolitanism and the National State* (Princeton, NJ: Princeton University Press, 1970).

Meinecke, Friedrich, *Die Entstehung des Historismus*, ed. and introduced by Carl Hinrichs (Munich: Oldenburg, 1965).

Meinecke, Friedrich, *The German Catastrophe. Reflections and Recollections* (Boston: Beacon Press, 1950).

Meinecke, Friedrich, *Historicism. The Rise of a New Historical Outlook*, trans. J. E. Anderson, Foreword by Isaiah Berlin (London: Routledge & Kegan Paul, 1972).

Morrison, Hugh, *Louis Sullivan: Prophet of Modern Architecture* (New York: Norton, 1962 [1935]).

Mujica, Francisco, *History of the Skyscraper* (New York : Da Capo Press, 1977).

Müller, Adam, *Elemente der Staatskunst* (Berlin: Haude und Spener, 1968).

Müller, Roland, *Das verzwistete Ich. Ludwig Klages und sein philosophisches Hauptwerk 'Der Geist als Widersacher der Seele'* (Bern: Lang, 1971).

Murphy, Peter, *Civic Justice: From Greek Antiquity to the Modern World* (Amherst, NY: Humanity Books, 2001).

Murphy, Peter, 'Friendship's eu-topia', *South Atlantic Quarterly* 97: 1 (Winter 1998), pp. 169–86.

Murphy, Peter, 'Marine reason', *Thesis Eleven* 67 (2001), 11–38.

Murphy, Peter, 'Metropolitan rhythms: a preface to a musical philosophy for the New World', *Thesis Eleven* 56 (1999), pp. 81–105.

Murphy, Peter, 'Romantic Modernism and the Greek Polis', *Thesis Eleven* 34 (1993), pp. 42–66.

Murphy, Peter, 'The seven pillars of nationalism', *Diaspora: A Journal of Transnational Studies* 7:3 (2000).

Nancy, Jean-Luc, *The Inoperative Community* (Minneapolis: University of Minnesota Press, 1991).

Neumeyer, Fritz, *The Artless Word: Mies van der Rohe on the Building Art* (Cambridge, MA: MIT Press, 1991).

Nevin, Thomas, *Ernst Jünger and Germany. Into the Abyss 1914–1945* (Durham, NC: Duke University Press, 1996).

Nietzsche, Friedrich, *Beyond Good and Evil*, trans. with commentary by Walter Kaufmann (New York: Vintage Books, 1966).

Nietzsche, Friedrich, *The Birth of Tragedy and the Case of Wagner*, trans. with commentary by Walter Kaufmann (New York: Vintage Books, 1967).

Nietzsche, Friedrich, 'Der Fall Wagner', in *Werke in zwei Bänden*, Vol. II (Munich: Hanser, 1967).

Nietzsche, Friedrich, *The Will to Power*, ed. Walter Kaufmann, trans. Walter Kaufmann and R. J. Hollingdale (New York: Vintage Books, 1968).

'Nihilismus', in Joachim Ritter and Karlfried Gründer (eds), *Historisches Wörterbuch der Philosophie*, Vol. 6 (Darmstadt: Wissenschaftliche Buchgesellschaft, 1984).

Nipperday, Thomas, 'Auf der Suche nach der Identität: Romantischer Nationalismus', in Nipperday, *Nachdenken über die deutsche Geschichte* (Munich: Beck, 1986), pp. 110–25.

'The Oldest Systematic Programme of German Idealism', in Ernst Behler (ed.) *Philosophy of German Idealism* (New York: Continuum, 1987), pp. 161–3.

Panofsky, Erwin, *Renaissance and Renascences in Western Art* (New York: Harper & Row, 1972 [1969]).

Pevsner, Nikolaus, *A History of Building Types* (Thames & Hudson: London, 1976).

Popper, Karl, *The Open Society and its Enemies* (London: Routledge, 1947).

Potts, Alex, *Flesh and the Ideal. Winckelmann and the Origins of Art History* (New Haven: Yale University Press, 1994).

Rather, L. J., *The Dream of Self-Destruction. Wagner's 'Ring' and the Modern World* (Baton Rouge: Louisiana State University Press, 1979).

Raulet, Gérard, *Humanisation de la nature, naturalization de l'homme. Ernst Bloch et le projet d'une autre rationalité* (Paris: Klinksieck, 1982).

Reed, T. J., *Schiller* (Oxford: Oxford University Press, 1991).

Reijen, Willem van, 'Die Dialektik der Aufklärung gelesen als Allegorie', in Willem van Reijen and Gunzelin Schmid Noerr (eds), *Vierzig Jahre Flaschenpost: Dialektik der Aufklärung 1947 bis 1987* (Frankfurt am Main: Fischer, 1987), pp. 192–209.

Reiss, Hans, *Political Thought of the German Romantics 1793–1815* (Oxford: Blackwell, 1955).

Richir, Marc, *Du sublime en politique* (Paris: Payot, 1991).

Rifkin, Jeremy, *The Age of Access: The New Culture of Hypercapitalism* (New York: Tarcher/Putnam, 2000).

Roberts, David, *Art and Enlightenment: Aesthetic Theory after Adorno* (Lincoln: University of Nebraska Press, 1991).

Rosen, Stanley, *G. W. F. Hegel. An Introduction to the Science of Wisdom* (New Haven: Yale University Press, 1974).

Rosenblum, Robert, *Modern Painting and the Northern Romantic Tradition. Friedrich to Rothko* (London: Thames & Hudson, 1975).

Rossi, Aldo, *The Architecture of the City* (Cambridge, MA: MIT Press, 1984).

Röttges, Heinz, *Nietzsche und die Dialektik der Aufklärung* (Berlin: de Gruyter, 1972).

Santner, Eric L. (ed.), *Hyperion and Selected Poems* (New York: Continuum, 1990).

Scharfschwerdt, Jürgen, *Hölderlin. Der Dichter des deutschen 'Sonderwegs'* (Stuttgart: Kohlhammer, 1994).

Schelling, Friedrich Wilhelm, *Of Human Freedom*, trans. James Gutman (Chicago: Open Court, 1936).

Schelling, Friedrich Wilhelm Joseph, *System of Transcendental Idealism* (1800), trans. Peter Heath, introduction Michael Vater (Charlottesville: University of Virginia Press, 1978).

Schelling, Friedrich Wilhelm, *The Philosophy of Art*, ed., trans. and introduced by Douglas W. Stoll (Minneapolis: University of Minnesota Press, 1989).

Schiller, Friedrich, *Naive and Sentimental Poetry and On the Sublime*, trans. with introduction by Julius A. Elias (New York: Ungar, 1966).

Schiller, Friedrich (1759–1805), *On the Aesthetic Education of Man, in a Series of Letters*, ed. and trans. with introduction by Elizabeth M. Wilkinson and L. A. Willoughby (Oxford: Clarendon Press, 1992).

Schlegel, Friedrich, 'Dialogue on Poetry', trans. Ernst Behler and Roman Struc, in A. Leslie Willson (ed.), *German Romantic Criticism* (New York: Continuum, 1982), pp. 84–133.

Schleiermacher, Friedrich Daniel Ernst, *On Religion. Speeches to its Cultured Despisers*, ed. Richard Crouter (New York: Cambridge University Press, 1996).

Schmid Noerr, Gunzelin, *Das Eingedenken der Natur im Subjekt. Zur Dialektik von Vernunft und Natur in der Kritischen Theorie Horkheimers, Adornos und Marcuses* (Darmstadt: Wissenschaftliche Buchgesellschaft, 1990).

Schmidt, Jochen, *Die Geschichte des Genie-Gedankens in der deutschen Literatur, Philosophie und Politik 1750–1945* (Darmstadt: Wissenschaftliche Buchgesellschaft, 1985).

Schmitt, Carl, *Political Romanticism* (Cambridge, MA: MIT Press, 1986).

Schnädelbach, Hans, *Philosophy in Germany 1831–1933* (Cambridge: Cambridge University Press, 1984).

Schopenhauer, Arthur, *The World as Will and Representation*. Vol. I, trans. E. F. J. Payne (New York: Dover, 1969).

Schulze, Franz, *Mies van der Rohe: A Critical Biography* (Chicago: University of Chicago Press, 1985).

Schulze, Franz, *Philip Johnson: Life and Work* (Chicago: University of Chicago Press, 1994).

Scully, Vincent, *Architecture: The Natural and the Manmade* (London: HarperCollins, 1991).

Sedlmayr, Hans, *Der Verlust der Mitte. Die bildende Kunst des 19. und 20. Jahrhunderts als Symptom und Symbol der Zeit* (Frankfurt: Ullstein, 1959).

Sedlmayr, Hans, *Die Revolution der modernen Kunst* (Reinbek bei Hamburg: Rowohlt, 1953).

Shaftesbury [Anthony Ashley Cooper, 3rd Earl of Shaftesbury], *Second Characters, or The Language of Forms* (Cambridge: Cambridge University Press, 1914 [1711–13]).

Sharpe, Lesley, *Friedrich Schiller. Drama, Thought, and Politics* (Cambridge: Cambridge University Press, 1991).

Sontag, Susan, 'Approaching Artaud', in *Under the Sign of Saturn* (New York: Farrar, Straus & Giroux, 1980).

Spengler, Oswald, *The Decline of the West*, Vols 1 & 2, authorized translation with notes by Charles Francis Atkinson (New York: Knopf, 1926–8).

Stauth, Georg, 'Critical Theory and Pre-Fascist Social Thought', *History of European Ideas*, XVIII (1994), pp. 711–27.

Stern, Fritz, *The Politics of Cultural Despair. A Study in the Rise of the German Ideology* (Berkeley: University of California Press, 1961).

Strauss, Leo, *Liberalism, Ancient and Modern* (New York: Basic Books, 1968).

Strauss, Leo, *Natural Right and History* (Chicago: IL: University of Chicago Press, 1953).

Strauss, Leo, *The City and Man* (Chicago: Rand McNally, 1964).

Strauss, Leo, *Thoughts on Machiavelli* (Glencoe, IL: Free Press, 1959).

Strauss, Leo, *What is Political Philosophy? and Other Studies* (Glencoe, IL: Free Press, 1959).

Tacitus, Cornelius, *Histories*, IV, trans. K. Wellesley (Harmondsworth: Penguin, 1975).

Talmon, J. L., *Romanticism and Revolt. Europe 1815–1848* (London: Thames & Hudson, 1967).

Taylor, Charles, 'Inwardness and the culture of modernity', in Axel Honneth *et al.* (eds), *Zwischenbetrachtungen. Im Prozess der Aufklärung. Jürgen Habermas zum 60. Geburtstag* (Frankfurt: Suhrkamp, 1989), pp. 601–23.

Taylor, Charles, *Sources of the Self. The Making of Modern Identity* (Cambridge, MA: Harvard University Press, 1989).

Travers, Martin, *Critics of Modernity. The Literature of the Conservative Revolution in Germany 1890–1933* (New York: Lang, 2001).

Tzonis, Alexander and Liane Lefaivre, *Classical Architecture: The Poetics of Order* (Cambridge, MA: MIT Press, 1986).

Villa, Dana R., *Arendt and Heidegger. The Fate of the Political* (Princeton: Princeton University Press, 1996).

Wagner, Richard, 'Beethoven', in *Gesammelte Schriften und Dichtungen*, ed. Wolfgang Golthe, Vol. 9 (Berlin: Bong, n.d.).

Wagner, Richard, *Judaism in Music and Other Essays*, trans. William Ashton Ellis (Lincoln: University of Nebraska Press, 1995).

Wagner, Richard, *Oper und Drama* (Stuttgart: Reclam, 1984).

Wagner, Richard, *Opera and Drama*, trans. William Ashton Ellis (Lincoln: University of Nebraska Press, 1995).

Wagner, Richard, *Prose Works*, Vol. I, trans. William Ashton Ellis (London: Kegan Paul, 1895).

Wagner, Richard, *Selected Letters of Richard Wagner*, trans. and ed. Stewart Spencer and Barry Millington (London: Dent, 1987).

Weber, Max, *The Protestant Ethic and the Spirit of Capitalism* (London: Allen & Unwin, 1976).

Weeks, Andrew, *Boehme: An Intellectual Biography* (Albany: State University of New York Press, 1991).

Weeks, Andrew, *German Mysticism from Hildegard of Bingen to Ludwig Wittgenstein: A Literary and Intellectual History* (Albany: State University of New York Press, 1993).

Weil, Simone, *The Intimations of Christianity among the Ancient Greeks* (London: Routledge, 1957).

Whiffen, Marcus, *American Architecture since 1780* (Cambridge, MA: MIT Press, revised edn, 1992).

Wijdeveld, Paul, *Ludwig Wittgenstein Architect* (London: Thames & Hudson, 1994).

Willson, A. Leslie (ed.), *German Romantic Criticism* (New York: Continuum Books, 1982).

Winckelmann, Johann, *History of Ancient Art*, trans. Alexander Gode, 4 vols (New York: Ungar, 1968).

Winckelmann, Johann, *Reflections on the Painting and Sculpture of the Greeks* (London: Routledge, 1999).

Wittgenstein, Ludwig, *Tractatus Logico-Philosophicus*, trans. D.F. Pears and B.F. McGuinness (London: Routledge, 1961 [1921]).

Wolin, Richard (ed.), *The Heidegger Controversy. A Critical Reader* (Cambridge, MA: MIT Press, 1993).

Wood, Roger, *The Conservative Revolution in the Weimar Republic* (London: Macmillan, 1996).

Yack, Bernhard, *The Longing for Total Revolution. Philosophic Sources of Social Discontent from Rousseau to Marx and Nietzsche* (Princeton: Princeton University Press, 1986).

Index